Reencounters

In the series *Asian American History and Culture*, edited by Cathy Schlund-Vials, Shelley Sang-Hee Lee, and Rick Bonus. Founding editor, Sucheng Chan; editors emeriti, David Palumbo-Liu, Michael Omi, K. Scott Wong, and Linda Trinh Võ.

ALSO IN THIS SERIES:

Michael Omi, Dana Y. Nakano, and Jeffrey Yamashita, eds., *Japanese American Millennials: Rethinking Generation, Community, and Diversity*
Masumi Izumi, *The Rise and Fall of America's Concentration Camp Law: Civil Liberties Debates from the Internment to McCarthyism and the Radical 1960s*
Shirley Jennifer Lim, *Anna May Wong: Performing the Modern*
Edward Tang, *From Confinement to Containment: Japanese/American Arts during the Early Cold War*
Patricia P. Chu, *Where I Have Never Been: Migration, Melancholia, and Memory in Asian American Narratives of Return*
Cynthia Wu, *Sticky Rice: A Politics of Intraracial Desire*
Marguerite Nguyen, *America's Vietnam: The* Longue Durée *of U.S. Literature and Empire*
Vanita Reddy, *Fashioning Diaspora: Beauty, Femininity, and South Asian American Culture*
Audrey Wu Clark, *The Asian American Avant-Garde: Universalist Aspirations in Modernist Literature and Art*
Eric Tang, *Unsettled: Cambodian Refugees in the New York City Hyperghetto*
Jeffrey Santa Ana, *Racial Feelings: Asian America in a Capitalist Culture of Emotion*
Jiemin Bao, *Creating a Buddhist Community: A Thai Temple in Silicon Valley*
Elda E. Tsou, *Unquiet Tropes: Form, Race, and Asian American Literature*
Tarry Hum, *Making a Global Immigrant Neighborhood: Brooklyn's Sunset Park*
Ruth Mayer, *Serial Fu Manchu: The Chinese Supervillain and the Spread of Yellow Peril Ideology*
Karen Kuo, *East Is West and West Is East: Gender, Culture, and Interwar Encounters between Asia and America*
Kieu-Linh Caroline Valverde, *Transnationalizing Viet Nam: Community, Culture, and Politics in the Diaspora*
Lan P. Duong, *Treacherous Subjects: Gender, Culture, and Trans-Vietnamese Feminism*
Kristi Brian, *Reframing Transracial Adoption: Adopted Koreans, White Parents, and the Politics of Kinship*
Belinda Kong, *Tiananmen Fictions outside the Square: The Chinese Literary Diaspora and the Politics of Global Culture*
Bindi V. Shah, *Laotian Daughters: Working toward Community, Belonging, and Environmental Justice*
Cherstin M. Lyon, *Prisons and Patriots: Japanese American Wartime Citizenship, Civil Disobedience, and Historical Memory*

A list of additional titles in this series appears at the back of this book.

Reencounters

*On the Korean War and
Diasporic Memory Critique*

Crystal Mun-hye Baik

TEMPLE UNIVERSITY PRESS
Philadelphia • Rome • Tokyo

TEMPLE UNIVERSITY PRESS
Philadelphia, Pennsylvania 19122
tupress.temple.edu

Copyright © 2020 by Temple University—Of The Commonwealth System
   of Higher Education
All rights reserved
Published 2020

Portions of Chapter 4 were previously published as
   Crystal Baik, "Unfaithful Returns: Reiterations of Dissent, U.S.-Korean Militarized Debt, and the Architecture of Violent Freedom." Copyright © 2015. Johns Hopkins University Press. This article first appeared in JOURNAL OF ASIAN AMERICAN STUDIES, Volume 18, Issue 1, February 2015, pages 41–72.
   Crystal Baik, "MAGO and Communal Ritual as Decolonial Praxis: An Exchange with Dohee Lee" in VERGE: STUDIES IN GLOBAL ASIAS, 2.2 (2016): 1–16.

Library of Congress Cataloging-in-Publication Data

Names: Baik, Crystal Mun-hye, author.
Title: Reencounters : on the Korean War and diasporic memory critique / Crystal Mun-hye Baik.
Other titles: On the Korean War and diasporic memory critique
Description: Philadelphia : Temple University Press, [2019] | Series: Asian American history and culture | Includes bibliographical references and index.
Identifiers: LCCN 2019005765 (print) | LCCN 2019981009 (ebook) |
   ISBN 9781439918982 (cloth : alk. paper) | ISBN 9781439918999 (pbk. : alk. paper) |
   ISBN 9781439919002 (ebook)
Subjects: LCSH: Korean War, 1950–1953—Social aspects. | Korean War, 1950–1953—Art and the war. | Koreans—Foreign countries. | Collective memory—Korea.
Classification: LCC DS921.5.S63 B35 2019 (print) | LCC DS921.5.S63 (ebook) |
   DDC 951.904/2—dc23
LC record available at https://lccn.loc.gov/2019005765
LC ebook record available at https://lccn.loc.gov/2019981009

*To those who are living under occupation
and those who remain separated, detained,
and displaced*

Contents

A Note on Transliteration and Terminology   *ix*

A Note on Methodology   *xi*

Acknowledgments   *xv*

The Delicious Taste of Army Base Stew: An Introduction   *1*

1   Militarized Migrations   *33*

2   Aurality   *67*

3   Returns   *97*

4   Durational Memory   *127*

    An Opening   *159*

Notes   *187*

Index   *219*

A Note on Transliteration and Terminology

All Korean words are spelled according to either the Revised Romanization system or the McCune-Reischauer system. I retain the spelling of Korean names as they appear in English-language publications, following the Western convention of given name preceding surname in reference to Korean diasporic subjects. For Korean historical figures and state actors, I follow the standard usage in East Asia, with surname preceding given name.

I use the term "Korean/Americans" rather than "Korean Americans" or "Korean-Americans." Following the work of Laura Hyun Yi Kang, I use the solidus between "Korean" and "American" to indicate the volatile making of "Koreans" into legible "Americans" within the fraught contexts of U.S. national politics and Cold War militarization. Thus, "Korean/American" does not signify a stable ontological status, fixed disciplinary subject (or object), or singular identity. Rather, it signifies my treatment of Korean/Americans as an unstable political, legislative, and epistemological category constituted through and conditioned by power.

A Note on Methodology

As an interdisciplinary and transnational study of the Korean War, *Reencounters: On the Korean War and Diasporic Memory Critique* draws on both cultural analysis of multimedia memory works and archival research and semi-structured interviews conducted in South Korea, Hong Kong, the United States, Denmark, and Sweden between January 2013 and August 2017. During this period, I traveled to South Korea and Hong Kong on two occasions to attend art exhibits and performances; conduct archival research; and consult with and interview Korean diasporic artists, curators, and public intellectuals. I also visited twenty-two sites, including institutional archives, museums, galleries, national memorials, and mass gravesites in Seoul, near the South Korean Civilian Control Zone, and on Jeju Island. My first visit, to South Korea and Jeju Island during the summer of 2013, lasted approximately four weeks; my second visit, to South Korea and Hong Kong during the summer of 2016, lasted five weeks. During this four-year period, I also organized or attended exhibits and performances related to this project in the Los Angeles metropolitan area; San Francisco; Washington, DC; New York City; Copenhagen, Denmark; and Mälmo, Sweden. During all of these endeavors, I collaborated and conversed at length with cultural practitioners whose work I take up in the subsequent pages.

In addition to these integral formal methods, I relied on improvised forms of engagement with cultural practitioners, curators, and archivists. These moments of engagement transpired through informal conversations that lasted several hours, e-mail correspondence, and touching moments of camaraderie shared with so many people throughout the five-plus years of research and writing in Asia, Europe, and North America. Though an official methodology may not typically include such off-the-cuff interactions, they proved to be just as intellectually meaningful and profound as the theorization stimulated by archival research and formal interviews. At times, the improvisational interactions contradicted what I had recorded or selectively remembered from my interviews, archival research, and site visits. In a surprising way, these points of disruption pushed me to reencounter what I *thought* I had read, heard, and touched. Indeed, I conceptualize these transient moments as openings that surface only through engaged practices of reorientation, accountability, and reciprocity.

I emphasize these precipitous moments of difference because I consistently spoke and corresponded with a small circle of mentors, peers, and cultural practitioners throughout the project. Every single artist, filmmaker, and performer who is substantively discussed in subsequent chapters contributed to this book through their correspondence and generous input.[1] Consequently, I address these cultural practitioners as *interlocutors* rather than as research subjects. A handful of mentors and peers also read segments of the manuscript, providing thoughtful feedback and asking vital questions at crucial stages of the writing. These moments of exchange complicated my analyses, providing variable points of reference. These shifting interactions remind me that scholarship is always already subjective and never removed from the contexts in which it is produced. Throughout this book, I mention the responses from my interlocutors within the primary text or through the feminist practice of citational reference.

In a more general sense, these feedback loops hold my scholarship accountable to a broader network of peers, readers, and cultural practitioners. Conversely, my interlocutors continually draw on my scholarship for their own inquiry-based reflection and research processes. By integrating feminist practices of reciprocity into my research methodology, I neither ascribe to the principle of "cultural authenticity" nor invest in notions of consensus and objective truth. Rather, by approaching research and writing as collaborative endeavors and slow methodical efforts, I accentuate the shared and, at times, unrecognized forms of labor that create critical intellectual work, as well as the necessity of vigorously contesting the neoliberal logics that saturate the world of publishing in and beyond the academy—a focus on speed and efficiency, a tacit belief in the importance of quantity over quality, and a dogged fixation on possessive "ownership" through the categorical production of intellectual property. This methodology allowed me to confront these pressures and reencounter research and writing as a shared, albeit uneven, process in which knowledge is co-created. By tracing the circuits through which intellectual knowledge crystallizes, my research acknowledges, as Nadine Naber observes, "the imbalances of power" implicit within academic labor and scholarship.[2] This self-reflexive process, I argue, is necessary to understand the meanings of decolonization within the context of knowledge production, commodification, and extraction within the settler academy.

As the work of James Baldwin, Walter Benjamin, Grace Lee Boggs, Frantz Fanon, Audre Lorde, Edward Said, Linda Tuhiwai Smith, and Lisa Yoneyama has taught me, enduring and endearing practices of self-reflexivity are necessary to trouble the destructive relationships of power that shape the academic-industrial complex. These self-reflexive practices refuse to be narrowly confined to a single action, because they encompass different ways of knowing, including modes of embodiment, sensorial impressions, and perception. In this way, the practice of being in but not of the university crystallizes through the ways we meet, approach, and (re)encounter one another within confined spaces of hierarchy, as well as through how we write about and reflect on injustices indicative of racial, gender, and sexual violence. These processes are, in fact, entwined. At the very least, the artists, activists, scholars, and peers I have conversed with throughout this research and writing process have permitted me to actualize a slow praxis of intentionality, reciprocity, and accountability—and to partake in my own process of unknowing and unlearning. For that, I am deeply humbled by and grateful for their wisdom and support.

Acknowledgments

The making (and remaking) of this book was possible only through a convergence of countless dialogues, support, and care that I received from so many peers, mentors, loved ones, and (non)institutional spaces. I first acknowledge the artists, oral historians, curators, and cultural workers who allowed me to engage their work. While I was unable to discuss all of their oeuvres in this project, my conversations with them greatly enriched my analysis. These individuals include Anna Jin Hwa Borstam, Erica Cho, Trine Mee Sook Gleerup, Sukjong Hong, Jane Jin Kaisen, Christine Sun Kim, Danny Kim, Gina Kim, Sunjung Kim, Dohee Lee, Deann Borshay Liem, Ramsay Liem, Minouk Lim, kate-hers RHEE, and Kim Stoker. In Chapter 2, I quote extensively from my 2016 interview with Sukjong Hong and Danny Kim, and I am grateful for their continued correspondence throughout this project. I am also grateful to Niana Liu and Cristiana Baik, who permitted to me use their beautiful photographs in the last chapter, "An Opening."

Much gratitude goes to the acquisitions, production, and marketing teams at Temple University Press (TUP), who made this process as joyful and seamless as it could have possibly been. I am especially grateful to Ann-Marie Anderson, Sara Jo Cohen, Gary Kramer, Ashley Petrucci, Joan S. P. Vidal, and the two anonymous readers who provided such thoughtful feedback on the manuscript. While Sara has since transitioned from TUP, I am eternally grateful for the resolute care she channeled into the manuscript. I am grateful to Cathy Schlund-Vials for her support and terrific sense of humor. Susan Deeks and Lisa Wehrle, with grace and patience, provided editorial support during the final stage of manuscript revisions. David Martinez provided stellar expertise as he worked on the book's comprehensive index. A hearty thank-you, as well, goes to Linda Võ, who first connected me with Temple University Press.

This project, in its earliest form, emerged from doctoral work pursued in the American Studies and Ethnicity (ASE) program at the University of Southern California (USC). I am particularly grateful for the generous input provided by Youngmin Choe, Macarena Gómez-Barris (my extraordinary chair), Jack Halberstam, Jodi Kim, and Dorinne Kondo. While Nayan Shah arrived at ASE during my last year in the program, I am grateful for his critical insights and mentorship. At various moments throughout my time at USC, Nitin Govil, Sarah Gualtieri, Neetu Khanna, Laura Pulido, and Laura Isabel Serna provided illuminating feedback—my sincerest gratitude goes to all of them. A shout-out goes to ASE's staff members, including Sonia Flores, Kitty Lai, and Jujuana Preston, for all their labor, administrative support, and encouragement. During my time at USC, I received generous research support and grants from the Center for Transpacific Studies (I thank Janet Hoskins and Viet Nguyen) and the Korean Studies Institute, as well as seed funding from the Radcliffe Institute for Advanced Study. During my first year at USC, I had the pleasure of taking Viet Nguyen's seminar "War and Memory," which provided intellectual grist for the questions posed in this book.

At USC, I am eternally grateful for the kindness and generosity of the comrades who sustained me during graduate school—especially Patty Ahn, Deborah al-Najjar, Umayyah Cable, Jih-Fei Cheng, Amee Chew, Sarah Fong, Feng-Mei Heberer, Jenny Hoang, Celeste Menchaca, Ho'esta Mo'e'hane, Anjali Nath, Mark Padoongpatt, Rebekah Park, Nic Ramos, Emily Raymundo, and David Stein. I am in awe of and inspired by their collective brilliance and commitment to intellectual rigor and justice. I would be remiss if I failed to mention the exemplary training I received from Columbia University's Oral History Master of Arts (OHMA) Program before I transitioned to USC. I am especially grateful to Mary Marshall Clark and Amy Starecheski and am moved by the imaginative, genre-bending creative writing and research of my fellow OHMAers, including Cindy Choung, Anna Kaplan, and Svetlana Kitto.

At the University of California, Riverside, I must acknowledge the shifting terrain of peers, mentors, and allies I have befriended these past few years. I am especially grateful to the faculty members of my home department, Gender and Sexuality Studies (GSST), including Juliann Allison, Alicia Arrizón, Amalia Cabezas, Katja M. Guenther, Sherine Hafez, Tamara Ho, Anthonia Kalu, Brandon Robinson, Jade Sasser, Chikako Takeshita, and Jane Ward.

Truly, I could not have asked for a more brilliant or supportive chair than Sherine. During my first few years at UC Riverside, Mariam Lam, Jennifer Nájera, Dylan Rodríguez, and Sarita See helped me navigate the professional maze that is academia; Sarita also read an early draft of a chapter and provided key feedback. I am grateful for my friendships with Megan Asaka, Donatella Galella, Emily Hue, Rita Kohli, Liz Przybylski, Jade Sasser, Stephen Sohn, and Jane Ward and for the heartwarming conversations we've been able to share these past few years. Although Maile Arvin and Eric Stanley transitioned to other institutions during my time at UC Riverside, I continue to be moved by their scholarship and courage. I am grateful for so many of the graduate students, both present and past, with whom I have had the honor to work in different capacities: Aaron Alvarado, Iris Blake, Tomoyo Joshi, Ren-yo Hwang, Beth Kopacz, Justin Phan, Loubna Qutami, J Sebastian, Luis Trujillo, and Wei-Chi Wu.

Chapter 3 of this book was first workshopped with a group of colleagues at UC Riverside through the research group Off Centers: Queer Racial Dis/Orientations (supported by the Center for Ideas and Society). Members include Donatella Gallela, Liz Przybylski, and Stephen Sohn. Laura Hyun Yi Kang also provided crucial feedback that reshaped the configuration of the manuscript. Stephen Sohn—who read integral components of this book—practices a model of care and mentorship that I am always striving to embody. A grant from the Danish Arts Foundation and a UC Riverside Academic Senate Grant and Hellman Fellowship provided support for fieldwork and research conducted in Korea, in Hong Kong, on Jeju Island, in Denmark, and in Sweden.

During the 2017–2018 academic year, I received a generous research fellowship from the Institute of American Cultures (IAC) at the University of California, Los Angeles, which allowed me to finish writing the manuscript. I am especially grateful to the wonderful faculty and staff affiliated with IAC and the Asian American Studies Center, including Melany de la Cruz-Viesca, Irene Suico Soriano, Karen Umemoto, and David Yoo. Throughout the intensive writing process, Keith Camacho, Grace Kyungwon Hong, and Kiri Sailiata provided much-needed moments of respite, camaraderie, and laughter. Chris A. Eng, Chris Fan, Feng-Mei Heberer, Joo Ok Kim, Andrew Leong, Cheryl Naruse, Vinh Nguyen, Travis Sharp, Stephen Sohn, Sunny Xiang, and Hentyle Yapp read multiple drafts of various chapters, and their insightful feedback sharpened and strengthened the manuscript. I am so grateful to them for their careful eye and intellectual labor.

Beyond UC Riverside, I am indebted to a circle of peers and mentors who not only buoy me in general but also encourage me to expand my understanding of creative intellectual work. In 2015 I attended a weeklong "Migratory

Aesthetics" workshop through Pennsylvania State University's Asian Studies Summer Institute. Little did I know, at that time, how vitally important this network of friends and mentors would become as an anchoring point during a particularly difficult period. Chris A. Eng, Chris Fan, Andrew Leong, Cheryl Naruse, Vinh Nguyen, Sunny Xiang, and Hentyle Yapp inspire me, to no end, with their sharp intellect and full hearts; they remind me that it is possible to pursue critical intellectual work in self-reflexive and ethical ways. Akash Belsare, Michelle Huang, and Leland Tabares provided crucial support during the weeklong workshop, and I continue to be awed by their emerging scholarship. I could not possibly overstate my respect and affection for Tina Chen. Her genuine commitment to cultivating lateral relationships of support, camaraderie, and exchange for and among junior scholars beyond institutional spaces is exemplary and all too rare in academe. Throughout the writing process, so many friends, mentors, and interlocutors provided meaningful input, encouraging words, and guidance over shared meals, coffee, e-mails, and Skype hangouts. So much gratitude goes to Javier Arbona, Jih-Fei Cheng, Michelle Cho, Sarah Fong, Feng-Mei Heberer, Christine Hong, Jane Jin Kaisen, Caren Kaplan, Joo-Ok Kim, Anjali Nath, erin Khuê Ninh, Yumi Pak, Leigh Patel, Stephen Sohn, Jane Ward, and Judy Wu.

Throughout the years, I have cultivated a robust network of chosen family members who ground me with their love and friendship. I have immense respect for Lisa Ahn, Janet Curran, Katherine Foo, Joo Han, A. Naomi Jackson, and Susie Yeo—all of whom I met decades ago in Williamstown, Massachusetts, a tiny hamlet nestled in the Berkshires. While our contact throughout these years has come in ebbs and flows, our points of convergence are always full of life, laughter, and joy. In Los Angeles, I am entirely grateful for (including those who have moved away recently) Lian Cheun, Megyung Chung, Mimi Kim, Tina Kim, Sarah Mountz, Mari Ryono, Preeti Sharma, Elizabeth Sunwoo, and Eric Wat. I thank them for the radical advocacy, organizing, writing, and care work that they all do. When I teach and write, I often think of them and their work.

Last, but by no means least, I acknowledge my family. Even through illness, my father, In Ki Baik, in his relentless support of me, still offers to attend my lectures at UC Riverside, while my mother, Young Ok Baik, continues to be an ever-present force in my life. Both of my vastly talented sisters, Cristiana Baik and Coleen Baik, contributed to this project: Cristiana provided photographs and wrote the poem "Wreckoning" for this book, and Coleen provided the artwork for the cover. The artwork is a creative remediation of a black-and-white photograph taken during an era of military dictatorship in South Korea. In the image, my mother, then in her late teens and wearing a subtle smile, is walking along the Han River with a group of friends. Only decades later would I be able to apprehend and feel the full weight of that photograph in regard to the tumultuous history it indexes and the innumerable ways that war, division, and colonialism have shaped my parents' lives. And while war remains outside the legible frame of our family's "immigration" history, the photograph reminds me of the inescapable ways in which division is absolutely central to our militarized migration. Daniel Ichinose is all things that I could have ever asked for and more in a life partner: his patience, thoughtfulness, brilliance, sense of humor, and commitment to justice are reaffirming. I am also grateful for the deep love provided by Travers and Juanita Ichinose and for the effervescence they have brought into our lives through Teo and Asha. Any errors in this book are my own.

Reencounters

The Delicious Taste of Army Base Stew

An Introduction

In the corner of a gallery room is a small video monitor placed inside a U.S. military C-ration can. Since the video installation is propped on top of a low eating table, viewers must squat, kneel, or sit to peek into the can's metallic interior. As the audience looks on, a time-lapse scene glows on the screen: American cheese, Spam, and Campbell's Pork and Beans appear neatly arranged across a table covered with a green-and-blue checkered cloth. While fragmented comments in English and Korean are heard throughout the video, a pair of hands dexterously deposits the food into a large pot simmering with tofu, *kimchi* (pickled cabbage), and water. Through a rapid sequence of close-up shots, the camera captures the softening of the foods as they melt and disappear into the bubbling red mixture. Abruptly, the cooking demonstration ends, only to be looped again and again for passing spectators.

Titled *BooDaeChiGae* (2005), this video installation by Ji-Young Yoo hints at the beginnings of the Korean War, as well as its indiscernible implications in contemporary social life.[1] *Budae jjigae* (a word that translates as "army base stew" in English) first surfaced in Uijeongbu, a city north of Seoul and home to an installment of the U.S. Second Infantry Division. Following the outbreak of full-scale combat fighting on the Korean Peninsula in 1950, starving Korean civilians scavenged military bases for leftovers, excising Spam and other processed meat from heaps of garbage and mixing their coveted findings with vegetables, noodles, and water to create filling stews. As the number of American soldiers stationed in Korea soared during the next two decades,

View of *BooDaeChiGae* (video monitor, Korean rice paper, table, C-ration cans, 2005).
(Courtesy of artist Ji-Young Yoo. Photograph by Ramsay Liem.)

Inside the C-ration can in *BooDaeChiGae*.
(Courtesy of artist Ji-Young Yoo. Photograph by Ramsay Liem.)

the popularity of budae jjigae also grew. Symbolizing American abundance in the face of scarcity among Koreans, canned meats became sought-after commodities in the black market, so much so that the South Korean government deemed the smuggling of Spam a crime punishable by imprisonment or even death. As Grace Cho notes, American products such as Spam also hint at a sexualized web of taboo relations, given that Korean women romantically associated with U.S. soldiers gained access to food exclusively sold at military retail stores or the Postal Exchange (PX).[2] To support their families, some resold tins of Spam for lucrative profit in Seoul's wealthiest districts, while others crafted makeshift versions of army base stew following their migrations to the United States as the married partners of U.S. servicemen.[3] In the ensuing decades, these very same women would become the primary visa sponsors of family members attempting to settle in the United States. While these fragmented stories of deracination, displacement, and migration resist forming a single or coherent narrative, budae jjigae's racialized and gendered origins index the diversified ramifications of an unfinished, transnational war. Enduring and traversing borders, budae jjigae embodies militarized occupation and precarity, as well as improvised survival. Paradoxically, it has morphed into what some now describe as a delectable "East-West fusion dish" served at late-night dive bars, trendy restaurants, and homes across the United States and South Korea.

I open *Reencounters: On the Korean War and Diasporic Memory Critique* with a description of *BooDaeChiGae* because Yoo's work poignantly captures a juxtaposition of diffused consequences taken up in the pages that follow. Namely, by moving away from spectacular forms of militarized violence solely affixed to combat warfare, this book concerns itself with a more complex range of conditions characteristic of a suspended seventy-year conflict. This analytical shift from the extraordinary to the ordinary is crucial, given that the Korean War's extended life engenders diasporic repercussions that are integral rather than exceptional to daily life: while armed fighting on the peninsula was halted by a 1953 armistice, efforts to definitively end the war with a finalized peace treaty co-signed by North Korea, China, and the United Nations Command (led by the United States) never came to fruition.[4] Reflective, then, of the war's status as to-be-concluded, Yoo's *BooDaeChiGae* gestures to how the militarized origins of mundane objects, everyday relations, and social phenomena remain murky, if not unintelligible, to contemporary audiences. As expressed by Sarah Park on the online commentary board for *Still Present Pasts,* Yoo's installation performs a disturbing disjuncture between the habitual ways we casually perceive and consume everyday commodities and the devastating histories of violence, loss, and survival embodied by those very objects: "Among my Korean American friends, this dish is really popular because it is both easy to make and delicious. Until I saw this exhibit, I never realized how this dish is a symbol of the Korean War."[5] Attending to the sedimented consequences of the Korean War, this book examines how accumulated forms of racialized, gendered, and sexual violence are recodified, across space and time, into bureaucratic immigration policy, multigenerational familial relations, and profitable enterprises removed from the immediacy of warfare. As the visual artist and writer Sukjong Hong discusses in Chapter 2, the Korean War is no longer just a "bomber jet," but surfaces as the foods we consume, the spaces we inhabit, the immobilities that mark our lives, the personal histories we are unable to access, and the people we are forbidden to or cannot name.

To both track and trouble these muddled distinctions between "wartime" and "peacetime" (as Mary Dudziak might put it), this book pulls together an interdisciplinary archive of diasporic memory works, including oral history projects, time-based performances, and video installations that activate *reencounters* with the Korean War.[6] Here, reencounters as a concept captures how diasporic memory works catalyze moments of return and remembering that denaturalize naturalized temporalities, solidified presumptions, and historical knowledges. More specifically, diasporic memory works mediate epistemological openings by gesturing to radically different memories of survival, refusal, and resurgence that exceed Cold War historical narrations of the United States as the benevolent liberator of Korea. Indeed, in the twenty-first century, the Korean War's protracted entanglements are irrefutably linked to a globalized Cold War logic that banalizes the Korean conflict as an altruistic action that only U.S.-centered diplomacy can resolve. As we shall see, this naturalized telos and temporality of the Korean War—as a drawn-out "action" that, nevertheless, is slowly inching toward a conclusion punctuated by U.S. victory—assumes that militarized division is essential for rather than oppositional to American hegemony in the North Pacific. In response to this damaging logic, reencounters actuate subversive memories of recalcitrance and insurgency that discompose the Cold War façade of American benevolence.

These "othered" memories, then, pave the way for potential moments of accountability necessary for healing among affected subjects. In this context, healing is incommensurate with a curative stance solely dependent on a politics of (inter)national recuperation and definitive resolution. Rather, I argue that profound healing germinates when the subjects of war are able to explicitly name, work through, and account for a concatenation of violent consequences while reckoning with irretrievable losses that (inter)national politics can never fully rectify. While this process of "working through" is informed by confrontations with militarized colonial violence, it also provides the foundational means for what Dorinne Kondo describes as reparative creativity.[7]

Kondo begins with Melanie Klein's psychoanalytic focus on the individual subject's "depressive position," a stance that registers the graduated phases an infant must navigate to come to terms with the "real of separation" from the mother. Extending beyond the insulated realm of mother-child relationships, reparative creativity, writes Kondo, is a social process of "working through" that materializes through intentional acts of artistic imagination. Yet while these acts encompass difficult if not painful reckonings with structural inequities, they also catalyze healing among impacted subjects.[8] More precisely, Kondo argues that it is this arduous and fraught labor of "working through" that provides the groundwork for the reparative. In light of Kondo's astute observations, this book considers the multitude of ways in which healing commences when subjects, through re-memberings mediated vis-à-vis diasporic memory works, refuse *and* insist beyond the U.S. state's narrative concerning the Korean War. *Reencounters* therefore catalogues a resignification process insofar as cultural workers and transnational audiences are moved to reconsider what they are seeing, hearing, and touching. By facilitating these moments of uncertainty, even of unknowing, diasporic cultural works underscore the blatant contradictions of American liberalism while activating other mnemonic potentialities that exist in tension with and against the militarized "division system" in Korea.[9]

As detailed later in this Introduction, reencounters as a concept offers three core considerations that deepen existing studies of the Korean War in transnational American scholarship. First and foremost, this book moves away from generalizable trauma-based approaches that dominate much of Asian/American cultural studies on the Korean militarized conflict. While in dialogue with productive terms such as "intergenerational hauntings" and "postmemory," trauma-based framings, I argue, at times obscure the specific conditions of the ongoing Korean War. Second, while state-facilitated arbitrations for Korean peace are centered on the United States, genuine peace, security, and healing cannot be premised on the United States' continued presence in the peninsula, a provision demanded by the U.S. government to end the Korean War. Rather, by turning to the everyday as a vital terrain of mnemonic intervention and remembering otherwise, this book demonstrates the prominent role played by the United States as the chief architect of violence and insecurity in Korea and the North Pacific. Relatedly, as Lisa Yoneyama discusses in her work, I assert that Korean decolonization and true justice exceed the delimited realm of high-stakes (inter)national political negotiations overwhelmingly dominated by a small circle of patriarchal state actors.[10]

Third, by conversing with a rich genealogy of transnational American scholarship that addresses the machinery of U.S. militarized governance and colonial ambitions in Asia, this book draws on the cultural as a generative arena for political critique. The cultural, as Raymond Williams reminds us, cannot be reduced to "finished products and activities" indicative of isolated positions; nor is it shorthand for mimetic practices of poetics and representation.[11] On the contrary, the cultural is a vibrant politicized realm shaped by contemporary relations of power and social conditions, even while it encompasses a confluence of vestigial and emergent formations. In conversation with Williams's commentary, scholars such as Sarita See, Mimi Thi Nguyen, and Cathy Schlund-Vials insightfully mobilize cultural forms and practices to identify the collateral damage inflicted by U.S. intervention in the Philippines, Vietnam, and Cambodia, respectively.[12] See, for instance, deploys the concept of disarticulation to describe how Filipinx artists produce a "visual and rhetorical grammar" to eviscerate the logic of American militarized colonialism in the Philippines.[13]

Nuancing such an argumentation, this book examines how U.S. militarized occupation generates its own seeds of demise, so to speak, by paradoxically producing *diasporic excesses,* or non-normative subjectivities and spaces deemed expendable to the U.S. and South Korean national agendas. Diasporic excesses activate cultural practices of resistance and regeneration that refuse to be narrowly confined to the arena of militarized security and state-adjudicated justice. This book's diasporic memory works therefore do not merely attend to the violent foreclosures or impossibilities of U.S. militarized empire—a rhetorical move that tends to treat U.S. governance as a stable or homogeneous "thing" that is all encompassing and exacting in its formidable power. Instead, I underscore how political, cultural, and social alterities always already exist in relation to and alongside dominant forms of power, which resonates with Macarena Gómez-Barris's description of the smaller gestures or micro-spaces of resistance submerged within, against, and beyond (settler) colonial infrastructures.[14]

In part, the capacity of diasporic memory works to facilitate reencounters relies on their characteristics as *aesthetic mediations*. While this book's selection of diasporic memory works is quite eclectic in form, praxis, and medium, these cultural sources share an overarching set of qualities: they are multisensorial multimedia projects that crystallize through dissolving lines, cacophonous sounds, and divergent temporalities. Emerging more as experiential processes than as inanimate artifacts, diasporic memory works demonstrate how the aesthetic, or *aisthesis*, encompasses the expansive realm of the senses, embodiment, and perception.[15] My interdisciplinary use of this concept is informed not by the Kantian discourse of beauty or the disciplined bounds of art history, but by a much more capacious engagement that segues with Sylvia Wynter's theorization of cultural forms as "deciphering practices": through perceptual means, aesthetic mediations facilitate reapprehensions of surrounding phenomena and codified knowledges.[16] In this way, *Reencounters* underlines the disconnections between how war's structural elements are commonly perceived and the "bodily ontologies" that constitute their becoming in the world.[17] To be clear, my focus on the ontological does not oppose epistemological concerns. Instead, the ontological and epistemological are interrelated, since the former is accessible only through a preexisting matrix of organizing principles. After all, the ways in which subjects, phenomena, and histories are seen, touched, and encountered in the world—or the "traditional patterns of assigning meaning to that which appears to our senses"—rely on a prevailing nexus of power, knowledge, and meaning making.[18]

In conceptualizing diasporic memory works as aesthetic mediations that enable self-conscious reckonings with Cold War dominant history, I find Jill Bennett's articulation of *casus* a generative starting point to challenge the assumed links between perception and signification. I am drawn to Bennett's incisive commentary precisely because her expansive scholarship takes cues from varied (inter)disciplines—ranging from art history and critical theory to affect studies, visual culture studies, sociology, and performance studies—only to theorize *beyond* the discrete bounds of such knowledge regimes. In attending to aesthetics as the dynamics of form, Bennett draws on the casus, or "the case, happening, instance," as a methodological approach to examining a "concrete problem" through expressive culture.[19] Using an inductive process, Bennett insists that cultural works are characterized by their capacity to convey the "nature of experience and presumption," rather than their "subsuming experience" under a calcified theory "imported from the outside."[20] Cultural works as aesthetic mediations, then, "bring experience to bear" to produce "different material and immaterial ways of connecting."[21] At their most dynamic, aesthetic formations induce enlivened, if not confounding, encounters that unmoor normalized assumptions. Consequently, by treating these interactive moments as the driving engine for epistemological openings, Bennett insists that we are able to ask what "art and imagery *does*—what it *becomes*—in its very particular relationship to events."[22]

Yet Bennett refrains from equating aesthetics to a "single ideal of 'activist art'" or rendering cultural production as a serviceable action that fulfills an insular political objective.[23] On the contrary, aesthetic mediations are "points of orientation" because the focus of study is not the artworks per se but how they direct audiences toward a cascading of divergent memories and interpretations.[24] In this way, it is the activated space of encounter that foregrounds the contradictory elements of hegemonic discourse. To demonstrate this condition, I return to an earlier observation regarding Sarah Park's interaction with *BooDaeChiGae*. In her response to Yoo's video installation, Park's expressed memories are less about the nostalgic particularities of cooking army base stew than about the perceptual dissonance that surfaces as she reconciles the pleasurable experiences of eating budae jjigae with its links to warfare. By defamiliarizing the familiar, *BooDaeChiGae* intimates how popular narrations of war, including heroic depictions of American soldiers and liberal stories of multiracial love, are interlaced with discordant memories of continued military presence, peninsular division, racial and sexual violence, and fugitive survival. This montage of historical fragments foregrounds the incongruent memories and dissident elements that bleed into the here and now. Park's reencounter with army base stew resonates with Bennett's commentary by reflecting the multifaceted, multitemporal dynamisms at play within a cultural work: aesthetic mediations function less as a preserved record or flashback of a fossilized past than as an experiential means of reinhabiting a past that fuses into the present. In this way, reencounters do not necessarily "restore subjective experience to history" but "[generate] new ways of being in the event."[25]

Extending Bennett's consideration of aesthetics in relation to history, memory, and temporality, I underscore that reencounters do not merely destabilize the everyday through modes of rupture and deconstruction. What emerges in the wake of such unsettling moments instead are *alternative* iterations of historical time and political possibility that exist relationally with and against Cold War historiography. Here alterity refers less to wholly imagined pasts or futures untethered from the lifeworlds we inhabit than to how radically different renderings of the past(s) and present(s) already dwell within the embodied realm of lived experience. Such memories, however, remain illegible to the dominant language and framing logics of Cold War historiography. Diasporic memory works, therefore, draw our attention to contradictions and critical oppositional memories that trouble the Cold War temporalization and prolongation of the Korean War as a good and just project.

As Yoneyama, Jodi Kim, and Heonik Kwon remind us, the Cold War *should not* be treated as a congealed period that commenced with the end of World War II and culminated with the fall of the Berlin Wall in 1989.[26] Indeed, given the protraction of Korean division and the absence of peace treaties among Japan, Russia, and North Korea, the very suggestion that we live in a "post"–Cold War moment reflects what Yoneyama describes as a "geographical provincialism" associated with the Western Hemisphere.[27] Emerging instead as an assemblage of epistemes, nationalistic feelings, and geopolitical relations of power, the Cold War is a shape-shifting system of governance and knowledge production that situates the United States as the noble defender of global capitalist freedom, democracy, and autonomy. In a related sense, the Cold War positioning of the United States as an altruistic power is associated with a conceptualization of modern time that idealizes the U.S. state as a paternalistic anticolonial power devoted to rehabilitating "less developed" nations in desperate need of political tutelage.

Far from functioning as an abstraction removed from the grist of contemporary life, the liberal logic of Cold War American exceptionalism is deployed by the U.S. state to rationalize the devastating costs paid by civilians who must live alongside the U.S. military for their own "security" and "protection." Consequently, the United States' prolonged presence in sovereign spaces, including South Korea, naturalizes an incremental timeline in which American occupation is recoded as a transitive move necessary for the maturation of "developing" nations. Relatedly, American militarized excursions into sovereign territories provide necessary security for allies partnering with the United States against the global "War on Terror."[28] Through this circuitous reasoning, the entrenched Cold War discourse of American goodness and its implied matrix of positive effects and affects—or as Mimi Thi Nguyen describes it, the feelings of love, gratitude, and indebtedness associated with America's "gift of freedom" to the world—are used to further bolster the U.S. military's geopolitical investments in South Korea and elsewhere.[29]

While the U.S. state has stood by this lofty tale of altruism for the past seven decades, these imperatives are blatantly upended by contradictions that tell us otherwise. As Inderpal Grewal states, many within and beyond U.S. territorial borders criticize America's "legitimacy as a proponent of freedom and democracy given its history of wars and colonialism, [and] of being a racial settler state."[30] Certainly, in relation to Asia, glaring conflicts emerge as one barely scratches the surface of Cold War historical discourse. In Korea, the U.S. military's on-the-ground practices repudiate the state's justification of its presence on the peninsula to protect South Koreans against vicious attacks by the communist Democratic People's Republic of Korea (DPRK). The United States, in fact, indiscriminately perpetrates racial, sexual, and gender violence against Koreans under the guise of benevolence and protection. Manifestations appear when one knows where to look—for example, in the inequitable terms of the U.S.–South Korean Status of Forces Agreement (SOFA), which dictates the conditions of U.S. occupation; in the all-too-common incidences such as the 1992 murder of the military sex worker Yun Kumi by an American soldier; or in the evictions of farmers to allow for the construction of military bases. In each of these instances, it is imperative to inquire into the valence of meanings associated with "peace" and "security"—and more precisely, *whose* interests and safety are prioritized and protected and *who* or *what* is deemed expendable to American global securitization. As Chandan Reddy puts it, the United States' grandiose vision of Cold War security is built on and "with violence," since U.S. governance shares a symbiotic relationship with modes of racial and sexual brutality perpetrated against subjects deemed dispensable to U.S. geopolitical interests.³¹

In a conjunctive sense, I also point to how Cold War geopolitics has failed to produce an outcome long prophesized by the United States: North Korea's total collapse and its unequivocal absorption into a global capitalist infrastructure. Exemplified by the belabored history of triangulated negotiations between the two Koreas and the United States, as well as vociferous civilian protests against U.S. military interests, the thwarting of an idealized Cold War trajectory is underscored by feelings of exhaustive wariness, postponement, and déjà vu. To illustrate this chronicity, we might briefly sketch out the repeated cycle of diplomatic arbitrations among South Korea, North Korea, and the United States in the past twenty-five years. In 1991, the two Korean states signed an inter-Korean agreement on reconciliation and nonaggression; however, the agreement was undermined by U.S. concerns over the DPRK's nuclear arms program. In 2000, North Korean and South Korean leaders met during a historic inter-Korean summit to jointly sign an eight-point peace declaration that the Bush administration eventually rejected. In 2002 and under the banner of the global War on Terror, the U.S. government recognized North Korea as part of the "axis of evil," along with Iran and Iraq. More recently, the April 2018 meeting between DPRK leader Kim Jong-un and South Korea's President Moon Jae-in reaffirmed a two-state commitment to establishing peace on the peninsula, despite the Trump administration's constant threats against North Korea. In each of these instances, the United States has *deterred* rather than *facilitated* direct North Korean–South Korean negotiations for peace.

This chronic cycle of negotiations alternates between the threat of resuscitated armed conflict and peace, serving as a sobering reminder of the United States' tenacious hold on Korea. It also accentuates how Korean and Korean diasporic refusals discompose such hegemonic relations of power. That is, the inherent contradictions of Cold War telos and temporality, as sharply foregrounded by Korean and Korean diasporic critiques, demonstrate how the vital terrain of cultural and social life coheres as fertile ground to enact critical memory interventions. When we return, again and again, to a range of obscured subjectivities, militarized bodies, and occupied spaces with a renewed commitment to remembering otherwise, we receive opportunities to "sever any simple connection between seeing and revealing."³² Consequently, as points of *disorientation,* diasporic cultural works mediate, as Walter Benjamin might suggest, vexed memories that contravene Cold War political discourse's cemented portrayals of a foregone past and inevitable future.³³ Conjuring contradictory memories precluded from dominant historiography, this reinterpretation of the past as plural transforms one's orientation toward the future insofar as the present moment embodies a pressing sense of multiplicity that cannot be easily pacified. For Yoneyama, this dialectical approach to history, so characteristic of Benjamin's perceptions of historiography, "reclaims missed opportunities and unfilled promises in history" so that "historical knowledge [will] remain critically germane to present struggles for social change."[34] Just as *BooDaeChiGae* registers enduring histories that exceed how the Korean War is popularly scripted for an American public, this book is attuned to a curation of memories that provide complex portrayals of how diasporic subjects survive, live, and create beyond the devastating ruination of war. I argue that when it is performed enough, the Cold War's rhetoric of American exceptionalism—no matter how uniform, polished, or natural it may seem—reveals its own confused gaps that permit us to remember otherwise.[35]

Reencounters and Trauma-Based Frameworks

Throughout this book, I treat the Korean War's calamities less as exceptional aftereffects than as structuring conditions of contemporary life. This approach reflects how the systematization of accrued impacts, or what Lauren Berlant describes as crisis ordinariness, produces an arresting juxtaposition between explicit forms of militarized brutality and more muted expressions of violence that reflect the Korean War's paradoxical status as ever present *and* forgotten, as a political entanglement *and* an anticommunist victory, and as continuing *and* to be ended.[36] In other words, this book does not catalogue how subjects of war move on following the shock of a single event. Instead, *Reencounters* attests to the complicated ways in which the protracted Korean War contributes to the forging of social life in South Korea and North Korea, the United States, and other spaces. As Marisol de la Cadena states, to "speak conceptually" is to "speak *with* the empirical and at times, with what escapes the empirical."[37] Along the same vein, my conceptual use of reencounters gestures to how seemingly soft or mitigated forms of violence, including political economic conditions and social formations, are anchored in militarized histories that are difficult to initially diagnose or recognize.

Addressing the Korean War's effects through the prism of reencounters provides a key contribution to transnational American studies—and, in a narrower sense, to Korean War memory studies—by moving beyond a singular focus on trauma-related concepts such as intergenerational hauntings and postmemory. In choosing this approach, I do not intend to deny or obscure the irreparable harm produced by the Korean War across time and space. Reencounters as a concept, in fact, indexes the damaging consequences of a conflict that continues to affect millions of lives on and beyond the Korean

Peninsula. Rather, in suggesting this shift in foci, I underscore how trauma-based framings that foreground the psychic afterlife or "postmemory" of a catastrophic event do not fully capture the historical, social, and political complexities that characterize the contemporaneity of the Korean War.

To elaborate on this observation, I briefly refer to how trauma-based concepts are dominantly deployed within Korean War memory scholarship. As further unpacked in Chapters 2–4, cultural studies of the Korean War primarily address the conflict's repercussions as spectral traces that evade sociological instruments of ethnographic documentation (or hauntings) or as hidden imprints energetically inherited by younger generations (or postmemory).[38] For scholars, including Grace Cho, the ghostly ramifications of the Korean War do not simply reference missing or deceased bodies; they also register the "unexamined irregularities of everyday life."[39] More precisely, Cho's compelling use of hauntings accentuates how the fragmented remnants of imperialism and war, including the experiences of Korean "comfort women" and military sex workers, remain ever present in our daily orbits as invisible or barely discernible traces.[40] In another critical scholarly work, Daniel Kim draws on the concept of postmemory (which I expand on shortly) to track how the horrifying experiences of the Korean War are vicariously felt by second-generation Korean/American narrators. Due to their own temporal and geographical distance from the Korean armed conflict, these young narrators can "map" the war's lingering effects only through tentative acts of imagined approximation.[41] In effect, these distinct yet related concepts of hauntings and postmemory push against the oft-cited portrayal of the Korean War as "over" or "forgotten" by challenging the rational ordering of linear time into discrete epochs of past, present, and future.

In fruitful conversation with these key analyses, this book provides a different entry point to examining the Korean War's persisting effects and affects. Namely, I attend to durable repercussions that are readily seen, heard, and felt by different publics but are intuited or named as something else altogether. My focus, therefore, is not so much on the invisible or lingering remnants of war that exist beyond an ocular scope or the traumatic secrets vertically passed down from one generation to another. As Ruth Leys attests, generalizable descriptions of unresolved pain seamlessly transferred to younger generations reproduce ahistorical accounts that essentialize trauma as a "timeless entity with an intrinsic quality."[42] Instead, by foregrounding the messy vicissitudes of the Korean War, I investigate the morphing conditions and causal effects that continuously transfigure militarized subjects, spaces, and phenomena into seen yet illegible manifestations of war in the first place. As Judith Butler suggests, the question of recognizability, or how we comprehend things as they are, registers the "general terms, conventions and norms" that "prepare a subject for recognition."⁴³ Consequently, to be recognizable is not a self-evident or an a priori status but a position that is historically, socially, and politically constituted. A central point of this book, then, is to scrutinize how the by-products of war are alchemically transfigured through the bureaucratic language and beautifying practices of contemporary governance and political subjectivity.

Chapters 1 and 2, for instance, discuss how post-1950 Korean militarized migrations are repackaged into successful U.S. immigration histories, while Chapter 3 addresses how the Korean War's racialized gendered subjects, including transnational adoptees, are reclaimed by the South Korean state as welcomed "returnees" and vibrant contributors to the country's economy. Chapter 4 considers how militarized colonial outposts such as Jeju Island are recalibrated into desirable tourist destinations, and the book's concluding chapter problematizes the ways in which North Korea is portrayed as both an abstracted sign of communist evil *and* a popular object of comedic relief gleefully consumed by Americans. These discussions elucidate the structural processes that sublimate the Korean War's manifestations into commonplace knowledges, desired commodities, and economic returns, and these chapters deploy a range of diasporic memories to contest such logics.⁴⁴ In prioritizing legibility and recognition rather than visibility and invisibility, *Reencounters* wrestles with a profound question posed by Simone Browne in reference to the nature of war, racial and sexual violence, and neoliberal surveillance in the twenty-first century: "Is [something] really invisible or is it rather unseen and unperceived by many?"⁴⁵

Located within a broader discursive context, the prevalence of trauma in Korean War memory studies reflects the significant impact of European Holocaust studies in the United States since the late twentieth century.⁴⁶ In this lineage of scholarship, which includes interdisciplinary works by Giorgio Agamben, Cathy Caruth, Shoshana Felman and Dori Laub, Marianne Hirsch, and Primo Levi (to name a few), the Holocaust is explicitly identified or intimated as the paradigmatic experience of catastrophe in the modern era.⁴⁷ Consequently, these works situate the difficult work of remembering, or memory work, within the context of the Holocaust. For instance, Hirsch uses the medium of photography and the family album to relay the belated quality of trauma as it relates to the Holocaust. As Hirsch explains, the circulation of Holocaust family photographs as "trace" or "fetish" signify how these visual objects paradoxically embody elements of life and death.⁴⁸ Here she draws on Roland Barthes's description of the photograph as a "carnal medium" that serves as a material connection to a loved one who has passed—and, more specifically, the portrayal of a disappeared family member in a domestic setting far removed from the Nazi concentration camp. Hirsch portrays the

Holocaust family photograph as a document that "capture[s] that which no longer exists," as well as "the desire and the necessity, and at the same time, the difficulty, the impossibility, of mourning."[49]

In part, this perceived difference between what is depicted in the photograph as a relic of the past (a portrait of a loved one) and what the photograph signifies in the here and now (the annihilation of that very person) is conditioned by the temporal distance that marks the entwined acts of looking and remembering. Coining the term "postmemory" to signify such a process, Hirsch underscores how this concept "characterizes the experience of those who grow up dominated by narratives that preceded their births" and "whose own belated stories are evacuated by the stories of the previous generation shaped by traumatic events that can be neither understood nor recreated."[50] Put differently, postmemory captures the deferred quality of a past trauma that is psychically passed onto and vicariously felt by younger subjects. These younger generations therefore bear the ethical brunt of parsing through a traumatic collection of disruptive memories, or mnemonic "leftovers," that preceded their own births and consciousness.

In the past twenty years, Hirsch's conceptualization has been taken up by scholars concerned with conflicts beyond the Holocaust, including the Korean War. Such interdisciplinary leaps attest to the important insights that postmemory offers. Yet I suggest that applying postmemory from one historical and disciplinary context to another ineluctably produces discursive gaps that obfuscate the particularities of the Korean conflict in at least two crucial ways. First and foremost, the Korean War is *not* a hidden afterlife that dwells in the contemporary moment solely through psychic and emotional traces. The Korean War remains a tinderbox with life-threatening implications, as clearly demonstrated by the Trump administration's renewed threat of nuclear warfare in 2017 and 2018, and preceded more specifically by Donald Trump's assertion that the United States would "totally destroy" North Korea if tested or pushed.[51] While it is true that younger Koreans did not directly experience the armed conflict waged between 1950 and 1953, trauma-based frameworks assume that it is primarily the psychic and emotional traces of a "past" violence that gnaw at the seams of daily life. In contrast, I explore the radically different and divergent relations that multigenerational Korean and Korean diasporic subjects share with the unfinished war, which *cannot and should not* be limited to the period between 1950 and 1953. Refraining from describing the Korean War as an event that can be accessed or "known" only through its invisible residues, I examine diverse manifestations that congeal as political, social, and affective formations seemingly removed from the context of war.

Second, by exploring how the Korean War inhabits and habituates the everyday, *Reencounters* contends with how war functions as a normative element rather than a disruptive force of neoliberal life. Certainly, this observation is not unique to the Korean War but intimates the state of permanent war in which the world finds itself, albeit with uneven implications for differently racialized populations. For Catherine Lutz, militarization in the United States, or the "contradictory and tense social processes in which civil society organizes itself for the production of violence," entails more than the allocation of resources toward brute violence.[52] As an administrative process, it also encompasses the most bureaucratic of tasks, spanning from the crafting of sizable defense budgets and the hammering out of national policy agendas to the robust build-out of public health, educational, and economic infrastructures, which consolidate the territorial interests and political stakes of the United States. In fact, the U.S. military-industrial complex commenced with the beginnings of the Korean War and expanded during America's intensive involvement in Southeast Asia from the 1950s to the 1970s.[53] In the twenty-first century, warmongering and war making in all of its variable forms are complicit with the formulation of political and economic affairs, ranging from resource extraction, land speculation, and tourist industries to corporate production, commodity consumption, and the technocratic logistics of circulating goods across the globe.[54] Because war is so thoroughly "threaded through the fabric of contemporary life," the effects of militarized intervention, occupation, and conflict are seemingly "everywhere and nowhere at all."[55]

This book thus foregrounds the destructive ways in which the *longue durée* of the Korean War embeds itself within the "non-militarized" systems of international migrations, political partnerships, and national economies. In particular, by underscoring the collapse between militarized and civilian life, *Reencounters* recounts the tragedy of the Korean War less as a cataclysmic trauma that breaks from the status quo of American (inter)national policy than as a damaging node within a much longer trajectory of governance that traces back to the U.S. state's duplicitous role as both adjudicator of formal justice *and* propagator of violence. Given this context, I posit that trauma-based concepts inadequately account for U.S. militarized empire and its continual enactments that exceed the normative temporal delineations around the Korean War.

Cold War Historical Discourse and Critical Revisionisms

Before elaborating on my selection of cultural memory works through the feminist analytic of the diasporic, I would like to sketch out the dynamisms of knowledge production underpinning Cold War and Korean War memory scholarship in the past thirty-five years. To clarify, this overview does not comprehensively survey Korean War memory studies in the United States. Instead, it situates this book's diasporic memory archive within a transnational and interdisciplinary field of intellectual, activist, and cultural production that challenges the core tenets of Cold War political discourse and historical narration. In particular, it elaborates on the logic of militarized security and peace as it relates to the United States' intervention in and occupation of Korea.

As astutely observed by Christine Hong, the Korean War is remembered in the United States through a Cold War historical lens.[56] In short, this narratology recognizes the Korean War as a necessary "police action" taken by a benevolent U.S. military to safeguard the freedom, self-determination, and liberty of the Korean people against the evils of communism.[57] During the past seven decades, popular media has reified and reproduced these perceptions in productions such as American television shows (*The Big Picture, M*A*S*H*), a bevy of studio-produced films (*Battle Hymn* [1957]; *War Hunt* [1962]; *The Manchurian Candidate* [1962]; *Inchon* [1982]), and dozens of comic book series.[58] The Korean War Veterans Memorial in Washington, DC, however, may best exemplify these sentiments. Opened to the public in July 1995 and located on the far western edge of the National Mall, the memorial includes nineteen stainless steel statues of male soldiers; a mural wall consisting of black granite panels with more than 2,400 overlaid photographs of Army, Navy, Marine Corps, Air Force, and Coast Guard personnel; and a small pool hugged by a semicircular wall inscribed with the phrase "Freedom Is Not Free."

Other inscriptions include one stating that America's "sons and daughters" were sent to Korea to "defend a country they never knew and a people they never met." Justified by a diligent desire to remember—or, more precisely, to *not* forget—the Washington, DC, memorial suggests that the clichéd discourse of the Korean War as forgotten is not so much about the absolute erasure of the conflict from public culture and memory. Instead, the incessant desire to selectively remember indexes the instrumentalized ways in which the contentious discourse of the Korean War as forgotten reconstitutes itself as a recuperative mode of remembering. This mode of remembering, then, atones for and reclaims American soldiers as heroic subjects worthy of National Remembering. Thus, for the American public, remembering the Korean War links to the sacrifices made by American soldiers on the behalf of a weaker nation unable to protect itself against the horrors and violence of communism.

Yet, as Hong puts it, two competing historical framings since the 1980s have challenged the sanctity of this Cold War discourse: (1) the emergence of critical revisionist accounts during the 1980s, which reexamine the complex

A view of the Korean War Veterans Memorial in Washington, DC, July 2016. (Photograph by the author.)

origins of the Korean War in relation to U.S. global ambitions, and (2) the testimonial turn of the 1990s, which centers on the eclipsed experiences of Korean civilians who survived the armed conflict and continue to live with the precarious consequences of U.S. military occupation. These overarching perspectives, of course, are not catchall categories belonging to a logical telos; nor do they supplant preceding interpretations, as attested to by the Cold War's tenacity in the contemporary moment. Instead, these alternative framings reengage the dialectics of knowledge production in relation to the Korean War and accentuate the social and political factors that led to the diversification of war memories since the 1980s.

In particular, while Cold War historiography narrates the Korean War as a Manichaean struggle between the good (the United States and the West) and the evil (the Soviet Union, China, and North Korea), the sweeping social movements and critical revisionist scholarship of the 1980s in Korea and Asia destabilized this dominant narration by questioning the implied asymmetrical power conditions between South Korea and the United States. In South Korea, the 1980s was a crucial decade of political activism and radical knowledge production that called for systemic changes within state governance and society as a whole. Galvanized by the South Korean military state's massacre of up to two thousand civilians in the Gwangju Uprising of May 1980, civilians organized a popular democratic uprising, the *Minjung*

(People's) movement, which agitated for the end of dictatorial rule and the ousting of the American military presence from the country. As Namhee Lee observes, the Minjung movement encompassed an intellectual dimension by reevaluating the normative logics of the state, including South Korea's beneficiary relationship with the United States, the privileging of economic development over distributive justice, and the statist anticommunist justifications leading to national division.[59] Eventually culminating in the first open presidential elections (1987) held in South Korea in nearly three decades, the procedural democratization of the country dovetailed with multiple calls by nongovernmental organizations, intellectuals, and activists to reassess unresolved matters related to Japan's colonial rule in Korea (1910–1945), including the unsettled plight of Korean "comfort women" forced into military sexual servitude by the Japanese Imperial Army during the Asia-Pacific War (1931–1945).[60]

In his groundbreaking U.S.-based scholarship published in 1981, Bruce Cumings also explores the multiple beginnings of the Korean War and the political stakes associated with the United States' military security presence in Korea.[61] Cumings argues that the long-standing history of American military occupation of Korea is anything but liberating or benevolent: motivated by the desire for global economic and political power through the brutal containment of communism, the U.S. Army Military Government in Korea (USAMGIK [1945–1948]) preserved rather than dismantled integral components of Japanese colonial rule in Korea, ranging from the centralized modes of governance and social organization (e.g., the family registration system) to a preexisting military sex economy.[62] Furthermore, Cumings gestures to the Cold War complicity of U.S. occupation and Japanese rule, or what Naoki Sakai and Keith Camacho and Setsu Shigematsu refer to as the "trans-Pacific arrangement" between the United States and Japan. The two countries collude through their competing *and* collaborative visions of militarized conquest, the mutual disavowal of colonial violence, and the forging of a neoliberal economy characterized by an imbalance of power relations among different nation-states.[63]

Spurred by this vital ground of social mobilization and engaged scholarship, the 1990s and early 2000s witnessed a burgeoning of divergent worldviews and historical narratives that further challenged the dictating bounds of Cold War knowledge production. These changes not only placed pressure on the prevailing presumptions of existing war historiography in South Korea and the United States. They also produced, as Yoneyama articulates, oppositional knowledges, activist practices, and memories that destabilized the foundational tenets of transitional justice formulated by international juridical establishments, including the United Nations, after World War II.[64]

Inspired by the intellectual work of the social historian Dong-choon Kim and the investigatory research conducted by the South Korean Truth and Reconciliation Commission (2003–2008), a decentralized web of personal memories, political investigations, and oral history projects centering on the experiences of Korean civilians, as well as public reports exposing U.S.–South Korean joint military atrocities, surfaced in Korea, Japan, and the United States.[65]

Within the transnational political sphere, these formal processes segued with the momentous, albeit temporary, thawing of inter-Korean diplomatic relationships at the turn of the twenty-first century. Encapsulated as part of South Korean President Kim Dae-jung's "Sunshine Policy," the revitalization of South Korean–North Korean relations during the early 2000s culminated in the first inter-Korean meeting in nearly forty years and the subsequent signing of the June 15 North-South Joint Declaration. In this declaration, the leaders of the South Korean and North Korean states (Kim Dae-jung and Kim Jong-il, respectively) agreed to "resolve the question of reunification independently" through the collaborative "efforts of the Korean people, who are the masters of the country."[66] Insinuated as a rebuking of U.S.-Soviet intervention on the peninsula, the declaration paved the way for more than two hundred inter-Korean family reunions coordinated by the North and South regimes in August 2000, half of which were held in Seoul and the other half in Pyongyang.[67] More recently, Moon Jae-in and Kim Jong-un, the leaders of South Korea and North Korea, respectively, met in April 2018 without the presence of a U.S. representative to pave a diplomatic pathway toward ending the Korean War. As discussed in Chapters 1 and 2 regarding Korean diasporic oral history projects that surfaced at the wake of the 2000 reunions, I refrain from designating these diversified accounts of the Korean War as "intact," "raw," or "objectively truthful" mnemonic records removed from political, social, and cultural contexts. Memories, after all, are always already mediated processes that reflect the conditions of a historical moment. Yet the multiplication of pluralistic memories of the Korean War in the late twentieth century and early twenty-first century undoubtedly exposes the political stakes associated with the maintenance and manufacturing of Cold War political discourse in the United States and South Korea.

While Hong refers to this last discursive shift as the testimonial turn, Yoneyama addresses the changes as part of the "post-redress moment."[68] Invoking the formal redress protocols pursued by the United States and the United Nations after 1945, Yoneyama is keen on addressing the unfinished business left in the wake of such formal arbitration processes, especially as the U.S. state's legislative, juridical, and political channels amplified the inequities it sought to reconcile and resolve. For example, the United Nations as an international institution historically has worked to protect and expand a global capitalist economic infrastructure and (neo)liberal modes of governance.[69] In the case of Korea, American and UN policies of intervention not only contained the spread of communism; they also knowingly suspended internal decolonization efforts spearheaded by leftist grassroots organizations, such as the Committee for Preparation of Korean Independence, set into motion at least a month before the U.S. military's arrival on the peninsula in September 1945.[70]

In light of these restitutive measures promulgated under the Cold War international regime, Yoneyama insists that scholars and activists alike must reevaluate the very meaning of true justice in opposition to the post–World War II's international nexus of governing rules and formal adjudicating processes. True justice, in other words, remains beyond the "force of law" in the Derridean sense, or outside of the extant system of juridical and legislative measures conceived by Cold War international institutions such as the United Nations and the U.S. nation-state.[71] Reassessing the relationship between the sovereign state and justice, Yoneyama reiterates that (inter)national modes of formal governance are unable to accommodate the unsettled grievances of transnational conflicts. They are unable to do so because the diasporic subjects of war are *transborder* figures who embody "insurgent memories, counter-knowledges, and inauthentic identities" antagonistic to "hegemonic post–World War II/Cold War epistemic and material formations."[72]

The remainder of this Introduction draws on Hong's and Yoneyama's crucial observations to parse out the diasporic underpinnings of this book's archive of cultural memory works. Foregrounding the linkages that bind the diasporic to the question of true justice, I consider how this book's memory works contend with the present- and future-oriented project(s) of Korean decolonization *beyond* the finite sphere of (inter)national state politics.

The Diasporic as Feminist Analytic

While this contextualization of political, historical, and scholarly discourse on the Korean War is incomplete, I use these genealogies of interdisciplinary scholarship and transnational activism to identify the key factors driving the emanation of diasporic memory works. This book's memory sources are eclectic in medium and format and signal the materialization of a Korean diasporic nexus across Korea, Jeju Island, Scandinavia, North America, and the Internet. They defy easy placement within any single national context, discipline, or aesthetic lineage. Yet as versatile cultural formations that emerged during a relatively condensed span of time (from 2001 until 2016), these mnemonic mediations are marked by the aforementioned shifts that gained traction between the 1980s and early 2000s. Consequently, as disconnected as they may appear to be, the memory works discussed here reflect the organic culmination, circulation, and sharing of critiques in relation to Cold War political discourse among diasporic cultural practitioners, intellectuals, and activists. Although my analysis attends to aesthetic practices located in particular social and cultural spaces, I underscore how theorization across media, sensorial platforms, and national spaces is necessary because the effects of war, militarization, and division are multimedial, multisensorial, and transnational.

In pulling together an interdisciplinary assemblage of cultural works rarely discussed in transnational American studies, this book's memory archive departs from existing scholarship on the Korean War, which tends to focus on literary sources and, to a lesser degree, filmic productions. In part, this shift in focus resonates with two crucial observations articulated by Sarita See: (1) the canonization of literary texts as the dominant site of cultural analysis among Asian/Americanists (although this is certainly changing); and (2) the presumption that cultural productions are "finished product[s]" removed from the "artistic communities and cultural moment from whence [they] came."[73] Thus, in deploying a methodological approach that highlights the "dialectical relationship between artists, texts and context" and through the selective curation of aesthetic mediations that belong to no one field, this book rubs against what might be described as the professionalized "disciplining" of Asian/American studies as a coherent field of study.[74] In part, to think and write through an interdisciplinary lens, as Laura Hyun Yi Kang reminds us, is defined not by the act of engaging or reading across multiple disciplines but by critically analyzing the "internalized rules and norms" that dictate the properness of a disciplinary object (what counts as a "real" oral history, performance or documentary project?).[75] Thus, while each chapter focuses on a particular cultural medium, my interdisciplinary engagement with diasporic memory works simultaneously perturbs the sustaining logics that reproduce disciplinary (and disciplined) work. This mode of research and writing resonates with the overarching goals of this project, given that the diasporic racialized and gendered subjects discussed resist the nationalistic "disciplining" of the U.S. and South Korean states. Centering the concept of reencounters as the primary concept of this book, I simultaneously consider the mnemonic potentialities associated with diasporic cultural works that are open-ended processes rather than closed objects. Given my intentional focus on how heterogeneous memories of war actualize a present- and future-oriented politics committed to true justice, this last point is especially integral to the composition of this book.

Exploring the precipitation of reencounters across a transnational geography, I conceptualize this book's memory sources as diasporic mediations that track the continuities and breaks of the Korean War's politicized terrain. Here my use of the diasporic stresses the nation-state's incapacity to fully account for the diffused consequences of the Korean War. In contrast to more traditional meanings associated with diaspora, such as the expulsion of a homogeneous ethnic people from an ancestral homeland, I deploy the diasporic as a feminist mode of analysis.[76] Drawing from women of color feminism and queer diasporic scholarship to conceptualize the diasporic, I attend especially to the pivotal role played by *relational differences* in the coalescing of social affinities and epistemes at odds with the heteronormative logics of the nation-state. That is, this book explores how transborder subjects and spaces marked by racial, gendered, and sexual difference are related through and because of the Korean War. As Grace Kyungwon Hong cogently argues, a women of color critique does not consolidate a naturalized sense of "essence"; nor is it a universal category that unifies all subjects perceived as "women of color."[77] Rather, by drawing on women of color feminism as a critical "reading practice," Hong engages the creative oeuvre of writers such as Cherríe Moraga and Audre Lorde to foreground the non-analogous yet interconnected ways in which varied subjects are racialized, gendered, and sexualized in proximity to one another within the hierarchal context of national citizenship.

To demonstrate the centrality of relational differences in the theorization of women of color critique, Hong deploys a close reading of an essayistic work by Moraga to flesh out a set of interlinked experiences that take place within the confines of a subway train.[78] While commuting on Boston's T line, Moraga witnesses the arrest of a young black man by a white police officer. She notes that the "day before, a 14-year-old Black boy was shot in the head by a white cop." Self-identifying as a Chicana lesbian who passes in her "white flesh" and "gold highlights," Moraga observes that "there are some women in this town plotting a *lesbian* revolution. What does this mean about the boy shot in the head is what I want to know."[79] For Hong, Moraga's lucid commentary illuminates how bodies contained within the train's interior are positioned differently in relation to "white domesticity, police brutality, and segregation." But through these differences, Moraga and the young black man are indelibly connected "by virtue of these relationships."[80] Deviating from the idealized American citizen defined as white, heterosexual, and male, the black rider's and Moraga's minoritized subjectivities demonstrate the profound ways in which the U.S. state emerges as the principal enforcer of violence rather than as a neutral arbiter of justice. Observing that Moraga's commentary "secures an understanding that different racial and gender formations are not produced in isolation, but relationally," Hong refuses to glorify "women of color" as the "purest, most revolutionary position."[81] Instead, as an intersectional mode of analysis, a women of color feminist framing contends with how race, gender, sexuality, class, and ableism function as interlocking vectors that are "mutually constitutive."[82]

Attentive to how different subjects occupy varied yet interlinked positions, women of color feminism identifies the paradoxical ways in which such bodies cannot be wholly disciplined or managed by the nation-state. Indeed, in the state's attempt to determine and police the borders of proper subjectivity, such regulations ironically produce non-normative formations or "deviant" socialities that surface as potential sites of struggle and alterity. Here women of color feminism's accentuation of coalition through difference and the radical possibilities generated by structures of power dovetail with feminist articulations of the diasporic. Fatima El-Tayeb describes how the diasporic registers a shifting populace, where transnational subjects are linked by a "contemporary condition" rather than a shared ancestry or common set of ethnocentric, physiological, and biological characteristics.[83] Instead of delimiting diaspora to state identitarian apparatuses—for example, legal citizenship and blood quantum—El-Tayeb calls on the diasporic to examine how non-normative racialized, gendered, and sexualized contingencies exist in tension with and in excess to state-sanctioned forms of recognizable personhood. More precisely, the diasporic encompasses strategies of disidentification that permit minoritarian subjects to survive and negotiate "a phobic majoritarian public sphere that elides or punishes the existence of subjects who do not conform to the phantasm of normative citizenship."[84] In this way, queer diaspora encompasses critiques that "[work] on and against dominant ideology" and cut through state-legislated categories of legal and legible identity.[85]

In generative conversation with women of color feminism and queer diaspora, I use the diasporic as a working analytic to track how the Korean War produces openings that puncture the normalized project of American militarized security in the North Pacific. Accentuating the long-term implications of the Korean War on and beyond the peninsula, this book explores how diasporic subjects occupy antagonistic positionalities in relation to and against the dominant politics and national cultures of the United States and South Korea. Marked, for instance, as racially, sexually, and politically deviant by the state, minoritarian subjects such as the biracial children of U.S. soldiers and Korean women, leftist rebels, or North Korean loyalists exist along the edge of normative citizenries insofar as their integration into the polity is only partially complete or altogether impossible. Yet by registering a dangerous sense of unknowability, illegibility, and incompleteness, a diasporic approach conveys two possibilities. First, the Korean War's production of non-normative bodies and categories generates *diasporic excesses,* or recalcitrant formations that refuse to be easily deciphered or tamed by the nation-state. In turn, these unruly diasporic elements, resulting from resistant "actions arising from concrete, structured conditions within and across defined locales," hint at the unstable footing of American militarized presence in Korea.[86] Second, by focusing on the synergetic sharing of a contemporary condition rather than the scattering of a homogeneous people from a romanticized homeland, the diasporic facilitates heterogeneous lines of affinity forged through, rather than in spite of, difference. This shift from (ethnic, national, and biological) sameness to critical difference, I argue, expands how we might conceptualize solidarity efforts against U.S. militarized investments in Korea.

In engaging memory works through a diasporic feminist lens, I approach the question of true justice—and more precisely, the question of Korean decolonization—in proximity to but also beyond the finite goals of national reconciliation, reunification, and autonomy. National reconciliation is absolutely crucial to addressing the most pressing concerns emanating from division, including family separations. But peace efforts that depend solely on the nation-state as the privileged mediator of true justice inadvertently amplify, rather than resolve, conditions of hegemonic violence. On the international stage, government representatives have long anchored peace negotiations on essentialized descriptors of proper "Korean-ness," including pure blood, cultural homogeneity, and shared ethnic attributes. As a result, the heteropatriarchal logics of national belonging are unquestionably upheld as normative values through which formal peace and justice are formulated and imagined. In the Panmunjom Declaration signed by North Korean and South Korean leaders in April 2018, for instance, national politicians emphasize the "blood relations of the [Korean] people" and the forging of a prosperous future reflective of the "whole [Korean] nation." Who, exactly, is recognized as part of the Korean "whole nation," and, conversely, which racialized and gendered subjects and grievances are always precluded from or perceived as irrelevant to such a discourse?

In a related sense, the United States treats the prospect of peace in Korea as a national security measure, with the U.S. government aiming to broker the skewed conditions for national reunification and militarized peace. As a means to ensure American hegemony in northeastern Asia, the U.S. government affixes formal peace in Korea to the total denuclearization of North Korea paired with the indefinite maintenance of U.S. military forces on the peninsula.[87] More blatantly, Korean decolonization is associated with the demise of the communist North Korean state regime and its successful integration into a neoliberal economic infrastructure, as observed in a 2014 statement delivered jointly by President Park Geun-hye of South Korea and President Barack Obama of the United States.[88] Within these well-defined,

U.S.-determined parameters, the multiple colonial origins of the Korean War remain unaddressed. At the same time, urgent questions related to the racialized and gendered differences of Korea and the Korean diaspora are relegated to the periphery, if they are acknowledged at all. By conflating genuine peace, true justice, and decolonization with national autonomy, American hegemony, and capitalism, we risk reproducing uneven power relations while reembracing monolithic renderings of Korean ethnocentric identity.

With these insights in mind, *Reencounters* is oriented around a different task: to move our focus from questions such as, "Who is the authentic Korean national subject?" or "How can we achieve American-approved reconciliation?" to self-reflexive practices, interdisciplinary methods, and cultural mediations capable of apprehending the making (and unmaking) of Korean diasporic militarized subjects and spaces. This reorientation depends on a more capacious definition of decolonization that confronts Korea's division system through a robust critique of its multiple colonial histories, including Japanese and U.S. imperialisms. Rather than aligning the term with the Westphalian logics of the modern state or post-1950 national independence movements mobilized against European imperial powers, this book approaches decolonization as a multiprong process that breaks down militarized colonial structures—social, epistemological, and psychic—while moving toward the actualization of true justice.[89] In the case of Korean decolonization, true justice points to a juxtaposition of conjunctive moves, including the unequivocal nullification of American hostilities toward North Korea, the removal of U.S. armed forces from northeastern Asia, reconciliation as determined by affected subjects, and the implementation of accountability measures necessary for deep healing. But, as considered in subsequent chapters, Korean decolonization is an extraordinarily volatile process that does not follow a progressive trajectory or gravitate toward an idyllic and preserved past. Instead, as an ebb and flow of converging efforts that exceed (inter)national state negotiations, decolonization embodies an extensive range of political, social, and cultural efforts that takes seriously the racialized, gendered, and sexualized effects of militarized colonial violence beyond the ethnocentric Korean "homeland." This reconceptualization of decolonization, I argue, is crucial to reencountering the Korean War's toxic effects across a transborder geography of diasporic bodies and sites.

Organization of the Book

The main body of this book is organized into four numbered chapters, followed by a concluding experimental essay. Chapter 1 provides a historical backdrop of the United States' militarized occupation of Korea to better track the heterogeneous implications of an unfinished war. Chapters 2, 3, and 4 each focus on a specific diasporic memory analytic or memory practice that facilitates reencounters with the Korean War. Encompassing a geography that consists of the United States (Chapters 1–2), Korea (Chapter 3) and Jeju Island and the transpacific (Chapter 4), this radiating spatiality reflects how the Korean War's ramifications, as well as strategies of remembering and resistance, should not and cannot be limited to the scale of the national. Although each chapter attends to a distinct geographical site, these identified locales are not insular or isolated. On the contrary, I examine how they operate as part of a transnational network of spaces linked through the geopolitical conditions of Korean division, American militarized occupation, and multiple colonialisms.

In Chapter 1, "Militarized Migrations," I consider the drawn-out implications of Cold War politics by examining the diasporic formation of a Korean militarized presence in the United States. Using legislative measures and oral histories as primary memory sources, the chapter provides a nuanced contextualization of the Korean War in relation to the Cold War narration of American benevolence and the apparatuses facilitating Korean migration following the 1953 armistice. As Ji-Yeon Yuh states, the Korean War's status in the United States is peculiar in the sense that Korean diasporic subjects are rarely defined as refugees escaping from the horrific ravages of war.[90] Instead, they are folded into a chronological timeline marked by displacement, resettlement, and successful integration into a national polity. Subsequently, Cold War historiography recognizes Korean diasporic subjects as hardworking *immigrants* pushed and pulled into the United States by the allure of abundant economic, educational, and professional opportunities.

In approximating the intersections of the Korean War, Cold War historiography, and Americanized political subjectivity, this book engages in productive dialogue with war and memory scholarship in Southeast Asian diasporic studies. In particular, I interrogate how Korean diasporic subjects are legislated through categories of political subjecthood disassociated from all traces of militarization.[91] As recounted in works by Yen Le Espiritu, Cathy Schlund-Vials, Mimi Thi Nguyen, and Ma Vang, the official categories of resettlement and refugee status are reserved for diasporic subjects "resuscitated" and "rescued" by the U.S. military from American-initiated wars in Vietnam, Cambodia, and Laos. In return, these "freed" diasporic subjects are bound to an indefinite cycle of costs determined by the U.S. state. Conversing with these pivotal insights, *Reencounters* addresses the regenerative life-forms of militarized conflict through the lens of the Korean War. It does so by attending to Korea's protracted militarized division, the temporal chasm that seemingly separates contemporary subjects from the conflict, and the striking ways in which Koreans are rarely recognized as refugees within dominant U.S. immigration discourses. Chapter 1 therefore reconceptualizes the everyday immigration of Korean diasporic subjects into a mode of *militarized migration*.

By identifying the connective tissue that sutures the Cold War to Korean diasporic trajectories after 1953, Chapter 1 also exemplifies how Cold War temporality is always already gendered to the degree that the chronological ordering of time segues with heteronormative expectations. In different ways, each of the following chapters indicates how this intersection of linearity, inevitability, and heteronormativity is essential to the consolidation of Cold War historical discourse. Chapters 1 and 3 examine how the U.S. and South Korean states seek to resolve the violent displacements of the Korean War by incorporating militarized migrants into nuclear heterosexual families or national citizenries. Chapters 2 and 4 indicate how memory and mourning practices are tacitly governed by social norms pertaining to proper masculinity and the patriarchal family unit in the United States and on Jeju Island. Thus, I draw on the critical work of Elizabeth Freeman to contextualize how linear time dovetails with heteronormative expectations to produce what might be conceived of as *Cold War chrononormativity*.[92]

While Chapter 1 introduces readers to how the Korean War's violent displacements are repackaged into sound bites of altruistic American intervention, Chapter 2, "Aurality," offers a direct counterpoint by reconsidering how diasporic memories reencounter and destabilize such dominant configurations. Drawing on the Intergenerational Korean American Oral History Project as an incubator for reencounters with the war, I examine how a cohort of Korean/Americans contend with the militarized repercussions of war, separation, and division within their families and beyond. An openended repertoire of multilayered facilitations rather than a closed repository of testimonies, the Intergenerational Korean American Oral History Project deploys practices of attentive listening to mediate two related tensions. On the one hand, the project challenges the Cold War schematics of power and representation that recognize the hypermasculine white American soldier as the heroic liberator of destitute Koreans. On the other hand, the project challenges two dominant tropes integral to existing Korean War postmemory scholarship: traumatic silence and intergenerational familial kinship. By troubling the commonplace rendering of these tropes through the co-production of different *and* shared knowledges, aural history reencounters cultivate diasporic lines of resistance and solidarity that exceed the ethnocentric confines of the nuclear family and nation-state.

While Chapters 1 and 2 examine the deracinated relocations of Korean diasporic subjects in the United States, Chapters 3 and 4 shift gears by examining a reversal of migratory movements. Chapters 3 and 4 explore the ways that diasporic subjects initiate literal and imagined reroutings to Korea to contend with America's prolonged militarized investments in northeastern Asia. Chapter 3, "Returns," expands on the previous chapter's discussion of non-normative genealogies and alternative social kinships by engaging katehers RHEE's documented performance *Sex Education for Finding Face in the 21st Century* (2002) and Jane Jin Kaisen's experimental film *The Woman, the Orphan, and the Tiger* (2010). Tracking the Korean War's manufacturing of adoptee subjectivities across Asia, the United States, and Western Europe, these diasporic memory productions employ the double entendre "returns" in two related ways. First, returns indicates a rerouting of sorts as Korean transnational adoptees raised in North America and Europe find themselves back in and reencountering South Korea. Second, as "excesses" removed from the South Korean populace, adoptee returns to Korea generate unforeseeable repercussions that register the triangulated relations among American humanitarian intervention in Korea, the transnational adoption industry, and the South Korean project of nation building. Thus, while RHEE's and Kaisen's works offer devastating commentaries on the precarious costs of the Korean War, these artists demonstrate how adoptee returns actualize resistance strategies that contend with the Cold War benefactor-beneficiary alliance between the United States and South Korea.

Chapter 3's focus on Korean transnational adoptions should not be interpreted as a tokenized gesture to simply include "adoptee perspectives" in this book. Instead, Chapter 3 challenges the very notion of a monolithic transnational adoptee identity, as do RHEE and Kaisen themselves, while pushing against the presumption that a coherent "adoptee artwork archive" exists to examine in the first place. Thus, in juxtaposing RHEE's and Kaisen's works with a selection of other diasporic memory sources, I demonstrate the connective tissue linking Korean overseas adoption to different U.S. and South Korean government enterprises and militarized subjectivities. In dialogue with other cultural memory works discussed in this book, I underscore how these two artists' diasporic memory productions unsettle dominant conceptualizations of "authentic Korean-ness" within national spaces and throughout the diaspora.

Chapter 4, "Durational Memory," considers how two diasporic artists, Kaisen and Dohee Lee, confront the militarized "present-pasts" of Korea and Jeju Island. Through the video installation *Reiterations of Dissent* (2010/2016) and performance *MAGO* (2014), Kaisen and Lee respectively punctuate how chrononormative time marshals the Korean War as a pacified past. Given its peripheral status within Cold War historical discourse *and* its key geopolitical location within America's "Asia Pacific," Jeju Island is an especially poignant space to examine the prolonged effects of the Korean War and the expansive build-out of an Americanized security infrastructure. Drawing on the Bergsonian notion of durational time, Chapter 4 examines how Kaisen's and Lee's cultural works unhinge the chronological notions of "past" and "present" through their coeval readings of two seemingly discrete events. These events include the April 3 tragedy (popularly known in South Korea as "4.3"), a U.S.–South Korean military campaign from 1948 to 1955 that decimated 20–30 percent of Jeju's civilian population and the more recent remilitarization of the island through the construction of a new naval base in the fishing village of Gangjeong. Tracking how the South Korean and U.S. states sanitize the 4.3 "incident" through the beautifying language of international tourism and national forgiveness, *Reiterations of Dissent* and *MAGO* elucidate the structural conditions that link the 4.3 massacre to the island's contemporary militarized buildup. Yet by producing an othered sense of unruly time at odds with national reconciliation, Kaisen's and Lee's works perform dissonant memories that do not assimilate into Cold War temporality. These cultural works therefore mediate decolonized meanings of solidarity and agency that trouble the project of American militarized security in Jeju, Korea, and the North Pacific.

In the last chapter, "An Opening," I engage one of the most maligned manifestations of the Korean War: North Korea. Commonly described as a menace to the global community and one of the most volatile countries in the world, North Korea is caricaturized by American media outlets as an object of ludic commentary and comedic relief for Western audiences. Mobilizing Édouard Glissant's analytic of opacity as a provocation, this concluding chapter destabilizes such ahistorical commentary while potentiating self-reflexive observations and moments of remembering otherwise. Centering reencounters as the primary method of analysis, I consider what it might mean to return to, reexamine, and untether ourselves from dominant media portrayals and Cold War political truths abundant within the American public sphere. Working through a composite of passing observations and questions, official statistics from the Korean War, borrowed poetry, and disparate imagery, this haphazard set of diasporic memory exercises does not aim to provide a singular counternarrative to the dominant stories told and retold about North Korea. Rather, as part of this book's diasporic memory archive and an exercise in remembering otherwise *through* self-reflexive questioning, this conclusion—or, more appropriately, this opening—asks readers to track how and what we know about North Korea, as well as the limitations of knowing and knowledge production that always already frame our perceptions of the DPRK.

In part, this (un)ending reflects the conceptual aims of this book. Namely, by taking up diasporic memory works that are open-ended—and, in some cases, literally unfinished—I deploy reencounters as an inquiry-based process that yields epistemological pathways to meaningfully engage the difficult questions posed in this book. To question is to reckon with how knowledge production reproduces its own set of blind spots associated with militarized colonial desires that seek to chart out and map, to surveil and enclose, and to make transparent for a consuming audience. This (un)ending also reflects my desire to examine the genre of the book conclusion. In most instances, the conclusion is written as an obligatory epilogue that offers some semblance of definitive closure to the text at hand. Given the fluctuating nature of the Korean War, a conclusion that serves as a platform for further questioning is more fruitful, if not imperative, for confronting the perplexing implications of this protracted conflict. My hope is that this experimental format will generate critical conversations on the intellectual work that a book conclusion should or is expected to do while calling for imaginative methodologies within transnational American studies.

1

Militarized Migrations

In a two-page *Life* magazine feature spread from November 1951, U.S. Sergeant Johnie M. Morgan and his Korean bride, Lee Yong Soon, are shown arriving in Seattle. Identified by some historians as the first Korean "war bride" to arrive in the United States, a smiling "Blue" (as the article refers to her) appears with perfectly coiffed hair wearing a cardigan and a knee-length skirt. A progression of seven photographs span from portrayals of an ebullient Yong Soon squeezed between her mother-in-law and Johnie to a demure Yong Soon correcting her husband's manners at his parents' kitchen table. This powerful visual narrative demonstrates the accelerated transformation of the Korean migrant into a good and capable American wife committed to mastering the recipe of her husband's favorite Carolina-style gravy.

Ostensibly, the article pays very little attention to Yong Soon's life "over there" in Korea. It only vaguely mentions the extenuating circumstances surrounding her initial encounters with Sergeant Johnie Morgan, as readers are told that she first met her American soldier as a "communications supervisor" for the U.S. military. Indeed, the accompanying 250 word article does not elaborate on the reasons for the U.S. military presence in Korea (remarkably, it never uses the word "war"). Rather, a sensationalized description of the armed conflict, replete with tragic details such as Yong Soon's determination to trek "200 miles" with "bare and bleeding feet" to reunite with her Johnie, becomes a convenient backdrop for a romanticized account of the couple's blossoming relationship crafted for a general *Life* readership. The ar-

Lee Yong Soon between her mother-in-law and U.S. Sergeant Johnie M. Morgan, *Life* magazine, November 1951.
(Courtesy of Magnum Foundation. Photograph by Wayne Miller.)

Johnie and Yong Soon praying at the kitchen table with Johnie's parents, *Life* magazine, November 1951.
(Courtesy of Magnum Foundation. Photograph by Wayne Miller.)

ticle culminates with an idealized consummation of Johnie and Yong Soon's heterosexual love: blissful marriage and the materialization of an American nuclear family.

Mobilizing this *Life* profile as a beginning point for discussion, this chapter explores the racialized and gendered transformation of Korean migrants displaced by armed conflict into naturalized American immigrants via the Cold War lexicon of heteronormative sexual intimacies, anticommunist fervor, and loyalty to the benevolent U.S. nation.[1] In particular, this chapter analyzes a set of policy decisions, legislative acts, and cultural discourses conjunctively implemented between 1945 and 1964 by the U.S. and South Korean governments to forge a synergetic political and economic alliance anchored in anticommunist rhetoric. The tumultuous interval between 1945 (marking the precipice of Korean division and American occupation) and 1964 (the year preceding significant changes in U.S. immigration policy) has proved foundational to the coalescing of a Korean diasporic presence in the United States and, to a larger degree, the development of what we now know and refer to as contemporary American immigration policy.

A critical revisionist rendering of this historical arc is also significant, given that prominent scholarship continues to portray Korean/Americans as a "post-1965" demographic safely removed from the devastating ramifications of the Korean War. In existing political science, sociological, and historical literature, both the 1945–1964 "wave" of Korean migrations and the definitive dates of the Korean War (1950–1953) are conceptualized as distant pasts delinked from a here and now shaped by the Immigration and Nationality Act of 1965. This legislation, in fact, is commonly described as a crucial policy that graciously opened American immigration to those hailing from non-Western countries.[2] Hence, despite Ji-Yeon Yuh's sobering reminder that "most, if not all, of Korean migration since 1950 can be traced to the war and its consequences," Korean migrations to the United States in and after 1965 are predominantly associated with nonmilitarized causal factors such as educational, professional, and economic opportunities.[3] Consequently, the implications of the Korean War are sanitized through the formal language of global freedom and mobility, individual autonomy, and voluntary immigration. As aptly demonstrated by Yong Soon's profile in *Life*, these migratory journeys are expected to culminate with the migrant subject's wholesale assimilation into the American(ized) heterosexual family and multiracial national citizenry. The conspicuous intersections of immigration, progressive temporality, and heteronormative sociality, then, might be referred to as Cold War *chrononormativity*, or the naturalized plotting of Korean immigration along a linear trajectory defined by heteronormative expectations.[4]

The chrononormative framing of the "pre-1965 Korean immigration wave" as an anterior relic of the past contributes to the popular discourse of "forgetting *as* remembering." Namely, it obscures the Korean War's far-reaching reverberations, which do not dovetail with a chronological timeline or resound with the formal definition of the refugee vetted by international institutions such as the United Nations. The United Nations correlates refugee status with one's level of exposure to clear and immediate dangers, such as physical warfare and political persecution.[5] Here Yuh's observations are once again instructive because she describes how this narrow definition masks the stratified complexities of *refuge* migrations, or myriad diasporic movements instigated by precarious repercussions linked to the Korean War and American military occupation. In the United States, these ongoing refuge migrations of Korean "military brides" and "the labor and professional migration of miners, doctors and nurses" (among others) do not typify or reflect more traditional conceptions of the war refugee.[6] Subsequently, such diasporic subjects are framed through the language of economic, educational, and family-related immigration. Given that the Korean War, in the past seven decades, has morphed from a full-scale armed conflict to an unresolved quagmire materialized through prolonged division, explicitly identifying and naming these muted yet enduring capacities is imperative.[7] Accentuating how subjects seemingly removed from war are always already touched by militarized violence, I extend Yuh's theorization of refuge migration by attending to diasporic movements as *militarized migrations,* a key term that indexes the racialized, gendered, and sexualized conditions underlying Korean diasporic trajectories. Specifically, I emphasize that the protracted history of Korean militarized migrations from 1945 to the present blurs the boundary between those seeking refuge from war and those recognized by the "receiving" state as bona fide immigrants (and the children of "assimilated" immigrants). This chapter therefore focuses on the continuities rather than the total breaks that bind the acutely felt aftereffects of militarized conflict to the long-term, structurally embedded political and social implications of a continuing war.

To track how Korean militarized migrants are reformulated into newly minted immigrants-cum-Americans, this chapter marshals an eclectic assemblage of memory sources. In the next two sections, I offer a historical backdrop that contextualizes the post–World War II American military occupation of Korea, as well as a critical analysis of a genealogy of legislative actions implemented by the United States between 1945 and 1964. Encompassing a composite of temporary emergency orders and transitory migration policies, these entangled apparatuses targeted Korean women recently married to U.S. soldiers, as well as the mixed-race or "GI" children (as they were commonly referred to by the U.S. and South Korean states) of American servicemen and Korean women primarily adopted by white families in the United States. Far from coincidental or accidental, the U.S. state's focus on these entwined sub-populaces register both the immediate outcomes of American occupation "over there" in Korea and the racial exclusivity of immigration and refugee policy "over here" in the United States.

But most important, I argue that the focus placed on these diasporic categories demonstrates a governmental logic that selectively identified which racialized and gendered subjects, even if "nonwhite," "different" and "problematic," could assimilate into and faithfully reproduce the American national populace. Situated within the larger agenda of American Cold War policy making, the emergency and temporary orders focusing on Korean migration reflect how the United States sustained its self-crafted image as the humanitarian leader of the "free world" through two contingent moves. First, the U.S. government justified its occupation of sovereign nations by emphasizing the need to save and protect effeminized countries against communism. Second, the state sought to assimilate into the American populace selective groups of diasporic subjects under the banner of liberal multiracial democracy. Registering the undeniable linkages between the transnational and domestic, these coeval sentiments coincided with the Cold War beginnings of model minority discourse, as Asian/Americans were progressively depicted as hardworking, passive, and obedient citizens committed to the American work ethic and steadfast anticommunist nationalism.

By offering this nuanced reading of legislative enactments, I examine official state policy encoded via legislative texts as part of Cold War historiography. That is, I emphasize how the legislative record functions as a site of history and subject making rather than as a disinterested platform that objectively mediates instrumental processes of policy making. As Chandan Reddy makes clear, the "naming of the law [as] an archive" intimates how "law organizes social and historical differences in ways that promise both membership and knowledge of difference."[8] Therefore, my analysis of state policies tracks how the privileged ledger of government decisions renders a selective cohort of Koreans as viable Americans by premising their citizenship on racial, gendered, and sexual difference.

With this context in place, the last two sections of the chapter address the present-pastness of these racialized and gendered policies in the contemporary lives of Korean/Americans. I underscore how these temporary policies were not so ephemeral or transitory but produced a lasting imprint on *permanent* immigration legislation. To flesh out these continuing implications, I offer a close reading of Eun-Joung Lee's and Min Yong Lee's oral histories included, respectively, in the digital archive Legacies of the Korean War (2014–present) and the thirty-minute documentary *Memory of Forgotten War* (dir. Deann Borshay Liem [2013]).[9] I analyze these particular oral histories for several reasons. First, as separate interviews conducted with a father and daughter who migrated to the United States after 1965, the narratives poignantly capture common themes, including racialized and gendered norms, that appear in other oral histories in Legacies of the Korean War and *Memory of Forgotten War*. These overlapping concerns range from the chaotic consequences and resonating tensions of family division across national and familial lines to the silences that permeate the everyday lives of Korean diasporic subjects. Second, Eun-Joung's and Min Yong's dialectical narratives produce contradictory knowledges that register a disjuncture between official forms of legislated knowledge sanctified by the U.S. government and radically different knowledges that diverge from and contradict these ideological accounts. In that sense, I attend to Eun-Joung's and Min Yong's oral histories as diasporic excesses that refuse to be wholly absorbed, integrated, or supplanted by dominant discourses of the Americanized Korean War. My discussion of oral history as a diasporic memory praxis continues in Chapter 2, albeit through a different project and analytical framing.

While I refrain from mobilizing oral history accounts as pure voices that monolithically challenge state interpretations, I emphasize that the vernacular knowledges shared and produced by Legacies of the Korean War and *Memory of Forgotten War* register a prominent lacuna within the general American public. Simply put, heterogeneous representations of the Korean War narrated by those who survived the armed conflict or continue to live with its material, social, and psychic ramifications are rarely found within the U.S. public sphere. Indeed, as is adamantly argued in this book, the obscuring of Korean diasporic narratives from American history textbooks and popular media depictions point to a grossly asymmetrical terrain of memory production in the United States. Given the instrumental role that Korean division plays within America's global security infrastructure, each of the following chapters underscores the ways in which Cold War historiographical accounts of the Korean War are affixed to and replenish U.S. military, political, and economic motivations in the North Pacific.

Origins of First Contact

As noted in the previous section, the aggregation of emergency orders and legislative processes that paved the way for Korean migrations to the United States immediately following World War II pertained to two related populations: Korean women who married U.S. servicemen stationed in South Korea and the mixed-race children of primarily white and black U.S. soldiers and Korean women adopted by families in the United States.[10]

The U.S. government's focus on these racialized and gendered cohorts of migrants is unsurprising insofar as the American military occupation facilitated intimate relations between U.S. soldiers and Korean women. Following the arrival of seventy thousand American troops in the southern half of Korea in September 1945, the U.S. Army Military Government in Korea (September 1945–August 1948) was established under a three-year trusteeship arrangement with the Soviet Union, which occupied the northern half of Korea.[11] While the number of U.S. military personnel was reduced to 22,823 after the South Korean state was established in 1948, the number again ballooned in early 1950 when skirmishes between the South and the North escalated along the international border marked by the 38th Parallel.[12] Following the signing of the Korean armistice in 1953—which again placed a temporary halt on the conflict without ending the war—national division and U.S. martial presence became permanent on the peninsula. As of August 2017, the U.S. military remains the only external force in Korea, with 23,468 soldiers scattered across eighty-three designated military bases and affiliated sites on the peninsula and in the semiautonomous province of Jeju Island.[13]

This shift of the U.S. presence from short-term to long-term occupation was accompanied by a domino effect. With the arrival of U.S. troops in southern Korea, temporary living quarters on military bases previously controlled by the Japanese Imperial Army, such as the colonial garrison in Yongsan, Seoul, became makeshift living quarters for American soldiers. The occupation also led to the hasty buildup of accommodations, businesses, and entertainment venues catering to U.S. soldiers. As Katherine Moon, Cynthia Enloe, and Mark Gillem observe, the evolving nexus of commercial districts that crystallized around U.S. military bases, commonly referred to as "camptowns" in English and as *gijichons* in Korean, encompassed a mishmash of service- and entertainment-oriented businesses, including brothels.[14] Still in existence today, military brothels materialized as spaces of gathering and leisure for soldiers, so much so that camptowns in South Korea are synonymously referred to by some as red-light districts. During the early 1960s, the number of Korean female "entertainment" workers licensed with health certificates, which permitted them to work in designated camptowns, reached an apex, with approximately thirty thousand workers. In the ensuing decades (1970–1990), the number of those licensed as entertainment workers dwindled to about twenty thousand.[15]

While existing literature affirms that most Korean women who married U.S. soldiers and migrated to the United States were part of the *gijichon* economy in one form or another, the mere presence of the U.S. military in South Korea generated other venues for social interface between locals and soldiers. These included civilian employment on and around American military bases as translators, teachers, secretaries, accountants, and cooks.[16] As Lee Yong Soon ("Blue") did, some Korean women worked as so-called communications supervisors for the U.S. military (an occupation associated with bilingual language skills); others worked as military language instructors, among other positions, in South Korea and the United States.[17]

The repercussions of these racialized, gendered, and sexualized intimacies between U.S. servicemen and Korean women were swift and hypervisible. Nearly 84 percent of the fourteen thousand Koreans who entered the United States between 1951 and 1964 were spouses of American soldiers or Korean and multiracial children adopted by American families.[18] With a total Korean population in the continental United States in 1950 of fewer than eight thousand, these militarized migrations substantively changed the existing Korean/American demographic. In the ensuing decades, the number of gendered migrations would exponentially increase: between 1950 and 2000, nearly 100,000 Korean women migrated to the United States as the fiancées or wives of American servicemen, with approximately four thousand women arriving annually between 1970 and the late 1980s.[19] Since nearly 20 percent of Korean/Americans today can trace their militarized migration history to Korean war brides, these earlier migrations had a significant impact when one considers the making of a contemporary Korean diasporic presence in the United States.

In addition, the sexual encounters between U.S. servicemen and Korean women materialized through the appearance of a multiracial population as thousands of children were conceived between Korean civilians and white and African American soldiers. Tobias Hübinette, Eleana J. Kim, Kim Park Nelson, and SooJin Pate describe how the South Korean state, as well as the U.S. government, perceived this multiracial population as a potential threat for different reasons.[20] South Korea treated multiracial children as obstacles to the realization of a viable ethnocentric nation anchored in the ideological notion of "pure" blood. The U.S. state contended that these children could be easily mobilized by the Soviet Union and other communist regimes to undermine the United States' self-crafted image as a just, democratic, and moral force committed to a free capitalist world.[21] As detailed in Chapter 3, the South Korean government under the pro-American administration of Rhee Syngman (1948–1960) treated these so-called GI babies as unwanted excesses that needed to be quickly removed from the national interior to build a racially homogeneous citizenry based on the principle of "one nation, one race."[22] Conveniently, Rhee's desire for extraction overlapped with the growing demand for adoptable children in the United States—not only from Korea but also from Japan, Europe, and elsewhere—between 1950 and the early 1960s, with adoption requests almost doubling during this time.[23] With the domestic shortage of "adoptable" children in the United States, Korea emerged as a rich source for international adoption. Buoyed by advocacy provided by the South Korean state, (inter)national aid and welfare agencies, and American evangelicals such as Harry and Bertha Holt (who eventually adopted eight multiracial children and established the first Korean transnational adoption agency still in existence today), almost 5,400 children from Korea were adopted by American families between 1951 and 1964. Approximately 3,500 of these children were identified by the state as the mixed-race offspring of Korean women and U.S. soldiers.[24] From 1950 to 2000, the number of adoptees abroad would swell, with nearly 150,000 Korean children adopted by families in the United States.[25]

Cold War American Benevolence and the Making of Korean "Immigrants"

The material and social repercussions of U.S. military intervention and presence in Korea mark the emergent beginnings of U.S. Cold War immigration policy. In light of the racialized exclusivity of extant refugee policies and legislation, the U.S. state passed a series of emergency orders and "non-quota" amendments between 1945 and 1956 to accommodate the accumulating requests of American soldiers seeking to bring their Asian spouses from Japan and Korea to the United States. More specifically, the U.S. government established a narrow set of legislative exceptions to facilitate the militarized migration of Asian war brides and Korean transnational adoptees.

In the aftermath of World War II, newly created international bodies were just forming official refugee policies. In 1951, the United Nations formalized the protocol for refugee status by establishing the UN Convention Relating to the Status of Refugees. Yet signatory nations such as the United States were given the option of extending refugee rights exclusively to Europeans.[26] Consequently, refugee policy after World War II became, de facto, a *European* refugee policy. Influenced and indelibly informed by UN protocols, the United States, decades later in 1980, passed the Refugee Act to amend the Migration and Refugee Assistance Act of 1962 and the Immigration and Nationality Act of 1965. On paper, the government framed the Refugee Act as an altruistic response to the urgent needs of millions displaced by more than two decades of brutal warfare across Southeast Asia, including in Vietnam, Laos, and Cambodia. But on the ground, more than 90 percent of those granted asylum in the United States until the mid-1980s were from the Eastern European communist bloc.[27]

U.S. immigration legislation largely echoed the racial exclusivity of these early refugee policies. Although the United States incrementally liberalized immigration laws starting in the early 1940s, it retained the national origins quota, a system that predominantly favored Western European immigrants and severely curtailed Asian immigration until the quota's revocation in 1965.[28] Due to this policy gap after 1945, the U.S. government implemented an improvised succession of provisional orders that permitted select migration of those directly associated with the U.S. military stationed in Korea and Japan, including soldiers' fiancées, new spouses, the biological children of soldiers, and so-called orphans, or "waifs," adopted by U.S. soldiers and servicemen. In 1947, for instance, the state had amended the War Brides Act (Public Law 271, expired in 1948) to circumvent the national origins quota, allowing Korean and Japanese spouses of U.S. servicemen to migrate and move to the United States with their husbands.[29] In 1952, this measure was incorporated into the Immigration and Nationality Act as a non-quota provision, with the hopes of neutralizing existing racial restrictions within federal immigration policy. Throughout the 1950s and early 1960s, concomitant policies related to overseas adoption were also institutionalized. In 1953, the U.S. government promulgated the Refugee Relief Act (RRA), which allotted four thousand over-quota visas to orphans age ten and younger. Implicitly, the vast majority of issued visas were for Korean and Japanese children unable to enter the United States because of racially restrictive immigration and refugee policies.[30] When the RRA expired in 1956, it was eventually replaced by permanent international adoption policy in 1962, which excised the word "refugee" from its legislative text.

It is necessary to scrutinize the broader motivations behind the U.S. state's decisions to facilitate these specific migrations. The U.S. government framed these makeshift orders as altruistic reflections of its unwavering commitment to global freedom and racial equality, but an examination of these Cold War policies suggests otherwise. As Christina Klein, Nikhil Singh, and Jodi Melamed point out, the hegemonic position of the United States as a global power after World War II situated it in a delicate, if not awkward, geopolitical position.[31] Although President Harry Truman's administration advocated globally for democracy and liberty against the "terror and oppression" of communist regimes, the U.S. government's domestic policies of racial segregation, immigrant exclusion, and state violence sorely contradicted these idealized principles—an embarrassing discrepancy that, much to Truman's chagrin, did not go unnoticed by the Chinese and Soviet governments.[32]

In response, the U.S. state decided that an effective method to deflect critiques of racial violence and maintain its reputation as a global humanitarian force was to accept and assimilate minoritarian "others" into its national polity.[33] The U.S. government sought to incorporate racialized subjects into existing social structures through official policies of desegregation and de jure integration while also cautiously liberalizing federal immigration policies. But tellingly, the U.S. state failed to address more radical critiques regarding the systemic and structural nature of racial violence articulated by African American and global South activists. Seeking to rectify and resolve racial "problems" without disrupting extant hierarchies of power, the U.S. state ultimately left intact a governing and surveillance infrastructure anchored in white supremacy, heteronormative ideals, and anticommunist principles.[34]

Thus, in conversation with this broader agenda of Cold War political sentiments, we might surmise the strategic interests informing the U.S. government's decision to allow Korean military brides and adoptees to emigrate. In effect, the facilitation of these particular militarized migrations empirically bolstered the U.S. claim of benevolent governance, internationally and domestically. Gradually coinciding with the model minority discourse during the 1960s—which pitted Asian/Americans against other racialized subjects by propping them up as model minority citizens capable of climbing the socioeconomic ladder without government aid—the continuing arrival of Korean women and children on America's shores reflected the dual-sided logics of Cold War geopolitics. On the one hand, the U.S. state framed American military occupation in Korea as a benevolent action necessary to contain communism and support global peace. As pithily stated by the legislative authors of the RRA, "Friendly international relations engendered by America's helping hand stretched out to these children [is] a forward step toward better international understanding and lasting peace in the world."[35] On the other hand, these military interventions were directly linked to a liberal domestic discourse of racial acceptance, assimilation, and cultural plurality, as the militarized diasporic subjects of American occupation eventually found their way to the colonial metropole. The United States, then, obligated itself to generously accept these "poor and destitute" subjects with open and compassionate arms.[36] In the case of Korea, these Americanized sentiments of generosity and humanitarianism reflect the overarching racialized and gendered relations between the two countries. Even now, the United States continues to personify itself as the "big brother" and militarized guardian of South Korea, its "younger sibling."[37] In a tacit sense, Korean diasporic children and women were always already perceived as effeminized subjects who could be effectively tamed, disciplined, and integrated into the domestic bounds of the American dominant milieu, defined as white, middle-class, and heterosexual.

In a related sense, the capacity of Korean women and children to successfully integrate into the American populace depended on their steadfast ability to quickly forget the Korean War. Consequently, even as women's and children's presence in the United States served as a conspicuous reminder of U.S. intervention in Korea, such dynamisms were recognized only when they further affirmed Koreans' willingness to transform into grateful and obedient Americans. One example of such a new American is Maria Cho, who in a 1962 *Los Angeles Times* article pairs her desire to forget and forever leave Korea with her enthusiasm for the United States. Elaborating on her plans to bring her parents to California so they "can see the beauty of this country," Cho describes her commitment to speaking with American women's groups to better educate "[them] of the evils and the workings of communism."[38] In another *Los Angeles Times* article published a decade earlier, in 1951, the author claims that eleven "Asiatic war brides" (ten Korean and one Chinese) who flew to their American homes left behind "bitter memories" of communist violence, war, death, and other hardships.[39] As testament to their new futures as Americans, upon their arrival the women exchanged their "ethnic" clothing for Western garb—smartly tailored suits and blouses, to be exact. Concomitantly, the U.S. Congress characterized Korean orphans as impressionable vessels or "blank slates" who could be easily molded into Americans. In documented conversations among members of the U.S. House Subcommittee on Immigration, Korean overseas adoptees are frequently described as the "best possible [U.S.] immigrants from the standpoint of their youth, flexibility, and lack of ties to any other cultures."[40]

Of course, the state exceptions made for Korean brides and children were qualified by the American government's decision to strategically embrace those it deemed the right kinds of Korean immigrants. And even in these cases, national acceptance was laced with a nagging sense of ambivalence and suspicion, indicated by the presumed *short-term, tentative,* and *temporary* status of these emergency measures. The loosening of immigration and refugee restrictions after 1945, in fact, was tempered by anticommunist surveillance and monitoring measures designed to "weed out" those the government deemed as deviant. Carl J. Bon Tempo argues that immigration and refugee policies implemented during this period were shaped by a pervasive paranoia that equated steadfast Americanism with steadfast anticommunism.[41] As discussed later in this chapter, Tempo's observation is affirmed by the cluster of anticommunist policies and surveillance practices jointly implemented by the United States and South Korea after 1948, which continue to affect those residing on the peninsula, in the United States, and beyond.

Simultaneously, while the American public seemed to welcome Korean women and adoptees, unsettling questions regarding the newcomers' on-the-ground assimilation, sexual (im)propriety, and conjugal intimacies remained unabated. As Susan Koshy and Susie Woo keenly observe, the positive Cold War messaging of multiracialism could not quell all of the rampant anxieties related to illicit racial and sexual "mixing," especially since antimiscegenation policies remained on the books until 1967, when the U.S. Supreme Court struck down such laws in the *Loving v. Virginia* decision.[42] Exacerbated by rumors that newly arrived spouses had been military prostitutes, Korean brides such as Lee Yong Soon disappeared from the public eye following the spectacular media coverage of their initial "homecomings." In effect, the gendered migration of Korean war brides alluded to a larger dilemma associated with Asian women, who were doubly constructed by American popular culture as sexually exotic, threatening, and licentious, as well as properly domesticated, feminine, and delicate.[43] Yet while American popular culture largely fetishized Japanese war brides rather than their Korean counterparts (again, presumably due to prevailing suspicions of immorality and sexual vice), the Orientalizing stereotypes affiliated with Asian women en masse—as permissive, self-sacrificing, and exceedingly obedient to their husbands—were elastically applied to Koreans.[44] It would be possible, with hard work, perseverance, and diligence, for Korean women to transform into good American wives and mothers loyal to the U.S. nation-state.

In contradistinction, Korean adoptees more easily reflected and soothingly bolstered the U.S. state's focused messaging around American benevolence and generosity against the travails of communism. But as Woo points out, the carefully culled story of the Korean orphan whose parents were cruelly killed by communists during the war was an easier "sell" than the story of mixed-race children abandoned by their GI fathers and ostracized Korean mothers who struggled to make ends meet.[45] Indeed, despite being labeled "waifs" by the American media, most adopted children after 1955 were *not* war orphans at all. Subsequently, the national story of the "Korean orphan" was defined by a bevy of common tropes: "the miserable Asian orphan; the child rescued by a valiant American family; and the completely assimilated Americanized adoptee."[46]

To a certain degree, the transformation of Korean women and children into proper Americans complicated their murky status as *not* quite refugees and *not* quite immigrants. Existing beyond the normative parameters of refugee and immigrant status, these two groups occupied a gray zone of ambiguity. Unlike Southeast Asians who were formally categorized by the U.S. government as refugees after 1980, Koreans were simultaneously perceived by the American public as refugees, immigrants, *and* quasi-Americans (or, at the very least, Americans in the making).[47] Within this zone of multiple identifications, desires for immediate refuge and safety from war overlapped with other factors, such as the yearning for professional employment and socioeconomic mobility, love, and marriage and the desire to leave South Korea altogether. For instance, while Yuh cautions against affiliating all Korean camptown workers with a homogeneous set of characteristics, her rich oral histories with Korean women who married American soldiers and migrated to the United States between 1950 and 1989 suggest a demographic pattern. In these interviews, the vast majority of *gijichon* laborers had limited access to formal education, came from financially precarious backgrounds, acted as parents to younger siblings, and were displaced by multiple colonial powers, including Japanese and American occupations.[48] In that sense, those interviewed by Yuh often perceived marriage to U.S. soldiers, or militarized migrations mediated through the legible category of heterosexual marriage, as an accessible pathway to "move out" of the entrenched violence produced by war.[49] As we shall see, this nebulous collapsing between the militarized conditions of war and other motivations is apparent in the oral histories of Eun-Joung and Min Yong Lee.

"We Are Here Because You Were There": Oral Histories and Militarized Migrations

While a recalibration of these early policies may seem tangential to Korean militarized migrations after 1965, it is critical to emphasize how the core elements of these emergency temporary orders, manufactured during a time of heated conflagration in Korea, became permanent elements within contemporary immigration policy. In other words, the temporary policies enacted immediately after 1945 to facilitate selective Korean militarized migrations—and, by extension, the transformation of Koreans seeking refuge from war into quasi-American immigrants—provided both a precedent and a blueprint for future immigration legislation passed in the United States. Ironically, while refugee policies in the United States historically have served to counter and neutralize racially restrictive immigration policies, provisional orders that surfaced to counter the racialized exclusions of emergent refugee policy have constituted the ideological backbone for U.S. immigration legislation implemented after 1960.

The Immigration and Nationality Act of 1965 (the Hart-Celler Act), for example, replaced the national origins formula with a seemingly egalitarian quota system that designated a uniform number of immigrant visas (20,000) for each country outside the Western Hemisphere. Often coupled with the Civil Rights Act of 1964, Hart-Celler is generally accepted as a watershed bill that miraculously opened immigration to populations around the world, radically shifting the demographics of the United States to generate a more racially and ethnically inclusive "melting pot." However, this myopic rendering of the Hart-Celler Act obscures other key elements of the bill, including the permanent codification of "temporary" racialized and gendered policies enacted after 1945.[50] Such policies include the privileging of heteronormative relations for family reunification, anticommunist surveillance and security protocols, and a seven-category system that prioritizes those who can prove their productivity as hardworking Americans, including professionals possessing specialized skills or those capable of meeting the demands of state-defined labor shortages. In short, Hart-Celler metabolized earlier assumptions of the state regarding which migrating populaces were (un)worthy of compassion, aid, and entrance into the United States.

To track the repercussions of these policies on everyday life among Korean diasporans, I shift to a set of oral histories included in Legacies of the Korean War and *Memories of Forgotten War,* both introduced earlier in the chapter. As foregrounded in the Introduction, the early 2000s witnessed reenergized efforts to establish Korean diasporic memory archives centered on civilian experiences of the war in the United States and South Korea. Encouraged by renewed talks between the North Korean and South Korean governments in the early 2000s, Korean/Americans born decades after the 1953 armistice began to share their family experiences of war, division, and family separation, first in ethnic print media and later through a circuit of academic conferences, activist-oriented events, art and educational exhibits, and other social gatherings.[51] In 2003–2004, Ramsay Liem, a Korean/American scholar and antiwar activist, collected more than three dozen oral histories with Korean/Americans residing in the greater Boston and San Francisco

Bay areas. This initial batch of interviews eventually served as the impetus for the *Memory of Forgotten War* and Legacies of the Korean War projects, as well as the *Still Present Pasts* exhibition discussed in the Introduction. Currently, Legacies of the Korean War includes twenty-two oral history interviews conducted with Korean/Americans by a small team of interviewers, including Ramsay Liem and the filmmakers Deann Borshay Liem and J. T. Takagi, while *Memory of Forgotten War* makes use of original source materials and interviews collected for the Legacies project.

Here I turn to Eun-Joung Lee's oral history.[52] Born in Seoul in 1973 and immigrating to the United States with her parents and older sister in 1976 (her youngest sister remained in Korea until 1979), Eun-Joung was interviewed in 2015 in Oakland, California, by Borshay Liem and Takagi. Identifying herself as a 1.5-generation Korean/American (i.e., born in South Korea but raised in the United States), Eun-Joung intimates the consequential ways in which the Korean War has permeated her "post-1965" life in the United States. Within the first few minutes of the interview, Eun-Joung gives the following complicated statement, which is developed later in this chapter:

> What is my relationship to—to [the war] and what does it mean for me now? In the context of who—who I am? It's not this remote part of me. I mean, it's [*pause*], I would not exist had the Korean War not happened in the way it had.... If the Korean war hadn't happened [the way it did,] then [my sisters and I] wouldn't exist in this form.

Eun-Joung's profound questioning of her own existence, her ontological relationship to the Korean War, and the connections to her family within the context of militarized division accentuate the intersubjective qualities of oral history. Note that I approach the oral history interview as a meta-space that generates critical reencounters with a life event that otherwise might not be intentionally shared. Producing what Ronald Grele portrays as a "complex web of interpretation," the oral history does not culminate as a rational progression of thoughts; nor does it coalesce as a chronologically organized history.[53] Rather, as a dialectical praxis of meaning making, the oral history is forged through a haphazard range of contradictions that reflect the sinewy fusing of past and present—and, in this case, the "present-pastness" of the Korean War. Hence, as Eun-Joung's narration jumps from her family's militarized migration to the United States to the fractured relations within her family to her own subjectivity, her complex life history provides a localized rendering of the Korean War that focuses on her family's multifaceted experiences of everyday division.

Early in the interview, Eun-Joung comments that she is hungry for these intimate accounts of war precisely because as a young person, she was unable to connect the formal history of the Korean conflict she learned in college to the textured lives of her parents:

> Even when I was in school in Chicago in college, I majored in—in East Asian history at first and we learned about—you know, we covered the Korean War in our East Asian civ class. But even at that point, it didn't occur to me to go back to my parents and say, "Sit down, let's—let's talk about the war."

Eun-Joung's passing observation regarding the disjuncture between the official history enshrined in textbooks and the embodied experiences of the Korean War is quite telling because it hints at alternative, even subversive, knowledge that exists in excess to and outside the canonized knowledge (re)produced by institutions such as the university. Eun-Joung's comment resonates with what Michel Foucault describes as subjugated knowledges—or "disqualified" and "naïve" knowledges situated "low down on the hierarchy, beneath the required level of scientity."[54] These localized oral histories perform two critical functions. First, they provide interlocutors with a sense of historical agency as they narrate the Korean War through their own subjective lens; and second, they point to macro-relations of power that manufacture Cold War historical narratives privileging the United States as the savior and benefactor of Korea.

The entanglement of divergent knowledges, both "official" and "local," in Eun-Joung's oral history narrative appears in her first description of her family's militarized migration in 1976 from Seoul to Atlanta, where her mother's sister already resided:

> I don't think I remember precisely the event of immigration. I was three years old, so it was 1976, and what I've been told in terms of the reason why we moved—why we immigrated [*narrator pauses*]. My mother's side of the story is that it was the Vietnam War and people in Korea were nervous that the war would spill back over into Korea. People were feeling unstable with the Vietnam War going on, and my mother was trained as a nurse. And so, that's what enabled us to get a visa fairly easily and immigrate to the U.S. because there was a shortage of doctors and nurses in the U.S. at the time. My father's story of why we immigrated to the U.S. is that he was a very young professor at Dongguk University, a professor of Buddhist philosophy.

At first blush, Eun-Joung's description of her family's experiences reads as a post-1965 narrative of economic migration insofar as professional opportunities "pulled" and "pushed" her family to voluntarily move to the United States. Having moved to Atlanta more than a decade after the 1965 Immigration and Nationality Act was implemented, Eun-Joung's family benefited from the occupational preferences established under the act. Migrating as a nuclear family from a fervid anticommunist ally of the United States, Eun-Joung's family further benefited from the sentimental and political ideals encoded within a Cold War genealogy of legislative actions, as discussed earlier in the chapter.

Eun-Joung's family's move to the United States was also bolstered by a synergetic set of migration policies implemented by the South Korean state. Under the helm of President Park Chung-hee (1961–1979), South Korea adopted an industrialization model based on the principle of *pukak kangbyŏng* (rich nation, strong army), derived from the Japanese military's nationalist agenda of *fukoku kyohei* (rich nation, strong army) and *shukusan kogyo* (production promotion) enacted during the Meiji Restoration era.[55] Inspired by the militarized ideals of efficiency, discipline, and anticommunism, the South Korean government, with substantial financial backing from the United States and Japan, enforced a sequence of five-year economic plans that propelled the country into an unprecedented era of rapid economic growth. As part of these governing schematics, Park, in 1962, devised emigration policies and guest worker programs in European countries (especially Germany), the Middle East, and throughout the Americas that encouraged South Koreans to become productive workers and permanently resettle abroad.[56] Prioritizing a wide range of laborers, including medical professionals (such as Eun-Joung's mother), these emigration policies stimulated national economic growth through global remittances provided by international Korean workers while also controlling the explosive growth of the country's population through the extraction of bodies from South Korea.[57] These coeval policies of extraction and migration between the United States and South Korea were extremely successful: between 1965 and 1979, more than 260,000 Koreans moved to and resettled in the United States.[58] A biopolitical tactic of governance anchored in the vigilant monitoring of its populace, the South Korean state's removal of excess bodies from the national interior builds on preceding policies of extraction stemming from the Korean War—most notably, the extrication of orphans-cum-adoptees from the country. Eventually, these variegated policies of removal and resettlement coincided with the codification of family-planning practices in which the South Korean state increasingly depended on emigration as an apparatus for national population control.[59]

But Eun-Joung's description foregrounds other obscured motivations for her family's militarized migration. In fact, these personal sentiments are not so easily catalogued or captured by official statistics and immigration categories, such as occupational preferences and family reunification policies. Eun-Joung referred to her mother's heightened concern over renewed fighting in South Korea as a catalyst for her family's departure from the country. This reference resonates with Yuh's conceptualization of refuge migration, given that Eun-Joung's mother, among other Koreans, expressed an acute desire for genuine security, safety, and a "stable environment that doesn't feel like it's always threatening to explode."[60] In broad terms, this sentiment points to an omnipresent apprehension linked to the prolongation of the Korean War. While full-scale fighting ended in 1953, Koreans on both sides of the 38th Parallel continue to live in a state of constant vigilance due to the absence of a definitive peace agreement and the prolonged presence of the U.S. military in the South. Demonstrated by the Trump administration's incitement of polemical flames with North Korea in 2017 and 2018 and the subsequent heightening of tensions between the North and South, the threat of warfare is always a possibility and, at times, seemingly imminent.

In an even less obvious manner, Eun-Joung's commentary registers the pivotal role played by the ever profiting, ever accumulating business of global warfare. The observation of Eun-Joung's mother's anxiety that "war would spill back over into Korea" from Vietnam underscores America's elongated history of militarized and colonial ambitions in Asia, as well as the intimate political relationship forged between South Korea and the United States through the machinery of war. As Jodi Kim reminds us, the intervention of the United States in Korea and its more than two decades of military involvement in Southeast Asian affairs from the early 1950s to 1979 were preceded by the government's "acquiring" of the Philippines in 1898 as victorious spoils from the Spanish-American War.[61] In private conversations held with Joseph Stalin during the Yalta Conference of February 1945, President Franklin D. Roosevelt referred to the U.S. "expertise" in the Philippines, an American colony until 1946, as an exemplary paradigm for future trusteeships that would be established in Korea and the (then) French territories of Vietnam, Cambodia, and Laos.[62] As Korea and Vietnam were geographically divided along Cold War ideological lines in 1945 and 1950, respectively, they became entangled in global polemics waged by international powers amid the wreckage and ruins of an all-consuming world war.

Yet Eun-Joung's triangulation of South Korea, America, and Vietnam inadvertently registers both the asymmetrical relationships among these countries and the specter of complicity between the former two nations. Between 1961 and 1980, the accelerated growth of the South Korean economy under the American-backed dictatorship of Park depended on the country's participation in militarized conflicts abroad as a staunch anticommunist partner of the United States. Jin-kyung Lee, Heonik Kwon, and Charles Armstrong confirm that the Vietnam War proved an especially lucrative undertaking for South Korea: between 1964 and 1973, Park contributed more than 300,000 combat troops to fight alongside American soldiers in Vietnam—the second-largest allied unit after the South Vietnamese Army and a detachment celebrated for its callous treatment of North Vietnamese soldiers and civilians.[63] In return for such service, the United States agreed to finance the modernization of South Korean urban infrastructure, support the training of its military forces, and provide multimillion-dollar contracts to Korean corporations across the globe—a total package worth more than $5 billion.[64] Unexpectedly, Eun-Joung's juxtaposition of immigrant life with the racialized, gendered, and classed implications of U.S. immigration policy and American presence in Southeast Asia underscores how her family's viable life in the country is conditioned by a logic of precariousness associated with the durable history of U.S. militarized aggression in Korea and Asia.

Eun-Joung's narrative, then, demonstrates the ways in which the post-1965 militarized migrations of South Korea are anchored in the reverberating consequences of the Korean War, American militarized occupation, and synergetic migration policies coalescing in the United States and South Korea. The overlapping of these different factors becomes more evident when Eun-Joung transitions into a discussion of her father's experiences in South Korea and the United States. An affable professor well liked by his students and colleagues, Min Yong was ultimately denied tenure by Dongguk University and eventually left Korea due to a suspicion that the university had discovered his family affiliations with the North. Eun-Joung notes, "He, you know, was at the top of his school, top of all of his classes, but he was denied tenure and he believes it was because of his family background and ties to North Korea. . . . [T]he academic community [in South Korea] knew about that and didn't want to help his career."

To unpack the sobering implications of Eun-Joung's observation, I now shift to segments of Min Yong's oral history, interwoven throughout the documentary *Memory of Forgotten War*. Interchangeably speaking in English and Korean, with more complicated descriptions of the war offered in the latter language, Min Yong describes his militarized migration and the division of his family in relation to the Korean War. With fighting breaking out along the 38th Parallel in 1950, when Min Yong was just nine years old, three of his six siblings—his eldest brother, a younger brother, and a younger sister—aligned themselves with communist ideology and the North Korean state. Following the death of the eldest brother at the hands of an anticommunist youth group, Min Yong's younger brother and sister departed for the North before the border was permanently sealed. Both have remained in North Korea for more than sixty years, with his brother passing away in the early 2000s.

Fearful of her children's connections to North Korea, Min Yong's mother submitted a new entry into the South Korean family registration system (*hojeok*), a state practice retained from the Japanese colonial era. In it, Min Yong and his three other sisters are listed as the only children within the household. Min Yong explains his mother's decision to create a wholly new genealogy, saying in Korean (translated via English subtitles):

> My mother went to City Hall and created a new registration. It included my late father [and] my mother and listed me as the eldest and only son. And my two [*sic*] sisters.[65] That was our new family registration. If I revealed that I had family in North Korea, or that I had any kind of family relations in North Korea, I would be immediately ostracized by Korean society.

Given the crucial role played by anticommunist ideology in the historical formation of South Korea, Min Yong's concerns about surveillance and rejection were not unfounded. Just after the departure of his siblings to the north, South Korean military police officers appeared at his home to ask questions. He relates (in English):

> I felt scared. Several times policemen came to my house and then woke up our house, and then search everything. All of the sudden I belong to a criminal family. And since then, I don't want to reveal myself to anybody else. The neighbor, to friend, I want to conceal.

Within a broader context, the South Korean state sanctified a hypervigilant stance toward North Korea, with anticommunist sentiments infiltrating every facet of daily life, ranging from all levels of education to residential neighborhood programs that indoctrinated citizens in nationalistic rhetoric concerning the looming threat of communist espionage.[66]

Jungran Shin, another narrator interviewed by Ramsay Liem and Borshay Liem for the Legacies of the Korean War project, describes how her elementary and high school teachers frequently instructed her and her classmates to be "foot soldiers" for the South Korean state by reporting suspicious friends and family members to the police: "Whenever we [wrote] an essay, we would write something like . . . 'we will defeat the Communists and reunite our country.' . . . [W]e were constantly educated to report [to a government agency] whoever looked suspicious."[67] After 1953, the South Korean state expanded the reach of the National Security Act, initially passed by the government in 1948 to punish those suspected of organizing activities to undermine the state.⁶⁸ Following the successful coup d'état by the military strongman Park in 1961, the South Korean government implemented the Anticommunist Law, designed to punish those suspected of affiliations with North Korea (including family members and friends of targeted civilians). As Namhee Lee observes, these laws were devised not merely to target North Korea or "real communists" but also to identify any and all domestic dissenters unfaithful to Park's regime.⁶⁹

Although South Korea experienced a softening of these policies after its long transition to civilian rule in the early 1990s, its citizens and Korean diasporic subjects alike still contend with the damaging consequences of communist red-baiting. Indeed, the repercussions of the National Security Act, which still exists today, are transnational in scope and impact. Until fairly recently, South Korean citizens with family in the North were blacklisted from participating in public life: thousands were barred from government employment and unable to apply for positions with major corporations, while others were denied entry into the military academy.⁷⁰ Following the impeachment of South Korean President Park Geun-hye in March 2017, it was revealed that more than ten thousand Korean filmmakers, artists, and musicians had been placed on a government blacklist, with direct orders from Park to "intimidate" and "humiliate" the identified individuals for their leftist sentiments and critiques of her conservative government.⁷¹ In other notable cases that gained international media attention, the Korean/American peace activists Juyeon Rhee and Christine Ahn were barred from entering South Korea in 2016 and 2017, respectively, as they traveled to the country to protest the installment of THAAD (Terminal High Altitude Area Defense), a new American antiballistic missile defense system, in Seongju, South Korea. According to South Korea's Ministry of Justice, Ahn, a prominent diasporic feminist activist who was vociferously critical of the now ousted Park regime, was denied entry on "sufficient grounds" that her presence would "hurt the national interests and public safety" of the country.⁷² In this particular case, "national interests and public safety" are part of anticommunist rhetoric aimed at quashing dissenting opinions critical of the South Korean government.

Even while attempting to "start his life over" in the United States, as Min Yong puts it, the consequences of these institutionalized practices of surveillance, blacklisting, and exclusion from public life did not end with his family's departure from South Korea. The constant fear of being "discovered" or "found out" as a family member of North Korean "sympathizers" informed Min Yong's relationships with his family, acquaintances, and even strangers in the United States. For the next thirty or so years, Min Yong remained reticent about his experiences with the war, choosing to "hide [him]self" from his family, friends, and co-workers. He said (in English):

> When I meet friends and people, I'm cheerful, big smile. And then [when I'm] asked [about] some personal family story, then I just avoid or ignore telling some other things. . . . I never mention about my brothers and sisters who disappeared.

Ironically, Min Yong's decision to move his family from South Korea in search of safety and security is troubled by a U.S. history informed by an equally pervasive climate of anticommunism. The post-1945 liberalization of U.S. Cold War immigration and refugee policies overlapped with a new hierarchal system of preferences, requirements, and protocols meant to maintain a heteronormative, pro-American populace. The Immigration and Nationality Act of 1952, for example, granted the U.S. government the power to deport immigrants and naturalized citizens engaged in what it vaguely defined as "deviant behavior" and "subversive activities," spanning from those who espoused communist sympathies to those identified by the state as "sexually deviant" or "homosexual."[73] U.S. government agencies such as the Federal Bureau of Investigation (FBI) and the House Un-American Activities Committee also collaborated with the South Korean Central Intelligence Agency (KCIA) to monitor and deport Korean/Americans suspected of North Korean affiliations. For example, members of Los Angeles's Korean National Revolutionary Party, an organization critical of American policy in Asia, were questioned by the FBI and eventually deported from the country.[74] Hence, the coalescing of anticommunist governance in South Korea was not a discrete effort but part of the Cold War global surveillance system.[75] A former FBI agent named John L. ("Jack") Ryan echoes these binding sentiments describing South Korean and American collusion. In 1985, Ryan was charged with investigating a North Korean espionage incident involving several Korean students in Illinois.[76] The U.S. government's anticommunist interrogation of Korean/American students clearly demonstrated the convergence between "foreign policy of South Korea" and American Cold War domestic policy.[77]

In his oral history, Min Yong hints at these bipolar sentiments in the United States and the incessant red-baiting of those suspected of having communist ties, even among Korean/Americans themselves, saying (in Korean):

> If you found yourself agreeing with communism or socialism, then you would be immediately ostracized as a Kim Il-sung puppet. . . . And that may be the cause of all of this. By "all of this," I mean clos-

ing oneself off. Having to hide the ideals of an entire generation, my brother's included, is a kind of radical McCarthyism.

Consequently, Min Yong's "new life" in the United States is inevitably interwoven with this "old life" in Korea. Even Min Yong's ability to reunite with his siblings in North Korea is literally contingent on the intricacies of American bureaucratic governance and delicate mediation. With nearly all South Korean citizens barred from North Korea, Min Yong applied for and eventually gained American citizenship so that he was able to visit his family in Pyongyang, North Korea, in 2000. In the most mundane yet impactful of ways, American intervention plays an unequivocal role in determining the (im)mobility of Korean diasporic subjects seeking to reunite with loved ones across entrenched barriers, both geographical and metaphorical. Perhaps one of the most incisive examples of the binding impact of U.S.–South Korean political complicities is the entwinedness of anticommunist logics and the racialized and gendered discourse of American model minority citizenship. Here I return to Eun-Joung's oral history and her depiction of her childhood in Atlanta, an outlier insofar as most Koreans, during the 1970s and early 1980s, were migrating to coastal or midwestern cities such as Los Angeles, New York, and Chicago:

> I didn't know any other life than growing up in, you know, Atlanta in the late '70s. As far as I remember, I think I had a pretty happy childhood. My friends were, at that time—the schools that I went to were, you know, half white, half black, [and a] handful of Asians like us. And my friends were about, you know, equally half black, half white, and handful of Asians. And I think for the most part we had a good childhood. I know my father went from being a university professor to working at a cash register in the equivalent of a 7-Eleven. . . . So he did that for a couple of years, and my mom was a nurse, and they saved up enough money to open up their own small business.

At first glance, Eun-Joung's chrononormative narrative seemingly reinscribes a familiar understanding of immigration as a chronological, linear, and heteronormative progression through which subjects migrate to, settle into, and establish familial roots in new places. Through this temporalized and spatialized move, Eun-Joung's family fulfills the "American dream" by vertically traversing the socioeconomic ladder: while her father is demoted from a white-collar profession in South Korea to a blue-collar occupation in Atlanta's service sector, her parents eventually save enough money to purchase a small business. Relatedly, Eun-Joung's description, in certain ways, is framed through an aperture of middle-class, multicultural, and multiracial harmony: her "good" childhood is filled with friends who were "equally half black, half white," as well as Asian, while her parents are able eventually to enjoy the well-earned fruits of middle-class life in the United States, despite the dogged challenges they faced upon their arrival.

But several times in her oral history, Eun-Joung adamantly troubles this rosy depiction by referring to her parents' racialized experiences in the United States. Near the beginning of her interview, she recalls memories of accompanying her mother during her nursing visits to the homes of senior citizens and the tension that would surface as these patients derided her mother with racial epithets: "I didn't understand what was going on. I, you know, I didn't understand English, but I could tell that there was so much tension in that room, and only years later I came to understand that tension was racism; that they weren't treating my mom well." In other descriptions, Eun-Joung juxtaposes her father's reticence with the anticommunist climate in South Korea and the costs of exposure in the United States. For Eun-Joung, her father's hesitation to speak and share is not a symptom of forgetting but a mode of fragmented communication that resonates loudly and painfully within the domestic confines of their family. As Eun-Joung notes, her father's palpable silence is convincing evidence that her parents desired to start anew in the United States without "burdening us [Eun-Joung and her sisters] with the story [of the war]. It was too depressing."

If we are to reanalyze Min Yong's reservation to speak in relation to his public persona as an exemplary immigrant worker and a husband and father beyond blame (in other words, the popular perception of the Asian/American model minority), we might disarticulate the instrumental ways in which an arrangement of factors converge to constitute what the American public commonly perceives as good and acceptable immigrant behavior. As Victor Bascara smartly observes, the miraculous conversion of Asian/Americans from the "yellow menace" to proper national subjects who could be "incorporated, uplifted, apologized to, and at times, literally healed" works hard to uphold a discourse of benevolent progress, inclusion, and multicultural tolerance. In turn, these idealized principles were upheld and consecrated by Cold War America.[78] However, the stinging reminder that Korean/Americans are *here,* in the first place, because of the U.S. military's presence over *there* in a divided Korea, pulls apart this fabricated account of seamless assimilation, revealing what Bascara pinpoints as fracture points, or "contradictions embedded within American culture," in the "form of underdevelopment, exclusion, and intolerance."[79]

The connective tissue that sutures the Korean War to a collaborative set of anticommunist migration policies, U.S. militarized intervention in Asia, and the racialization of Asian/Americans as model minorities is raised by several other narrators in Legacies of the Korean War, including the transformative justice activist and scholar Mimi Kim. Mimi, whose father was separated from his family in the North during the armed conflict, reiterates the urgent need to examine the enmeshed dynamisms of war, power, and violence that enable and actualize Korean militarized migrations to the United States. Referring to how "this whole model minority idea that people all came over for better . . . opportunities" is so thoroughly engrained in the American popular imaginary, Mimi asks why so many people, including Asian/Americans, "buy into that": "Are we even talking about the Vietnam War? Do you remember why people, Southeast Asians, are here? And Koreans. I mean, I consider myself here because of the Korean War."

"It's Political"

While the bulk of Eun-Joung's oral history addresses her father's experiences of war and division, she also delves into the untidy implications of the Korean War for her own life. Rather than diagnosing these repercussions as unresolved hauntings inherited from her parents, I attend to them, as Lisa Yoneyama suggests in her work with Japanese atomic bomb survivors (*hibakusha*), as historical formations structurally reproduced by a protracted war engrained within the cultural, social, and affective lives of Korean diasporans across national and generational lines.[80]

In the most immediate sense, Eun-Joung refers to the reiterations of division within her own family life. Here I return to Eun-Joung's existential questioning of her own identity and relationships with family members within the context of the Korean War. When Eun-Joung's family migrated to the United States in 1976, her parents decided to leave their youngest daughter in Korea in the care of her grandmother; she joined her parents and siblings in Atlanta in 1979. As Eun-Joung explains, her overwhelmed parents were uncertain about whether they could manage the process of moving across the globe with three young children: "She was an infant. . . . [W]e learned later that was one of the hardest, most difficult decisions that my parents had to make. . . . [T]hey simply didn't feel that they could manage three children, three very young children, in the process of immigration to the U.S." For Eun-Joung, the temporary separation created tension within her family and a strained relationship with her youngest sister until they both reached adulthood. Describing her sister as temporarily abandoned by the family, Eun-Joung explains that the causal conditions informing her parents' decision, including economic uncertainty, social precarity, and the fear of red-baiting, are indelibly marked by the Korean War: "That's a direct legacy of the Korean War . . . my parents having to make this awful decision and her life being, you know—the course of her life being set by that decision. And I'm sure so many families have similar stories like that."

Throughout the oral history, Eun-Joung simultaneously intimates tensions with her father, who still refrains from speaking openly about the war with his family and close friends. When asked whether she discussed *Memory of Forgotten War* with her father, Eun-Joung laughs and conveys that she has received only "bits and pieces" of information from him. Even after Min Yong visited North Korea in 2000, Eun-Joung perused only a handful of photographs from her father's trip. Although Eun-Joung is well aware of and sensitive to the damaging toll of war on both of her parents, she expresses a profound sense of sadness and frustration that her father remains guarded about the war with his family: "I feel another level of sadness that he feels so restrained in being unable to talk about it inside his own family. . . . [D]on't be ashamed of [your involvement in the documentary]! It's something to celebrate." However, from Min Yong's perspective, we might surmise that his decision to remain mum about his family's fraught history is less about shame and embarrassment than an improvised strategy to protect his family and himself from potential violence inflicted by the South Korean and U.S. governments due to his personal connections with North Korea. Thus, rather than attending to Min Yong's silence as an inability or unwillingness to speak about a foregone past, I situate his reticence alongside and in relation to Cold War anticommunist political culture and discourse, which are still very much alive in South Korea and the United States.

Although Eun-Joung speaks to the confounding silences indicative of her communication with family members, it is critical to foreground how this hesitancy, even fear, to speak about North Korea inundates her narrative as well. Within a thirty-minute span of Eun-Joung's oral history, the words "It's too political" and iterations of this phrase appear eleven times. In every case, "It's too political" is code for the taboo subject of North Korea. Throughout the interview, Eun-Joung is clearly unnerved when the issue is broached by Borshay Liem and Takagi and frequently moves away from potentially triggering conversations that focus on North Korea and the damaging consequences of American military intervention. Instead, she opts for milder framings that depoliticize or "humanize" the Korean War:

> Any mention of North Korea or having any interest in North Korea is automatically, immediately deemed as pro-communist. . . . [I] somehow internalized at an early age that anything related with North

Korea was a taboo topic. I just felt that, you know, that's a topic that's—that's not easy to talk about, right?

This reluctance is more noticeable when Eun-Joung describes an interview conducted by the cable network CNN with her father regarding his appearance in the documentary for the commemoration of the sixtieth anniversary of the Korean armistice (2013). Prior to the interview, a CNN correspondent revealed to Eun-Joung that the network had selected her father as an interviewee because of his ability to discuss the war from a civil or "humanistic" perspective rather than from a caustic or "angry" position, as others featured in the documentary did. Concurring with this statement, Eun-Joung observes that her father's capacity to address the Korean War as a "humanitarian issue" rather than "making it into a political thing" provides a "good opportunity" for him to speak to a broader, more diverse audience about the overwhelming costs and consequences of Korean division.

In contrast, I suggest that we might reencounter Min Yong's framing of the Korean War *beyond* the binary of good and evil as an attempt to speak against and outside of Cold War historical writing. As a militarized migrant associated with North Korean family members, a diasporic subject who has experienced the toll of anticommunist surveillance, *and* an American citizen recognized as a model minority subject in the United States, Min Yong refuses to abide by an "us versus them" binary so essential to and necessary for Cold War historiographical writing. Rather, encompassing localized knowledges that trace the messiness, complexities, and micro-aggressions of a prolonged war, Min Yong's life history attends to—perhaps even upends—the feel-good linkages that suture the Korean War to the discourse of American benevolence and "humanitarian" sentiments. If re-rendered through this alternative frame, Min Yong's narrative decolonizes the dominant discourse of the Korean War, which champions the United States and South Korea as shining beacons of free democracy while demonizing North Korea as a savage communist regime responsible for warfare and division.

Coda

In this chapter, I engage the Cold War historiography of Korean militarized migrations to the United States in the past seven decades. While the temporal markers of "pre-" and "post-"1965 attenuate and distance the devastating pastness of the Korean War from the here and now, a synergetic reading of transnational legislative acts and on-the-ground practices, anticommunist discourse, and cultural sources tell us otherwise. The arbitrary designations "past" and "present" are not so much discrete temporalities as what Ann Laura

Stoler refers to as persistent "durabilities" of a militarized colonial endeavor that remains firmly in place.[81] While the Korean War, of course, ever shifts its "temporal, spatial and affective coordinates," its protean life has ensured that its most pressing repercussions gestate into forms and formations of violence that replenish themselves in the most bureaucratic, mundane, and subtle ways.[82]

In rereading the acute and gradual as conjoined rather than oppositional conditions, this chapter also links the immediate departures of Koreans from the peninsula following the outbreak of fighting to "post-1965" migrations that pundits and politicians alike describe as opportunities gifted by a benevolent America. Specifically, by intentionally renaming these immigrations "militarized migrations," I identify how the material and affective conditions of war refuge intersect with and fold into normative immigration categories that privilege white, heteronormative, and anticommunist ideals of proper Americanness. The narrow set of temporary emergency policies discussed in this chapter, as well as the inherent assumptions regarding who deserves entrance, aid, and compassion, served as harbinger and clearing ground for immigration changes that would affect Korean militarized migrations in the decades to come. In this way, the identifiable markers that distinguish the Korean refugee from the immigrant are confused, if not collapsed altogether. Yet as Min Yong's and Eun-Joung's oral histories attest, the speedy transformation of the Korean War refugee into the grateful, hardworking, and quiet model minority absorbed into the American populace is not always so seamless or smooth. Rather, the militarized terms and conditions propelling these diasporic movements precipitate in unexpected ways, defying the chrononormative expectations of linear, multiracial, and heterosexual integration.

With these tensions in mind, I circle back to the coverage of Lee Yong Soon in *Life*, a profile that erases and replaces Yong Soon's "old" Korean name with the "new" Americanized nickname Blue. I was unable to locate other substantive articles focusing on Yong Soon's life and marriage in the United States, but my research eventually led to the online portfolio of Wayne Miller, the contract photographer hired for the *Life* profile. While looking through a series of black-and-white images posted under Miller's Magnum Photos website, I came across one photograph that did not make it to the final two-page spread in *Life*.[83]

In the close-up shot, a smiling Johnie is lying in bed next to Yong Soon, who is dressed in a lace-collared short-sleeve silk top that exposes her bare shoulders and arms. Her left arm is casually propped over her husband's bare chest as her head comfortably sits on Johnie's extended arm. Depicting a snuggling Yong Soon and Johnie underneath disheveled covers, Miller's intimate portrayal hints at a possible post-coital moment as the camera's unwav-

Johnie and Yong Soon in bed, *Life* magazine, November 1951.
(Courtesy of Magnum Foundation. Photograph by Wayne Miller.)

ering gaze captures the resting couple as they move to clasp hands. It seems reasonable to conclude that this image was dropped because its suggestive, sexually tinged imagery might spur feelings of uneasiness and disapproval among *Life*'s overwhelmingly white, suburban, and middle-class readership.[84]

Here my reference to such negative feelings indexes the public's ambivalent attitudes toward Korean women and how Asian war brides tested the very limits of American generosity and goodwill. Korean militarized migrants were welcomed into the United States as long as they did not diverge from and threaten the white, heteronormative, and anticommunist social order. But for the American public, the suggested sexual liaisons between American soldiers and their exotic Korean wives were challenging to the degree that such illicit unions hinted at the inevitability of sexual "mixing" and the reproduction of a "mixed-race," nonwhite population that could compromise an all-American milieu. As possible consolation or salve to such anxieties, Korean women were expected to integrate into the American population as seamlessly, quietly, and quickly as possible. And yet, such hushed processes of assimilation were always already partial insofar as the perceived racialized and gendered difference of Korean militarized migrants marked them as potentially dangerous and not quite as American as apple pie. In this way, the militarized presence of Korean women in the United States gestures to a range of refutations: their *unassimilation* registers the damaging impact of American racial exclusivity, as well as militarized migrants' incapacity—and sometimes adamant refusal—to integrate gratefully into the folds of white America. In this way, the excluded image of Yong Soon and Johnie symbolizes the racialized, gendered, and sexual violence materialized by the Korean War, as well as notions of racial and gendered difference that fly in the face of America's fictionalized discourse of liberal inclusion and humanitarianism.

2

Aurality

If you practice listening, you hear so much.
—Ramsay Liem, "The Making(s) of Memory Archives"

Listening is an act of community, which takes space, time and silence.
—Ursula K. Le Guin, "The Operating Instructions"

In *Pianoiss . . . issmo (Worse Finish)* (2012), the sound artist Christine Sun Kim offers an arresting visual study of silence. Crowned with a single letter "P" on top, the triangular flowchart gradually cascades into a progression of descending steps, with each subsequent *p* level proliferating by a multiple of 3 (the second row multiplies into four *p*'s; the third, into 12; and so forth). Intimating the very title of the work—*pianissimo* in Italian means "very soft" or "very softly"—every layer of *p* amplification inversely corresponds with an implied volume: the more *p*'s there are, the quieter it becomes. And yet this muffling of sound does not erase all sonic traces. For Kim, a deaf artist who engages sound through visual, vibrational, and felt means, this representation of diffused sound visualizes the sonic shape of silence beyond absence or void. As Kim describes in a 2015 interview, her "*p*-tree" communicates that "no matter how many thousands upon thousands of *p*'s there may be, you'll never reach 'complete' silence."[1]

Kim's "*p*-tree" sketch readily demonstrates the previous chapter's discussion of the symptomatic implications of Cold War militarized violence and the permutations of silence embedded in Eun-Joung Lee's and Min Yong Lee's lives. As addressed in Chapter 1, Min Yong's identification of the Korean War as the connective tissue that links his "old" life in South Korea to his "new" life in the United States accentuates the binding implications of an unfinished war that transcends national and temporal distinctions. In essence, Min Yong describes how the chilling effects of the Korean War have

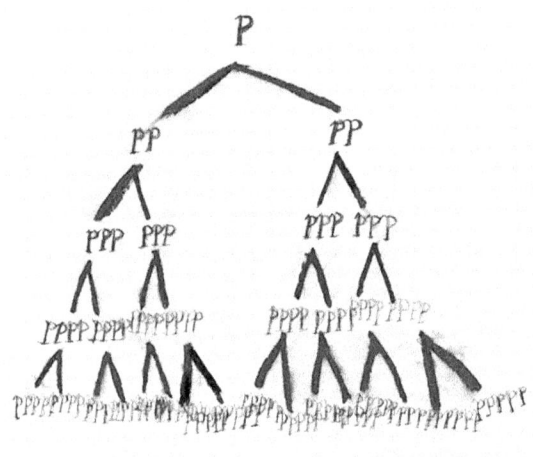

Sounds (P-Tree), charcoal and pen on paper, 2012.
(Courtesy of Christine Sun Kim.)

morphed into a pervasive quietness that infiltrates all facets of his family life. Min Yong's reticence also gestures to the engendering of silences among his daughters, including Eun-Joung. This disarray of burgeoning silences, emerging as fragmented knowledges of the war and denied access to family history, hints at the mundane ways in which the Korean War structures and permeates the everyday lives of Korean diasporic subjects.

Mobilizing Kim's drawing as a starting point, Chapter 2 deepens and departs from the previous chapter's examination of condensed familial silences among participants of the Legacies of the Korean War and *Memory of Forgotten War* projects. While Chapter 1 squarely situates oral history as a narrative text that communicates the muted oppressions of the Korean War, this chapter reorients oral history as a diasporic memory practice that suggests the unforeseen potentialities of branching silences. That is, rather than solely approaching silences as negative aftereffects of oppressive measures, this chapter considers how oral history's mediation of silence actualizes multiple forms of participatory remembering and political solidarities that push against the limits of dominant Cold War portrayals. In turn, oral history forges a horizontal radiation of coalitional affinities and listening spaces that refuses to be confined to the vertical lineage of heteronormative relations and blood kinship.

This reframing of oral history as a contested terrain of dialogical negotiations departs from established memory and trauma literature, which tends to characterize oral history as a testimonial platform—that is, oral history *as* testimony giving.[2] Within this psychoanalytical framing, a unidirectional dynamic crystallizes as a narrator speaks about a past event or "unclaimed" trauma to an interviewer, whose primary obligation is to listen and serve as a witness within the discrete space of the testimony. While this past event is a driving force in the narrator's life, this understanding of testimony giving underscores the unexplainable characteristic of trauma: it is unrecognizable to the narrator because trauma destroys any sense of intelligible and emotional coherence.[3] This calculus suggests that a subject's self-preservation depends on their capacity to disassociate completely from and silence the self at the moment of traumatic impact. Subsequently, survival is a hushed form of afterlife that culminates at the terminus of an event, even as lingering traumatic residues uncannily repeat through a cycle of emotional ruptures and psychic disturbances. The narrator then "breaks the silence" by speaking to a listening witness who becomes, as Dori Laub puts it, a "blank screen on which the event comes to be inscribed for the first time."[4]

In productive tension with this articulation of trauma, this chapter identifies the divergent ways in which a transient community of Korean diasporic *participants*—narrators who are also listeners—grapples with a convergence of militarized entanglements that eclipses any single account of survival. In other words, the living status of the Korean War necessitates different questions that exceed the aforementioned model of trauma. What does survival mean, and look and sound like, when the devastating event itself is prolonged? What obligations or stakes are associated with memory and remembering when the multiple traumas induced by war reflect rather than interrupt the everyday? And if we understand silence as a communicating discourse that speaks across multiple registers, what does the act of listening tell us about the tenacity of a pervasive war? By privileging listening as the pivotal mnemonic praxis of this chapter, I attune to the ways in which oral—or, more precisely, *aural*—history senses sonic shards that escape the conventional ways in which we might hear and remember war. Put differently, the aural capacities of oral history point to the urgent need to reencounter *pianissimo* resonances that are not always registered as "sounds of war" in the first place. Hence, while I do not romanticize aural histories as emancipatory formations delinked from enduring militarized colonial violence, these textured processes facilitate diasporic memories or "mnemonic sounds" that shift our analysis from individuated psychic imprints to historical and social formations implicated within the noisy composition of contemporary life. This reorientation exemplifies the myriad ways in which silence, as the feminist oral historian Luisa Passerini puts it, is "connected with remembering, not with forgetting."[5] Concurrently, by placing pressure on the aural dimensions of narrative and listening practices, this chapter builds on the heterogeneous scholarship of feminist oral historians, including Sherna Berger Gluck, Passerini, and Sady Sullivan, who accentuate the principles of relationality, ethical care, and radical empathy within the oral history process.[6] This last point is particularly meaningful as I consider the decolonizing possibilities associated with aural history.

To flesh out the agentive possibilities of aural history, this chapter carefully analyzes the Intergenerational Korean American Oral History Project, which was founded in 2012 by the visual artist and writer Sukjong Hong and the multimedia artist Danny Kim. The Intergenerational project conceptualizes aural history as a multilayered process that unfolds beyond the spatiotemporal confines of a single interview. To be clear, "intergenerational" and "generational" in this project do not signify categories of biologically related kin progressively removed from an original moment of trauma. Rather, as indicated by Hong and Kim, the vernacular use of these politically constructed terms refers to how and where project participants locate themselves within the historical terrain of U.S. immigration (e.g., "1.5 generation" refers to those born in Korea but raised in the United States, while "second generation" refers to those born and raised in the United States).[7] Ultimately, through the dynamic sharing of narratives that exceed rigid periodization, participants reconfigure "generational" into a politicized category constituted through social and experiential, rather than biological and genetic, means. Indeed, Hong and Kim are explicit about their framing of the Intergenerational project as a community-organizing process rather than as an institutionalized repository of fossilized memories. They describe how the Intergenerational project's aural history paradigm facilitates affinities without quarantining such relations to ethnocentric, nationalist, and embodied sameness. As discussed at length in the Introduction, I approach the diasporic as a feminist mode of critical analysis that situates vexed subjectivities in contradistinction to patriarchal articulations of national time, political citizenry, and public memory. Yet it is precisely these diasporic excesses, or "non-normative" social formations, that contend with the inner workings of Cold War historicism through alternative ways of listening and remembering. Thus, in conversation with critical refugee scholars such as Ma Vang, who foreground the "gendered formation" and "gaps" of Americanized Cold War historiography, I conceptualize aurality as a diasporic methodological praxis that potentiates solidarities *through* and *in tension with* difference.[8]

Drawing from an extended interview conducted with Hong and Kim in 2016, the next section of the chapter examines three framing principles of the Intergenerational project's narration-and-listening model. These interrelated principles include the collaborative dimensions of aural history, the centrality of differentiated listening practices to the interview process, and the multiplicities of silence. By foregrounding these praxis-oriented dimensions, I point to the ways in which the Intergenerational project unsettles the seeming cohesiveness or naturalized uniformity of Cold War historical memory. Considering how dominant political discourse in the United States persistently privileges a hypermasculine, hypernationalist ethos of anticommunism, U.S. exceptionalism, and American heroism, a participant's will and willingness to craft oppositional memories of the Korean War does not simply remedy the conspicuous gaps of Cold War knowledge production. These diasporic memories instead delineate the *always already evacuated status* of the official historical record. Reformulating aural history as a layered process that mediates reencounters with the Korean War, the Intergenerational project facilitates an intersubjective mode of inquiry through which participants contemplate their own sense of historical agency and political consciousness in dialogue with other narrators and listeners.[9] Insisting on the project's capacity to trouble the epistemological underpinnings of Cold War/Korean War knowledge production, I consider the crucial methodological implications of the Intergenerational project's aural history paradigm.

The third and final section of the chapter elaborates on the temporal elasticity of the Intergenerational project's narratives as memories are re-listened to, reinterpreted, and performed across different publics. Describing this continuum of interpretive moves as "re-performances," I foreground the fluctuations of mnemonic production through the reanimation of memories beyond the momentary space of the "original" interview.[10] While re-performance explicitly refers to the performance scholarship of Rebecca Schneider, the term also suggests Toni Morrison's conceptualization of *rememory,* or the tendency of incidences (in this case, the interview) to endure beyond a single moment in time.[11] In accentuating the regenerative properties of memory, the Intergenerational project attunes both to the uneven conditions and the liberating potentialities of radical knowledge production. In particular, the narrators and listeners conceptualize diasporic memory formation(s) as emblematic of an open-ended future.[12] Thus, re-performed memories do not resemble mummified inscriptions vertically imparted to and inherited by younger generations of biological kin. Instead, they are horizontal mnemonic sounds necessary for the imagining and imaging of a futurity unfettered by the strictures of a militarized here and now.

Beginnings

During an interview in June 2016, Sukjong Hong and Danny Kim discussed their intentions for jump-starting the Intergenerational Korean American

Oral History Project.[13] Hong and Kim are associated with Nodutdol for Korean Community Development, a politically leftist Korean diasporic organization and the sponsor of the Intergenerational project.[14] The majority of the project's first-generation participants are local members affiliated with Nodutdol and have a strong rapport with the organization's younger 1.5- and second-generation members, including Hong and Kim.[15] Given the politically sensitive, potentially distressing experiences shared during the narration-and-listening sessions, the nurturing of trust within the spatial confines of Nodutdol is a necessary anchoring point for the project.[16]

Hong herself has participated in several other oral history projects initiated by and beyond Nodutdol, including the *Still Present Pasts* exhibit.[17] Yet while Nodutdol has coordinated a cluster of short-term "mini-oral history gathering sessions," constraints such as limited staff resources and viable funding have prevented the organization from sustaining oral history projects beyond the real time and space of discrete interviews. As Hong states, "The projects, like one for the sixtieth anniversary of the Korean armistice [in 2013], were super brief and weren't collective. It was just somebody going over to somebody else's house, collecting this history, and coming back with this CD or tape. . . . And at the end, not all of *us heard* the oral histories" (emphasis added). The gravity placed on collaborative listening ("us" and "heard") underscores how the Intergenerational project's participants mobilize aural history as a critical participatory process rather than an insular volley between interviewer and interviewee.[18]

In broad strokes, the Intergenerational project aims to cultivate relationships through a shared sense of political consciousness; address controversial questions too unsettling to raise in public spaces; forge social bonds among participants; and build skills in interviewing, archiving, and documentation processes. Hong and Kim refer to these four interrelated elements as *organizing* communities, *disrupting* official narratives, *bridging* divides, and *generating* new potentialities, and they constitute the discursive backbone of the project. In the beginning of the project's conceptualization in 2012, Kim said, he was "looking to be a part of an oral history process that looks differently than other projects." When asked to elaborate, he explained his desire to partake in "an ongoing process" and to "be a part of a forming community that shares stories and thinks of ways to activate oral histories through tools like cultural practices."

Here my elaboration of the tentative beginnings of the Intergenerational project circles back to the contentious relationship between aural history praxis and the core tenets of Cold War historiography. If Cold War Orientalizing knowledges are reproduced through an authorial approach that privileges the white hypermasculine American soldier as the heroic liberator, a participant-driven aural history paradigm, as we shall see, breaks apart

**Intergenerational Korean American
Oral History Project Paradigm**

Peer Trainings

Second-Generation Story Sessions

First-Generation Interview Sessions

Community Listening Sessions

First-Generation/Second-Generation Bridging Session

Cross-Generational Story Exchange

Interpretive Workshops

Summary of the Intergenerational Korean American
Oral History Project's working paradigm.
(Created by the author.)

these assumptions by amplifying a decentered and polyvocal, polyaural approach to memory making among Korean diasporic subjects. Through this gradated narration-and-listening process, participants examine the striking disjuncture between their own understandings of the Korean War and the formal histories recodified by the U.S. nation-state and American popular media. Kim offered the following observation:

> These mainstream narratives, like the histories taught here in the U.S. around Korean history, are just lacking—if they're taught at all. It just seems like the U.S. is always framed as this benefactor or the benevolent, the central force that "helped" South Korea to overcome the war. And then Koreans immigrate to and become a part of America. I guess we wanted to provide different interpretations from folks who survived this moment but who are never even mentioned in this official narrative. So, yeah, the intention was to build what you might call a "people's history" that fights against this kind of script.

To build a "people-centered" history of the Korean War, Kim and Hong co-organized a series of study sessions during a four-month interval in 2012.[19]

Meeting at Nodutdol's office in Woodside, Queens, and at the homes of several members, participants collectively researched, read about, and analyzed various methodological approaches to oral history. For the project's participants, the forging of deinstitutionalized spaces of collaborative learning and listening is necessary to interrogating the methodological roots of oral history praxis in the U.S. academy, a practice that originally *supplemented* rather than *challenged* the dominant logic of institutional archives.[20] Relatedly, these "othered" spaces of learning foreground the reification of Cold War political discourse within the infrastructural confines of the academy.

While Hong and Kim refrained from portraying the university in homogeneous terms, their comments allude to the proclivity of professionalized spaces such as the university to manufacture discrete bodies of knowledge associated with differing degrees of expertise, rigor, and reason. In turn, it is these official corpuses of knowledge that are canonized, cited, reproduced, reprinted, and recirculated in the academic sphere and dominant culture. In contrast, "vernacular" knowledges co-produced by Intergenerational project participants exist on the fringe, or even outside, of institutionalized spaces; most researchers deem them "uncritical," "too personal," "emotional," and "unreliable."[21] And yet these alternative knowledges also convey the power differentials and partiality of Cold War political discourse. Thus, aligning with Fred Moten's and Stefano Harney's discussion of critical study in *The University and the Undercommons,* Hong and Kim mobilize collaborative learning to trace the entwinements of power, knowledge production, and the hierarchy of value affixed to divergent iterations of history.[22] For Hong, a reassessment of these discrepancies segues with other concerns identified by Intergenerational project members, including "what it means to do oral history in social movements as opposed to doing more 'professional' oral history."[23]

After reflecting on eight or so models of interviewing, participants were struck by approaches grounded in women of color feminism that prioritize a "coalitional politics of difference."[24] Specifically, by drawing attention to the overarching principle of collaboration through difference, participants expressed a desire to conceptualize a narration-and-listening model that would make space for rather than assimilate or erase the variegated knowledges, experiences, and subject-positionalities of project members. Following this gestational period of methodological exploration, participants co-determined project goals and intentions and conceptualized group protocols, including the prioritization of bilingual interviews and interpretation and distribution methods.[25] What eventually emerged is a still developing, multistep paradigm that encompasses an eight-part sequence of narration, listening, collaborative analyses, and public sharing sessions.[26]

The aural history interview, then, constitutes a memory-making *process* rather than a single *act*. These interrelated segments include peer-training workshops that facilitate the sharing of skills such as time coding and interviewing strategies, as well as two separate rounds of interview sessions. The first round takes place among Koreans born or raised in the United States, while the second round of interview sessions is conducted by these younger participants with elders who survived or were born immediately after the armed conflict. The process continues with a series of collaborative relistening workshops in which participants identify common themes and differences within each batch of interviews (Community Listening Session); clarify or add to what was already shared during the interview sessions (Bridging Session); and exchange multigenerational stories of war, migration, and survival (Cross-Generational Story Exchange). The final two steps of the aural history process include workshops in which participants interpret a curated selection of interview excerpts. In turn, these interpretations are shared with broader audiences through public performance, musical compositions, and short films.

The Intergenerational project's working paradigm of the multilayered interview engages core principles of oral history praxis, including *shared authority* and an *ethics of access*. For Michael Frisch, the concept of shared authority, or an insistence that all participants within a shared space are experts of their own experiences, necessitates a reevaluation of normative expectations that identify the interviewee/research subject as the authentic source of raw data and the interviewer/researcher as the trained expert who mines for and analyzes narratives.[27] In particular, this hierarchal relationship between interviewer and interviewee is destabilized by the multiple roles held by participants (as narrators *and* listeners) and the plethora of differentiated perspectives, knowledges, and orientations—intellectual, activist, and skills-based, as well as experiential and embodied—brought into the interview space. In contemplating the dynamics of power embedded in documentary film practice, Marit Corneil's scholarship approaches the ethics of access as a constantly evolving process of negotiation through which participants situate their skills, experiences, and access to cultural production apparatuses within larger socioeconomic, cultural, and political contexts.[28] In applying this principle to oral history, Elizabeth Miller observes that "grappling with larger representational questions as well as practical concerns" is essential to a process of redistributing rather than merely extending oral history training, production, and dissemination resources across a larger span of participants.[29] The Intergenerational project's model of narration and listening builds on these crucial principles to create and hold space for complex narrations perpetually omitted from official historical discourses in the United States.

Given its focus on the epistemological underpinnings, motivations, and high stakes of knowledge production, the Intergenerational project resonates with Linda Tuhiwai Smith's decolonizing methodology.[30] While Smith's work is in explicit conversation with indigenous peoples in and beyond Oceania, her attention to colonial violence within research methodologies, as well as the intimate linkages between epistemology and everyday discourse, reflects how Cold War historiography functions as part of a larger "division system" that names the United States as Korea's paternalistic liberator. This global system of bipolar division is replenished through conjunctive conditions, including the occupational presence of the American military in Korea and the North Pacific, systemic acts of militarized sexual violence perpetrated against "disposable" bodies, and the indefinite separation of families. For Kim and Hong, these aural histories provide an entry point and accessible platform for participants to "speak back" and against Cold War conditions of power. They also contribute to an alternative repertoire of diasporic memories at odds with naturalized portrayals of the Korean War in the United States. Within this social ecology of narration-and-listening spaces, Intergenerational project participants reencounter the "murkiness of who, exactly, is the enemy in ways that don't really come out in [American] history textbooks" (Hong).

Collaboration through Difference and Differentiated Listening

Despite the poignant ways in which the Intergenerational project provides meaningful opportunities for shared knowledge production, the exploratory process of conceptualizing a new aural history paradigm is replete with its own set of wrinkles or contradictions. The project raises a bevy of questions concerning social and epistemological differences among interlocutors, as well as the ethics of accessibility, which I address in this chapter's final section. In other words, the collaborative dimensions of the Intergenerational project are not commensurate with idealized notions of unanimity, consensus, and ethnocentric sameness. Instead, "collaborative" in this instance refers to an inherent messiness insofar as participants work through, alongside, and in tension with difference. These divergences are registered through participants' historical perspectives and embodied experiences of the Korean War, as well as their socioeconomic status, educational levels, language and listening capacities, and varied abilities.

My highlighting of collaboration through difference expands on an earlier description of participants' interest in women of color feminism. In particular, I reference the centrality of women of color feminist critique in the diasporic formation of the Intergenerational project's aural history paradigm. As Grace Kyungwon Hong and Roderick Ferguson point out, a women of color analytic foregrounds rather than obscures how "differentials" underlie "the vexed work of forging a *coalition politics*."[31] Framed differently, the pursuing of a collaborative narration-and-listening approach demonstrates how "difference between and within racialized, gendered, sexualized collectivities" functions at the heart of the political and intellectual work of the Intergenerational project.[32] This observation directs us to the tensions among participants, especially since multigenerational members have different experiences with and perspectives of warfare, displacement, and family separation. For instance, older participants speak of the disappearance of their spouses, parents, and close friends during the armed conflict, while others elaborate on the social and psychic impact of constantly living under a surveilling gaze in South Korea during the military dictatorship. As Kim observes, young participants born or raised in the United States decades after the Korean Armistice (1953), including him, express an ambivalent sense of "distance" or "separation" from these embodied experiences, even as they explain the different and diffused ways that they, too, are affected by the Korean War. Different participants thus express disparate knowledges of, and uneven exposure to, political activism and militarized violence. Sensitive to the triggering risks associated with sharing painful memories within a quasi-public space, Intergenerational project members navigate these moments of tension by "reflecting back" memories to participants with explicit statements of acknowledgment ("I heard you saying this"). This concept of reflecting back, as Kim explains, provides a "held" space for narrators to speak and be heard without insisting that they divulge "things they don't feel ready to reveal" or "really go deep into detail."[33] In this dialogical context, younger participants express both curiosity and interest in learning from older narrators to deepen their own understanding of the Korean War.[34] The Intergenerational Korean American Oral History Project, then, not only encompasses a pedagogical dimension. The interview process simultaneously reaffirms the subjugated knowledges of elders, who, as Hong puts it, "have the experience of others valuing a history that isn't really told anywhere else or is shut down by others."

These different forms of experiential, embodied, and discursive knowledge are further exemplified by the technical skills that participants bring into the interview space(s). Some members, for instance, are audiovisual artists; others are experimental video makers, zine artists, writers, researchers, or political activists. These differences are less about possessing discrete skills that contribute to the making of a homogeneous whole than about the incommensurability of historical experience and subject positionality. This attentiveness to difference, perhaps, is most evident through the praxis of differentiated aurality, or the conceptualization of listening as plural and textured. In contrast to a more traditional interview paradigm relegated to a researcher-narrator dyad, interviews conducted with participants within the Intergenerational project involve multiple listeners, usually three to four per session. In this context, listeners—primarily participants who identify as 1.5- or second-generation Korean/American—are also narrators to the degree that all members facilitating interviews are encouraged to share their experiences, anxieties, and questions during previous listening sessions tailored to meet the needs of young participants.

Kim and Hong explain that the implementation of a self-reflexive session specifically for young narrators and listeners serves several purposes. For one, it allows 1.5- and second-generation members to clarify their reasons for and stakes in becoming involved in the aural history project. Second, participants are able to share with one another their splintered and silenced knowledges of the Korean War or, as detailed later in this chapter, the "bits and fragments" of whispered information refracted through their family histories. Having opportunities to put into words their murky knowledges within a collaborative space impels an urgent sense of accountability, or what Leigh Patel theorizes as *answerability*: "being responsible, accountable and being part of an exchange."[35] Through this co-created sense of answerability, participants assume the responsibility of "being present during the interview process" and "listening to others as carefully as we can" (Kim). Consequently, a commitment to answerability requires participants to contend with the asymmetrical conditions of power that are inherent within oral history methodology. "Before asking someone else to share their story," Hong said, "it's important for those who want to participate to know what it's like to share their own story, to be heard, to be vulnerable and to have others listen to you and maybe misinterpret you."

The multiplicity of listeners within the interview space untethers the aural from the physiological boundaries of the naturalized body by exemplifying how textured listening is more than the accumulation of individuated sounds or "sonic reductions" instrumentally registered by the ear.[36] On the contrary, listening is a deeply subjective and multisensorial process sutured to one's orientation in the world. During our interview, Hong and Kim described one session in which a narrator touched on myriad experiences, ranging from acts of sexual violence perpetrated by the South Korean police force and army against friends and acquaintances to anxieties triggered by heighted anticommunist surveillance measures enacted under Park Chung-hee's Yushin Constitution (1972–1981).[37] During a debriefing session among listeners, it was evident to Hong and Kim that different members inhabiting the room attuned to divergent elements of the offered narrative. As Hong mentioned during our interview:

> Someone was attuned to [the narrator] speaking about gendered experiences of state violence. Someone else found the history of work and labor really key. And someone else was really interested in the mother-father [aspect] of the story. So it felt like with multiple listeners—depending on who you are, your own interests—there were multiple highlights and levels of emphasis that could be pulled out of this joint session.

The praxis of teasing out different elements of the same narrative, or differentiated listening, segues with a key question regarding language and bilingual abilities among participants. The majority of interviews conducted with first-generation narrators are primarily in Korean; questions related to bilingual capacity and translation are raised by young participants who may not be as adept at speaking or understanding Korean. Depending on their own familiarity or relationship with the Korean language, listeners will *hear* different nuances and *feel* different emotional resonances during the joint interview session. For Hong and Kim, the question of translation is a tricky one since it raises both pragmatic and conceptual concerns. (Who will translate? How does this act change the narrative, since translation is a meaning-making process rather than a neutral transaction?) These and other related inquiries address how different subjects communicate through and beyond verbal cues. But, as Hong and Kim emphasized, the Intergenerational project's narration-and-listening model provides space for negotiation and maneuvering, since multiple listening sessions following the first interview are integrated into the aural history paradigm. As a result, participants who are not wholly fluent in Korean are provided with different opportunities to relisten to narratives in collaborative settings. Hong offered this description:

> We try to stress that in [the interview] session itself, we'll try to give a summary translation so when there's a natural break, we'll get to the basic gist of the story. And also: it's not the end. We get together and listen to the narrative so there's time and moments where it will get translated in full or translated in depth and detail. So it's like the initial session is not the end at all of hearing the story. It's just the beginning.

For Kim, this crucial question of language and translation among listeners dovetails with the selective ways in which participants express their experiences with others and listen through and against assumed language limitations. In particular, he speaks to the "languaging" of narratives through emotional, physical, and gestural resonances. During one session in 2013, a first-generation narrator insisted on speaking in English, since several young listeners in the room had difficulty understanding the more technical aspects of the interview in Korean. In the process of speaking in English, however, the narrator struggled to explain certain events and historical concepts in detail. Ultimately, Kim felt as if nuances were potentially obscured because "certain things could not be articulated in the 'best' way given [that] they had to speak English." Yet rather than defining this Korean-to-English translation as a process of irretrievable loss, Kim observed that the narrator's improvisational way of communicating through gestural, tonal, and somatic cues was telling:

> It was interesting, this *feeling* that this interview could have been different in Korean. But also, the way [the narrator] explained in English, I think there might have been more emotion that was revealed in this way versus if they were speaking fluently in Korean. Because they're doing this in English, they had to use different ways of expressing or communicating with others—like hand motions, stomping their feet, closing their eyes, sighing and pausing, things like this. I'm guessing that in English, this narrator might have added emotion and body language to communicate.

Kim's reference to the connections between multisensorial listening and narration and emotional intensities underscores the project's mediation of affective contingencies.[38] That is, the interpretive readings of emotional vectors by narrators and listeners are crucial to how life histories are reencountered among participants. Here the affective or emotional exceeds the notion that the aural history interview is simply a "cathartic" space that permits the uninhibited releasing of repressed feelings (although in certain cases, this may certainly be the case). Instead, as the remainder of the chapter illustrates, a listener's capacity to gauge the bodily, verbal or emotional "signs" of an interview becomes one means of listening for and attuning to communicative silences embedded within shared histories. Perceived emotions within the interview thus demonstrate the degree to which affective dynamisms are integral to aural history methodology itself.[39] Framed in this way, the emotional undercurrents of an interview do not disrupt the remembering process. Instead, they are crucial to the production of diasporic memories. Aligned with Ann Cvetkovich's portrayal of an "archive of feelings," the Intergenerational project's repertoire of memories is a dialogical formation replete with "all kinds of affective resonances and not just clinical symptoms."[40]

"The Korean War Isn't a Bomber Jet Anymore": Listening for Silences

The discussion of narration and listening as a diasporic praxis, in conversation with and informed by women of color feminist theory, segues with the conceptualization of silence as a shape-shifting formation. I accentuate how aural history's mediation of silence engenders unforeseen possibilities, such as the actualization of diasporic solidarities and social affinities among Korean/Americans. Through collaborative discussions and analyses of silences that inform participants' lives, the Intergenerational project's sessions produce alternative social kinships in tension with the heteronormative conditions and contours of the ethnocentric nuclear family.

To clarify, my engagement with silence in relation to historical conditions of violence engages *and* departs from a Foucauldian analysis of silence. For Michel Foucault, silence is an element of power that indicates rather than opposes speech and proliferating discourse. Addressing the underpinnings of silence in conjunction with the Western modern state's disciplining, suppression and medicalization of sexuality throughout much of the nineteenth century, Foucault explores a dizzying gamut of mechanisms, discursive structures, and exhaustive details that congealed during an era of so-called sexual repression. Speaking loudly about its own condition of possibility, silence is "less the absolute limit of discourse . . . than an element that functions alongside the things said, with them, and in relation to them."[41]

As discussed in Chapter 1, this rendering of silence clearly resonates with narrators included in Legacies of the Korean War and *Memory of the Forgotten War,* speakers who are perceived as quiet and well-behaved model minorities in the United States. Interviewees' decisions to keep mum about their war experiences and shroud their familial associations in North Korea brush up against a transnational web of state policies, surveillance measures, and societal norms that threaten their material safety and dictate the conditions of (un)acceptable and (im)proper behavior. Several elders in the Intergenerational project also describe anticommunist monitoring as a fearful deterrent to openly speaking about the Korean War with their families; others express how divulging such entangled histories only exacerbates existing political discordance and hostilities within their social networks. In this context, silence is configured as an informed albeit limited strategy that permits narrators to practice a modicum of agency under extenuating circumstances. Indeed, Hong emphasizes that the familial silences discussed among young members—for instance, the refusal of parents or grandparents to share their experiences of division with their children and grandchildren—are not natural expressions of irreconcilable generational or cultural difference, as they are often interpreted by the public. Rather, such reticence is a sociohistorical formation anchored in the "idea of what can and can't be said out loud because of the Cold War's violence" (Hong). In this way, we might trouble how discrete acts of silencing and speaking are plotted along a linear trajectory: while the public commonly defines the former as an absolute sign of oppression or abject subjugation, the latter is formulated as an empowering decision that liberates all narrators from the oppressive chains of shame and fear. However, among Intergenerational project participants, this dichotomous articulation of silence and speech and the moral values affixed to each do not account for the complicated implications of Cold War dynamics that radiate from the domestic sphere, to one's community (however participants might define this), to the larger U.S. and South Korean societies.

Yet while Foucault describes silence as a "speaking discourse," his articulation seems to amplify silence's positive linkages with institutionalized forms of power: silence, as a by-product of power, remains within the discursive bounds of state discipline, regulation, and control. In contrast—and without minimizing silence's relationship with systemic forms of discursive and material violence—I want to consider how silence(s) confronted by Intergenerational project participants activate other potentialities. In line with the ways in which Passerini formulates multifaceted silences within oral history methodology, I look to how shared narratives and listening practices foreground silence's *agentive* capacities. More precisely, I am interested in silence's ability to open up and avail itself of new "ways of listening" and modes of relationality among aural history participants.[42]

During my extended conversation with Hong and Kim, I asked why it was crucial for them to gather cross-generational narratives of the Korean War beyond their own families. Both responded by describing a commonality linking narrations offered by participants. Nearly all of the young participants gesture to a threadbare, partial, or piecemeal quality to their knowledges of the Korean War. More specifically, young participants describe their own uncertainties regarding personal histories of war, separation, and division: during one session, some participants commented on an underlying sense of detachment from their family histories in Korea, while others expressed ambiguity about who, exactly (including themselves), belonged to and did not belong to their family history. Others referred to their frustrating struggles with the Korean language and their inability to communicate effectively with elders, while several participants described how gendered expectations strained relations with family members. For example, due to enduring norms of masculinity and strength attributed to cisgender men in their immediate families, participants pointed to the conspicuous absence of fathers, uncles, and grandfathers from fragmented discussions of the war. In turn, participants mentioned how these vexing silences intersected with different forms of suppression or silencing within their homes. Several participants mentioned that their queer or gender-nonconforming identities exacerbated already existing tensions within their families, contributing to a dejected sense of "unbelonging."[43] In the following excerpt, Kim elaborates on the concerns raised by 1.5- and second-generation participants:

> We gathered and shared our stories, we discussed our understandings of gaps within Korean history, what we understood to be true, and what we felt like was missing. We discovered a few common threads among our experiences—primarily, we knew to a certain extent, but not much more than that. There was this sense that there was still so much to learn. Basically, we discussed how hard it was to learn about the Korean War through our family members.

Yet among these young participants, this common experience of entrenched silence and silencing generated inquiries regarding the discursive limitations placed around the Korean War within their families. The realization that participants were not alone in their experiences of familial silence "sparked," as Hong notes, "a thousand of other questions" associated with immigration histories and ideological differences cutting across immediate and extended families. Thus, while participants often identified the biological family as a contentious space of political and ideological strife, they approached inter view sessions as alternative sites of sociality through which their incomplete stories and developing questions about family history could be shared without an obligation to resolve prevailing ambiguities.

By bringing their inquiries into bridging sessions and joint discussions, participants cultivate what Kim and Hong describe as a radically different conceptualization of intergenerational relations. Despite the divergent social, political, and historical conditions shaping subjective perceptions of the Korean War, participants identify how conspicuous silences are socially constructed, systemic, and endemic. In turn, the overlapping processes of sharing and listening produce a diasporic sense of kinship cemented through *social* rather than *biological* bonds. As participants encounter other narrators and listeners in the shared interview space and make themselves answerable to this collective, emergent social affinities concretize: "We were all responsible and accountable, collectively, as opposed to one person leading the way or one person saying that this is the way. We're constantly feeding off of each other and creating this vision together" (Kim). Horizontally extending narration-and-listening practices beyond the space of the biological family home, the Intergenerational project disrupts the normative ways in which certain concepts, such as postmemory, privilege or prioritize blood kinship as the primary genealogical vehicle through which memories of war are vertically or vicariously transmitted. The diasporic social relations that crystallize through these sessions are particularly meaningful, given that participants refrain from associating themselves with assumed notions of ethnic, filial, and national "sameness." Participants, in fact, have different or even conflicting understandings of what it means to be "Korean" or "Korean/American."

Below I include a quote from a narrator's commentary offered during a 2012 bridging session between elders and 1.5- and second-generation participants in New York City.[44] The narrator was born after 1953 and raised during the Park Chung-hee dictatorship before migrating to the United States. His voice in the audiovisual recording is interchangeably marked by inflections of anger, exasperation, and surprise; the narrator expresses both disbelief *and* relief at locating a space in which he is able to share his story without the fear of retribution or expulsion. Given the devastating history of communist red-baiting in South Korea and the United States, as well as the marginalization of political opinions and war experiences among Korean/Americans, the prospect of being listened to and heard is not insignificant. This particular narrator gestures to the social and emotional costs affiliated with his leftist political leanings within his own family and among other Korean diasporans who hold more conservative political beliefs in the United States:

> To me, the fact that there is even a space like this, this is an unbelievable space. I can't speak about things like this with my family. If I do, I become an outcast in my family. I get ostracized by my wife and son. They are OK with everything else, but when it comes to this kind of work, I am afraid [to speak about it]. And this is the present, what is going on now. Also, it's just not my family. Whenever I go out to rallies, there are those [right-wing] bastards chasing after us. . . . So this is one of the few times I can share and let this out. There is just no time to let my tears out.

This narrator's observation that there is simply "no time" to reveal or process emotions related to the Korean War is commonly shared among other participants. In recalling certain interviews with members of the Intergenerational project, Hong described a paradoxical gap between the affective presentation of speakers—smiling, laughing, or with calm facial expressions—and the substantive content of their narrations, which detail dead or missing family members, imprisoned lovers, and witnessed bombings by the U.S. military. As a listener, Hong felt that "at these moments, the storytelling and emotion—they didn't match the way that the person was sharing the story." Yet this perceived sense of disjointedness provides a meandering pathway for listeners to sit with and identify improvisational tactics mobilized by narrators to survive and navigate the war's immediate repercussions. As Kim put it, "They had to move on the best way they knew how. And most of the time, they didn't want to talk about the fighting because they thought, 'Well, what will talking ultimately do?'" Within this context, the Intergenerational project's sessions provide a moment of critical reflection in which first-generation participants are able to "stop, sigh, and shed tears because they feel like they haven't had time to cry all of these years" (Hong).

In other striking ways, the Intergenerational project's sessions reflect how the protracted Korean War imbricates itself within the mundane details of day-to-day life. Hence, what listeners might initially hear as a narrative devoid of "war content" registers the naturalized sedimentation of militarized violence in the realm of contemporary life. For Hong, repeatedly listening to aural histories over time demystifies the Korean War to the extent that these narratives emulate how experiences of deferred conflict and survival latch onto seemingly trivial tasks or commonplace objects: "The Korean War is not a bomber jet anymore. It's all of these other images that are much more complex than the horrifying things you see in newsreels." When asked to elaborate on this observation, she offered this extended explanation:

> It's interesting which gestures, moments really stick out in people's minds, how vivid their childhood is as war survivors. It's things like, one clip that we developed has to do with *hobak* [zucchini] leaves. And how they were used as medicine, how that was the only medicine around. And how they're used to patch up wounds. And so, [there's] this very interesting juxtaposition of medicine with a lot of other images, like around sewing and mothers. . . . Someone else talked about the way they do laundry: they take apart all the seams of the clothes and wash the pieces and sew them back together. A lot of these kinds of images are actually of survival: what children, what people, had to do to survive the war, the spaces that protected them, how this affected their brothers and sisters. . . . For me, I realized, "Oh, the war is ever present in these different ways for you."

Here the sensorial imagery evoked by Hong's thick descriptions—leafy *hobak* fibers covering blistering wounds, the restitched seams of clothing worn by tired bodies, the crevices that children crawl into for safety—underscores the thin boundary between the ordinary and spectacular in our reencounters with an extended war that refuses to desist. That is, the protracted status of the Korean War recalibrates the confounding repercussions of war *through* the vernacular language and framing of daily life. In this way, the immediate repercussions of war, such as the violent displacements of civilians, fresh bomb craters seared into the earth, and the frantic separation of families, are reconfigured by time and space into Korean immigration "waves," fragmented memories of family life, and the permanent absence of loved ones. Subsequently, the conspicuous silences embedded in these narratives, or the missing status of napalm bombs, barbed-wire fences, and soldiers, communicate an undiminished fullness that is not so much about a "post" memory of a forgotten war. Rather, these accounts of all that remains and all that is demonstrate the present-pastness of a war that bleeds into crevices and corners of the contemporary memoryscape.[45]

The Re-performance of Memories

The Intergenerational project's narratives emerge through collaborative rounds of listening and relistening; the process of archiving and sharing narratives with broader publics is just as multifaceted. For Hong and Kim, questions of archiving and documentation initially conjure the image of the dusty repository linked to "expert" knowledges produced by and for formally trained researchers. However, throughout our conversation this initial imagery fractured into a set of inquiries related to praxis and epistemology. Hong and Kim, for instance, expressed concerns about why and how certain paradigms (e.g., Cold War historiography) are legislated as "official" forms of knowledge while other embodied and social knowledges are discarded altogether. During other sessions, participants questioned the conflicting motivations propelling the creation of a Korean War memory archive: who is gathering, collecting, and organizing these memories and why? And how will these memories be marshalled and by whom? Reminiscent of Ann Laura Stoler's description of the archive "as process" rather than "as [a] thing," the Intergenerational project examines the catalysts behind Cold War knowledge production.[46] Given their commitment to using aural history as a relationship-building platform, participants define the project as a continuum of memory documentation, interpretation, and sharing practices that extend beyond institutional walls. Hong noted that participants "weren't necessarily interested in building a professional archive but wanted to imagine and organize a practice overall."

The actualization of memory as practice rather than memory as repository encompasses technical as well as epistemological concerns related to the accessibility of information. Kim described how the collection of interviews through (audio)visual means segues with the editing, storing, and cataloguing of interviews in a digitized archive. This method of organizing source materials, however, raises questions among older participants who might not be as familiar or comfortable with using digital tools. As Kim put it, the collaborative listening and analyses sessions were developed as one concrete method of "bringing the interviews back to elders and the folks we work with." Relatedly, public access to materials emerging from interview sessions is a key concern among Intergenerational project members. Since participants have not yet collectively determined how materials will be shared with a larger audience, the recorded interview sessions are currently unavailable for public listening. Hence, ongoing questions of safety, confidentiality, and trust complicate liberal notions of "open use" and "user engagement," which at times unequivocally associate intellectual freedom with unlimited access to information collection and consumption.[47]

These explicit concerns shaped my encounter with the Intergenerational project. Unquestionably, Hong and Kim were generous with their time and material sharing: I viewed audiovisual recordings of performances, selective clips from interview sessions, and a comprehensive document that traces the development of the project's interview model. But I was unable to access the bulk of original recordings from the narration-and-listening sessions. Because of my subject position as a researcher located outside the Intergenerational project's memory community, the quandary of restricted access forced me to grapple with several methodological questions and dilemmas. These predicaments include self-reflections on my privileged positionality as an academic, as well as the necessity to create improvised entry points to the project's vital work without feeling as if I was overstepping boundaries. For instance, instead of accessing these source materials, I interviewed and corresponded with Hong and Kim for more than a year through Skype conversations and e-mail while also organizing and attending a chain of oral history events.[48] These self-reflections regarding my presumptions about access and the intentional process of "stepping back" connects to the decolonizing methodology mentioned earlier. As Audra Simpson states, these felt tensions and refusals are not necessarily full "stops" or "impediments to knowing."[49] Rather, the perceived limitations placed on knowledge production or the disappointments we might feel when we are of unable to access information we desire say quite a bit about scholarly presumptions that bind "rigorous" research to the accumulation of official data. These presumptions, however, are also "expansive in what they do not tell us"—and if we listen carefully enough, "they tell us when to stop."[50] This impasse of limited access pressed me also to reconsider the damaging implications of Cold War polemics, which continue to inform participants' anxieties about personal memories circulating beyond closed communities of acquaintances, friends, and family members.

But as an intervention to Cold War knowledge production, the Intergenerational project aims to upend the dominant portrayals of the Korean War in the United States while also attending to the safety and shared concerns of its participants. Members address these goals by relistening to and interpreting oral histories through cultural works such as spoken word poetry, creative writing, visual arts, and experimental video shorts. Specifically, with explicit permission and input from narrators, participants collaboratively select segments from interviews to interpret, analyze, and share with larger audiences. In several cultural productions created by Intergenerational project participants, excerpts from different aural histories are remixed into a single performance, film, or multimedia piece. These reinterpretations retain the anonymity of narrators if so desired but also provide participants with opportunities to engage the public and generate nuanced meanings from source materials. The cultural productions are subsequently shared with audiences through performances held at Nodutdol's office, as well as public programming at local New York City branch libraries and community-based arts spaces.[51] Performing a curation of aural histories fulfills several goals co-determined by participants. First, this continuum of performed interpretations, or what Schneider refers to as a "re-performance," amplify the intersubjective dimensions of aural history.[52] Rejecting the notion that aural histories are unmediated accounts that capture an isolated voice, participants underscore how the interview space(s) co-produces synergetic knowledges among transient narrators and listeners. For older participants, the most important audience members they hope to reach are young Korean/Americans who have limited access to, or uneven knowledges of, the Korean War. Conversely, to have younger narrators "perform and tell [their] story," as Hong states, is an experience that has a deep impact for older members of the Intergenerational project.

Second, the articulation of aural histories as collaborative knowledges that are always already shifting intervenes in hegemonic spatiotemporal conceptualizations in which time and its narrative derivatives are situated within a "unidirectional . . . march toward an empiric future of preservation."[53] By extension, the experienced temporality of war, as elaborated in Chapter 1, does not align with a chronological linearity that culminates in happy homecomings, heteronormative reunions such as marriage, and a seamless incorporation into a welcoming national populace. Wartime instead troubles the chrononormativity of Cold War temporal progression by playing "forward and backward and sideways across."[54] Thus, demonstrating how the Korean War exceeds a linear timeline that automatically advances and moves on, the Intergenerational project's collapsing of past, present, and future through re-performance teases out the theatricality of temporality. Subsequently, through the performance of narratives that do not remain within the prescriptive bounds of "history proper," the subject of analysis becomes Cold War time itself. Third, the re-performance of aural histories recalibrates shared narratives as beginning points rather than endpoints to ongoing conversations that take place across varied audiences. The project's oral, aural, and written sources therefore are not intended to be listened to or read within a sterile reading room. Producing a genealogy of interactions beyond the written page, these narration-and-interview sessions impel listeners to become interlocutors and narrators of history and memory. As Hong puts it, the conjoined acts of hearing *and* retelling "transforms the person that's interpreting it."

Here I refer to an interpretive workshop that culminated among participants in August 2014. During the session, several members created experimental video shorts that were screened during organized events and performances at Nodutdol. In one four-and-a-half-minute video short, *Small House Burning*, a participant performs an excerpt from an elder's aural history narrative, which describes the U.S. military's incessant bombing of her home village in northern Korea during the armed conflict. In total, the U.S. Air Force dropped more than 635,000 tons of bombs in Korea between 1950 and 1953, including 32,557 tons of napalm. More than 90 percent of the bombings occurred in the northern half of the peninsula.[55] This diasporic narrative directly confronts and contradicts nationalist depictions of the U.S. military as the heroic savior of Korean civilians mercilessly killed by Chinese and North Korean communist troops. The participant uses spoken word poetry as the primary medium of narration, a form of performative poetics that, as Vinh Nguyen reminds us, "emphasizes sociality and social transformation."[56] Wearing black and standing against a dark backdrop, the performer locks eyes with the camera and speaks in a syncopated rhythm punctuated by moments of silence:

> *They blast off, bridge*
> *There was cement*
> *Cement bricks*
> *Flying and then hitting people*
> *Killing people, killing animals, cows*
> *And all over, blood*
> *Now yelling, screaming*
> *Peaceful farm town, suddenly hell*
> *My small house, burning.*

This spoken word poetry performance is intermixed with live acting, animation, and original music accompaniment, including *poongmul* (Korean traditional drumming) performed by participants. This layered multimedia

Still image from *Small House Burning*.
(Courtesy of Danny Kim, Nodutdol for Korean Community Development.)

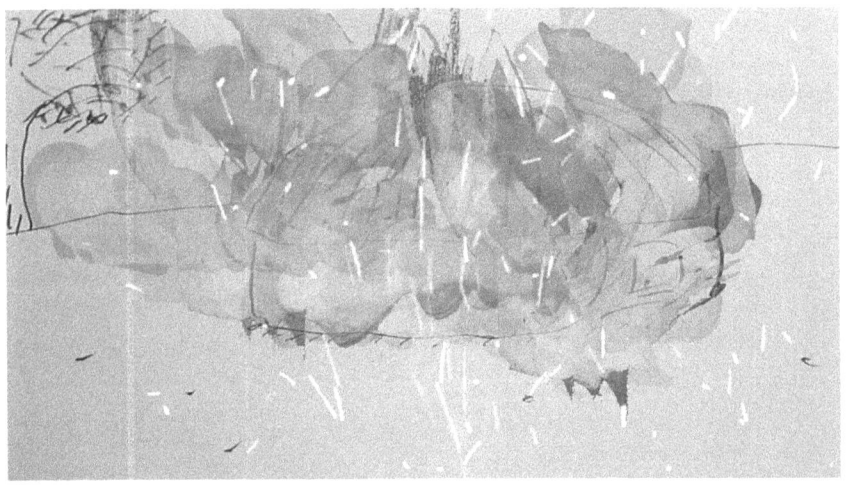

Still image from *Small House Burning*.
(Courtesy of Danny Kim, Nodutdol for Korean Community Development.)

rendering of the aural history, so full of fragmented sounds and silences, generates inflections in which cataclysmic moments are signaled by percussive emphasis, as well as perceived changes in volume and cadence.

For instance, the spoken line "killing people, killing animals, cows" is punctuated by a hissing rumble and moments of "pop" as the drumstick hits the *buk*'s (*poongmul* instrument) taut surface.[57] This last line is immediately followed by a half second of silence before the spoken word performer transitions into the next line ("And all over, blood"). Participants' readings of emotional cues within aural histories are signaled by these perceived shifts in volume, intonation, and rhythm. By jointly relistening to an interview several times, participants select excerpts to share with the public by identifying moments in which a narration seems especially passionate, tense, or stressful. "It's almost like these sessions were leading to different moments of climaxes scattered throughout the interview," Hong said. Participants explain how these catalogued moments of unvanquished anger, overwhelming sadness, or utter shock are "especially revealing" in what they relay (and do not relay) about the sustained horrors of aerial bombings, the destructive obliteration of entire villages, and the absent presence of disappeared family members. For Hong, these interlocking acts of interpretation, retelling, and re-performance are heuristic insofar as they compel participants to "make difficult choices in regard to what mattered, what's important, what emotionally stood out, and what moved them." In turn, performers "reactivate the narratives" and "make it so [they] can occur again for people." In this context, the emotional transformation of memory into a re-performance constitutes historical interpretation itself.[58]

The privileging of listening and retelling within the aural history process noticeably departs from existing paradigms of testimony giving. For instance, in her ethnographic work detailing the radiating memories of the atomic bombing of Hiroshima, Lisa Yoneyama explains how the testimony practices of the *hibakusha* (Japanese atomic bomb survivors) discourage audience members from actively participating in the narrative-making project. Yoneyama emphasizes that for many of these survivors, the "authenticity of [their] original experience" can be retained only through the preclusion of "arbitrary interpretations of willful audiences."[59] Situated as such, hibakusha narrators depend on the written medium as a preferred platform to share and circulate their memories.

In contrast, participants in the Intergenerational project emphasize that a collaborative aural history process permits one to acknowledge, grapple with, and make sense of the Korean War's insensibilities. To be located within and acknowledged by a community of listeners is a dialogical process that entails intentional feedback loops among members who co-inhabit a shared, albeit momentary, space. However, by approaching this continuum of interpretations through a diasporic analysis, I underscore that participants are not "copying," "imitating," or "reproducing" aural histories as they are. Rather, by prioritizing the meaning-making process over the calcification of "objective" or "truthful" facts so crucial to Cold War nationalist historiographies, Kim said, multiple iterations and interpretations of shared histories contribute to a coalitional politics anchored in difference. Indeed, the re-performances of these narratives within public spaces are intended to facilitate lively, if not difficult, dialogues among listening subjects who do not necessarily share national, ethnocentric, cultural, or political allegiances. Thus, emergent discussions do not preclude contradictory and divergent perspectives. In this way, the diasporic practice of re-performance models the untidy process of memory formation by accentuating the "dialectical relationship between memory and history, how memory becomes history, and how history becomes memory."[60]

In laying claim to the vital characteristics of re-performance, Kim depicts aural history as a mushrooming process that expands beyond the legible perceptions of the here and now. Describing aural history interviews as part of a "living archive as opposed to tapes or files on the shelf," Kim emphasizes that participants are "acting out the archive" and that the "archive *is in* the actual performance and practices [members are] engaging in" (emphasis added). By associating memory and aural history with re-performance, Kim resituates these shared narratives within a horizontal chain of future transfers that are "just as much about the present as they are about what we can't [yet] see or know." Thus, the Intergenerational project's ever expanding memory repertoire hints at participants who are not yet fully actualized or realized. As elaborated in Chapter 4, this speculative anticipation of the future through a recalibration of the past and present is a potent memory exercise for envisioning a demilitarized Korea.

This suggestion of the aural history re-performance as part of a diasporic memory repertoire dovetails with Diana Taylor's description of embodied memories as "vital acts of [performance] transfer" across time and space.[61] As aural histories are reinterpreted into performance, film, and other cultural productions, the processes of "selection, memorization . . . , internalization and transmission" engender their own "systems of re-presentation."[62] Framed differently, these regenerative acts of mnemonic interpretation produce new cultural inscriptions that take on narrative lives of their own. The Intergenerational project's narratives, therefore, are open-ended and unstable, given that their discursive content and aesthetic forms are always mutating: the indefinite cycle of re-performance "keeps and transforms choreographies of meaning."[63] This coalescing horizon of aural histories relays the "resiliently eruptive" or dissonant quality of fugitive memories shared and retold by diasporic narrators and listeners who are always already reappearing or on the brink of becoming.[64]

Coda

In this chapter, I consider the diverging variants of silence that seep into the aural histories mediated by the Intergenerational Korean American Oral History Project. Tracking silence's relationship to structures of violence, power, and oppressive apparatuses, the project nevertheless approaches silence as a textured formation that avails itself of unforeseen potentialities and moments of opening. In particular, Danny Kim and Sukjong Hong refer to how a collaborative interrogation of silences embedded within participants' daily lives engenders shared inquiries and intergenerational social bonds that exceed the biological family. Centering differentiated listening as a diasporic memory practice anchored in women of color feminism, the Intergenerational project reformulates memory as a multifaceted process delinked from established historiographical renderings of the Korean War in the United States.

My attentiveness to silence as a "speaking" discourse, a critical mode of remembering, and a condition of possibility extends *and* departs from existing literature that addresses the Korean War through the entwined logics of memory, deferment, and trauma. Namely, by insisting on a constellation of social, historical, and affective dynamisms, I emphasize that the Korean War's silences are more than spectral traces of individuated traumas that haunt the here and now. These silences instead indicate war's tectonic sedimentations that morph, condense, and multiply into normative formations. Thus, as briefly discussed in relation to Christine Sun Kim's "*p*-tree" sketch at the beginning of this chapter, diffused silences across time and space are less about absolute disappearance, erasure, or noiselessness than about a re-sensitization process that recalibrates a protracted war through the comforting and comfortable language of normal life. Contextualized this way, the Korean War's "quietness" is a profound repercussion and function of a slow, militarized violence that exerts itself in ever pressing ways.

In closing, I foreground how the generative elements of silence are sutured to the limitations of knowledge production. Returning to my reading of Simpson's work, I consider how an attentive listening practice feels for opacities that are tricky to comprehend or that exceed discursive categories of formal knowledge established by institutions such as the state and academia. These opacities refract the incommensurability affixed to an embodied experience located at the dense intersection of historical, social, cultural, and affective conditions. Silences, in other words, do not solely materialize as communicative slippages that remain unheard or "unverbalized." They are also vocalized, sounded, and spoken knowledges, or traces of knowledge, resistant to the logical "supremacy of reason," as Stoler might say.[65]

I was reminded of this during an oral history roundtable I organized at the University of California, Riverside, in February 2015. During the roundtable, facilitators from various oral history projects related to the Korean War—including not only Sukjong Hong but also Ramsay Liem and Christine Hong from the Legacies of the Korean War Project—discussed their experiences of grappling with and listening to a broad arrangement of life history narratives shared by Korean/Americans. In her commentary, Christine Hong shared a particularly moving narrative in which an elder close to her own mortality recalled her abrupt separation from her husband during the armed conflict and the excruciating panic she felt when she realized she would never see him alive again. During her interview, the elder stated, with irritation audible in her voice, that when she reencounters her husband in the afterlife, she will berate him by asking, "Why didn't you come looking for us?" As Hong observes, this line of questioning would land for the vast majority of listeners as a statement of anger, confusion, and blame—or, possibly, a proclamation of frustration, wistfulness, and sadness. In contrast, Hong characterized the elder's question as an idiomatic expression of boundless love, which may have been grasped by a handful of listeners equipped with a set of cultural knowledges and historical references. The elder demonstrated love by expressing her immense anger at the political circumstances that changed the course of her life; this quaking anger, however, was mediated through a sense of relief that she would soon be reunited spiritually with her beloved after this lifetime. This expression of longing, love, and reunification beyond formal political arbitration remains illegible to and beyond the reach of state recognition. In this way, the elder's narrative exemplifies how the diasporic memory practice of listening encompasses a self-reflexive negotiation between those sonic traces we are able to identify, scrutinize, and unpack and those other vocalized soundings that exceed the well-defined bounds of simple recognition, knowing, and definitive resolution.

3

Returns

> What if that other kind of return—things that come back, the act of going back—disturbs the chain of promised returns on investment?
>
> —Nadine Attewell and S. Trimble, "Introduction"

In the Netflix documentary *Twinsters* (2015), Samantha ("Sam") Futerman and Anaïs Bordier, Korean identical twins separated at birth, meet for the first time after nearly twenty-five years of separation.[1] Born in Pusan in November 1987, Sam and Anaïs were adopted and raised by white families in the United States and France, respectively. Serendipitously reunited via Facebook in 2012, Sam, an actress living in Los Angeles, and Anaïs, a fashion designer raised in Paris and living in London, return together to South Korea in 2013 as participants of a global conference organized by the International Korean Adoptee Association. At the commencement of the conference, South Korean President Park Geun-hye offered a warm message to hundreds of attendees through a prerecorded message, welcoming overseas adoptees back to their "home country" and encouraging them to "take pride in [their] mother country and to love it as well." Overwhelmed by Park's message, Anaïs describes a sense of exhilaration of being part of a global adoptee community while also expressing feelings of gratitude toward South Korea: "You feel like you're a part of something. . . . And to know you're in Korea and that your birth country cares about you as well, it's really moving." In their co-written autobiography, *Separated @ Birth: A True Love Story of Twin Sisters Reunited*, Sam expands on these shared sentiments as she writes, "So much care had been taken to make this conference special, and to have someone as important as the president of Korea welcoming us home was so moving. It reinforced the thought of how much love went into the process of adoption."[2]

This brief description of *Twinsters* introduces the entangled normative sentiments affiliated with Korean transnational adoption in South Korea and the United States. If observed and listened to carefully, the documentary's accounts of displacement, reunion, and personal gratitude register a scaffolding of vexed identifications that underlie the miraculous transfiguration of the war orphan into a cosmopolitan diasporic returnee. As discussed in Chapter 1, Korean children fathered by U.S. soldiers stationed on the peninsula after 1945 were depicted by American media as bereft orphans and destitute urchins in desperate need of Western love and humanitarian intervention. Extracted from the South Korean populace, these so-called GI babies or mixed-race children were ushered into the American populace, with the expectation that they would assimilate into a white, middle-class, heterosexual milieu and serve as a "cultural bridge" between Americans (the West) and Koreans (the East).[3] This racialized configuration of the Korean adoptee as a cultural translator par excellence dovetailed with the overarching discourse of the exceptional model minority in the United States, in which Asian/Americans were racially inscribed as exemplars of obedient and hardworking citizens capable of moving up the socioeconomic ladder without public assistance. Between 1958 and 2008, the number of Korean transnational adoptees would swell to more than 160,000, with close to 110,000 children adopted by American families and 50,000 more adopted by Western Europeans.[4]

Yet starting in the late 1980s, transnational adoptees resituated in North America and Western Europe began to return to the Republic of Korea (ROK, South Korea) in prominent numbers to search for their "pre-adoption" histories—trips that were unforeseen by the ROK government insofar as adoptions were *not* intended to be round-trip affairs. Included as beneficiaries of the Overseas Korean Act (OKA) in 1999, which extended long-term ROK visa and residence privileges to select diasporic subjects, transnational adoptees are now commonly perceived by the South Korean public as entitled Westerners associated with lucrative economic, social, and cultural capital.[5] By extension, adoptee returnees to the so-called Korean motherland index another remarkable transformation: the South Korean neoliberal state's recalibration of orphans-turned-adoptees into spectacular forms of human capital.

As Eleana J. Kim puts it, human capital under advanced neoliberalism is distinct from other modes of capital in that labor and value are indistinguishable from workers themselves. That is, rather than defining labor power as the "property of the 'free laborer'" that can be "exchanged for wages under capitalism," Kim argues, the social value affixed to transnational adoptees demonstrates how the "commodity owned by the worker [becomes] human capital . . . coterminous with the individual as producer and entrepreneur of the self."[6] Drawing on a Foucauldian analysis of biopower, Kim describes how human capital *is* the subject or the "set of skills and capabilities . . . 'modified by all that affects [the subject] and all that the [subject] effect[s].'"[7] Accordingly, by virtue of their association with the West and affiliated with characteristics such as upward mobility, English fluency, and a desirable urbaneness, adoptees-as-human capital are reconstituted by the South Korean state as productive ethnic returnees contributing to a deterritorialized national economy. The neoliberal designation of adoptees as human capital, of course, is not an inherent marker of authentic subjectivity. Instead, as Kim makes clear, such a designation reflects a "grid of intelligibility," or a field of power relations that (re)produces a nexus of knowledge-based and epistemic formations.[8]

Building on Kim's crucial insights regarding transnational adoption and human capital, I am interested in how these permutations of orphan-to-adoptee-to-returnee demonstrate the social and material linkages that bind the contemporary South Korean state to the profit-making industry that is war. More specifically, this chapter examines how adoptee returns, as embodied forms of diasporic excess, illustrate the degree to which South Korean nation building depends on and reproduces a persisting cycle of racial, gender, and sexual violence anchored in the enterprise of war. Indeed, as subjects whose global trajectories are indelibly connected to the Korean War and U.S. occupation, transnational adoptees and their ambivalent returns to the "ethnic homeland" are pervasive reminders that on the Korean Peninsula, there is no such thing as a postwar period. Thus, mobilizing these observations as beginning points for discussion, this chapter builds on core arguments offered in previous chapters. While Chapters 1 and 2 trouble the legislative reconfiguration of Korean militarized migrants into model minority subjects in the United States, this chapter addresses how transnational adoptees, primarily raised in the United States and Western Europe, are recomposed as model minoritarian denizens returning to the welcoming "mother country" that is South Korea. Taking on the concept of returns as a diasporic memory analytic, I especially attend to the contradictions, as well as the subversive potentialities, enacted by adoptee reroutings to South Korea.

Here I conceptualize "diasporic return" as verb and noun: a return registers a process of arriving at a destination or departure point while also signaling what Nadine Attewell and S. Trimble describe as "disturbing" elements affixed to this "act of going back." In our context, returns point to a condensation of unanticipated actions, memories, and feelings that crystallize as adoptees reencounter South Korea decades after their involuntary removal. In effect, these mnemonic and affective elements, or negative diasporic excesses, disrupt South Korea's attempt to smoothly rehabilitate the transnational adoptee from a surplus figure rendered expendable into a vital contributor to the global and national economy. Stripped from its militarized context, this kind of translation and transformation is delinked from any trace of war and militarized violence. The analytic of returns therefore clarifies the symbiotic relationship between disposability and productivity within the orphan-to-adoptee-to-returnee calculus: the value assigned to adoptee-returnees depends on their extraction from South Korea and the disciplining and re-domestication of their laboring bodies for the purpose of national economic development. Phrased differently, diasporic returns accentuate how the symbolic and material value attributed to the Korean transnational adoptee is inseparable from the destructive dividends of war, including displacement and social and material death. And yet, rather than narrowly consigning returns to an overdetermined discourse of unending debt and repayment, or what J. K. Gibson-Graham might refer to as a "politics of [continual] deferment," this chapter demonstrates how adoptee returns trouble the state's biopolitical arithmetic by rejecting South Korea's efforts to discipline, repossess, and rehabilitate.[9] Along this vein, I argue that the racialized and gendered presence of transnational adoptees in South Korea ruptures dominant rhetoric and established policies that have sought to erase adoptee subjectivities from public sight and dominant national history.

To attend to these acts of refusal through the diasporic concept of adoptee returns, I draw on two cultural memory works: kate-hers RHEE's documented performance *Sex Education for Finding Face in the 21st Century* (2002) and Jane Jin Kaisen's experimental film *The Woman, the Orphan, and the Tiger* (2010).[10] Distinct in their use of aesthetic strategies, RHEE's and Kaisen's works nevertheless amplify how adoptee returns, or the rerouting of adoptees to South Korea and the unruly excesses that accompany these reappearances, do not always affirm grateful sentiments or recover lost family origins. On the contrary, adoptee returns lead to very different discoveries that reflect the Cold War becoming of a pro-U.S., anticommunist South Korean state. Confronting this militarized history, RHEE's and Kaisen's works gesture to subjectivities marked as socially queer and superfluous to the dual projects of South Korean nation building and American humanitarianism. But in turn, these untamed excesses illustrate how the Korean War produces its own tensions and antagonistic formations, including racialized and gendered subjects who refuse to be appeased by state policies of resettlement and belated national citizenship. Adoptee reroutings, therefore, do not register a "going back" to an intact and forgone past but demonstrate how life-forms of war are continually regenerated and "returned" when the past remains fundamental to the here and now.

"Civil Diplomats": Korean Transnational Adoption as Political Economic Apparatus

Before discussing RHEE's and Kaisen's cultural productions, I want to briefly situate these artists' oeuvres in relation to the Korean War while also clarifying the conditions informing adoptee returns to South Korea—and, by extension, the emergence of vocal critiques of transnational adoption. In so doing, it is necessary to read the now well-established critique of American hegemonic power and Cold War Orientalist assumptions alongside a matrix of emergent policies, contradictory actions, and on-the-ground practices of the South Korean state, especially since transnational adoption fulfills related yet distinct objectives in the United States and South Korea.

As meticulously researched by Tobias Hübinette, Eleana J. Kim, Kim Park Nelson, and SooJin Pate, overseas adoption in South Korea, even before 1950, served three primary purposes under Rhee Syngman's pro-American presidency (1948–1960).[11] First, it allowed Rhee's administration to concentrate its resources and energy on national economic development while refusing to invest in a comprehensive social welfare system capable of supporting a general populace devastated by years of military conflict, including the destruction of more than 70 percent of the internal infrastructure in the southern half of the peninsula. Second, as most Korean overseas adoptees between 1950 and 1960 were the multiracial progeny of Korean women and U.S. soldiers, the removal of these racialized children from South Korea's interior—visible evidence of taboo sexual intimacy between U.S. soldiers and Korean women—permitted the Rhee administration to actualize a homogeneous citizenry based on the ethnocentric principle and the ideology of "one nation, one race" (*ilguk, ilminju*).[12] Although by 1960, the majority of Korean adoptees were *not* orphans or biracial children but were born to young single women, the policy of national extrication via overseas adoption allowed the South Korean government to manufacture a "pure blood" population under the banner of nation building. Eventually, these policies of removal solidified as part of the South Korean state's emigration, family-planning, and population-control policies, codified by the Park Chung-hee administration in the early 1970s. More than two-thirds of all overseas placements, in fact, occurred between 1970 and the late 1980s.[13] Third, the adoption industry proved extremely lucrative for South Korea. Formally facilitated through four state-elected public and private agencies, the adoption of close to 200,000 children between 1950 and 2010 produced more than $3.3 billion in hard currency for South Korea's economy.[14]

The growing visibility of the war orphan figure on the international stage reproduced racialized assumptions regarding South Korea's status as a "poor" and "developing" country that needed support from Western nations. But South Korea shrewdly benefited from these practices, especially as the state sought to strengthen its political alliance with the United States. As Korean children were incrementally absorbed into white, Christian, and middle- to working-class families in the United States and Western Europe, South Korea and the United States became entangled via the filial bondages of flesh and blood. Consequently, American popular culture symbolically portrayed South Korea as a loyal anticommunist ally of the United States and, more specifically, as a "little brother" to America's "big brother."[15] In nationally circulating periodicals such as *Time* magazine and the *New York Times,* and in Hollywood films such as *Battle Hymn* (1956) and the Army Pictorial Center's documentary series *The Big Picture* (1951–1964), the United States is represented as the paternalistic steward of South Korea. In turn, South Korea is depicted as a vulnerable child in desperate need of aid and protection. For instance, in *Battle Hymn,* a group of orphaned Korean refugees are miraculously saved by the Christian minister-turned-U.S. Air Force fighter pilot Dean E. Hess, played by Rock Hudson, at the height of the armed struggle between North Korea and South Korea. By the end of the film, these orphaned children have been whisked away from their bombed village and transported, via cargo aircraft, to the idyllic island haven of Jeju, patiently waiting to be adopted by their "forever" families. Yet as discussed in Chapter 4, Jeju Island also became an American target of anticommunist surveillance during the Korean War, with at least one-quarter of its civilian population killed by U.S.-trained South Korean armed forces and right-wing youth groups between 1948 and 1955.

Depictions of Korean transnational adoption often included oversimplified narratives of "search-and-reunion" that conclude with adoptees joyfully locating their birth families. In her nuanced critiques of such depictions, Kaisen observes how these filmic representations "thrive on tears" and the "excessive use of extra-diegetic sound in the form of melodramatic music."[16] Constructed through extreme close-ups that document highly emotional stories, these portrayals, as Kaisen explains, confirm one of two possibilities: the reincorporation of the adoptee returnee within the loving folds of the "sending country" (South Korea, in this case) or the returnee's rejection of the birth country and the reembracing of the Western "receiving country." As this language intimates, the notions of "sending" and "receiving" countries recall formal terminology associated with the global neoliberal business of importing and exporting national goods. Kaisen's commentary thus hints at how saccharine representations of tragic separation and family reunions ultimately obscure the core roots of transnational adoption, including American military occupation and South Korean nation building. As discussed later in this chapter, RHEE and Kaisen trouble these dominant representations of transnational adoption by disrupting the normative sentiments of American humanitarian love, South Korean generosity, and adoptee gratitude. The visual syntax and grammar of South Korea's poor orphaned children, however, is not merely symbolic or discursive.[17] The imagery reflects a much deeper Cold War American investment in South Korea as a key anticommunist ally serving American political and economic interests in the North Pacific. Under the military presidency of Chun Doo-Hwan (1979–1988), overseas adoption was depicted as "civil diplomacy." Korean children were named and recognized as "goodwill ambassadors" who cultivated positive communicative ties and cultural understanding between South Korea and the United States.[18]

Starting just before and during the 1988 Seoul Olympics, public critiques of Korean transnational adoption gained momentum, domestically and internationally. Negative international press, for example, characterized Korean adoptions as a "child exporting business," to which the South Korean state initially responded with appeasement tactics.[19] The government began to sponsor all-expense-paid "motherland trips" for select adoptees in the hope of reframing searches for birth families as belated homecoming trips for returnees interested in learning more about their "cultural and ethnic heritage."[20] Influential as well were internationally circulating films such as Suzanne Brink's *Arirang* (1991), a Swedish biopic based loosely on the life history of Brink, a Korean overseas adoptee raised in Sweden who endured domestic abuse and virulent racism in her adoptive country. By the early 1990s, the number of transnational adoptees returning to South Korea increased so much that adoption agencies and the South Korean state were overwhelmed with requests for birth records.[21] Spearheaded by adoptee activists, scholars, writers, and artists who traced the historical origins of overseas adoption back to the Korean War and U.S. military occupation, the South Korean government implemented legislative reforms in 1996 to better support the needs of adoptees, including a proliferation of "motherland" tours and the establishment of postadoption services to facilitate birth family location and searches.[22] Since the 2000s, other lobbying efforts by adoptee social networks and advocacy groups have led to a dramatic decrease in overseas adoption and the systemic integration of legal platforms supporting the rights of children and birth mothers.[23]

Consequently, the returns of thousands of adoptees to South Korea in the late 1980s coincided with the coalescing of nongovernmental organizations (NGOs) advocating for the political rights of transnational adoptees and their birth mothers, as well as the creation of adoptee-generated social spaces in and beyond South Korea. Deemed by Pate and Eleana Kim as a differentiated global network that is always already shifting, this dynamic adoptee "counterpublic" actively challenges hegemonic practices and social norms that associate Korean transnational adoption with the intoxicating feelings of love, gratitude, and compassion—an affective configuration unevenly taken up by Western aid workers, missionaries, and the American and South Korean publics since the establishment of an overseas adoption program.[24]

This counterpublic includes political discourses, public forums and gatherings, and critical scholarship related to Korean transnational adoption, as well as a vibrant assemblage of creative works and cultural productions by adoptees. Several converging factors have propelled these productions: the development of the Internet as a platform for diasporic communication, the coming of age of nearly 120,000 Korean children, and the organized presence of overseas adoptees in South Korea. RHEE's and Kaisen's artistic oeuvres surfaced alongside other artwork and cultural productions in the late 1990s. While certainly not an exhaustive list, earlier cultural works include the experimental video art of Mihee-Nathalie Lemoine and Kim Su Theiler; the curatorial projects and scholarship of Kim Stoker; the poetic and literary writing of Jennifer Kwon Dobbs and Jane Jeong Trenka; the radical performative portfolio of UFOLab (Unidentified Foreign Object) by visual artists in Sweden and Denmark, including Jane Jin Kaisen, Trine Mee Sook Gleerup, Charlotte Kim Boed, Anna Jin Hwa Borstam, and Jette Hye Jin Mortensen; and the documentary films of Deann Borshay Liem, tammy ko Robinson, Tammy Chu, and Jennifer Arndt-Johns.[25] As Pate puts it, this eclectic arrangement of diasporic visual, performative, and literary works by adoptees situated in very different geographical and cultural locales formulates a "much more complicated, fraught, painful and melancholy picture of adoption and identity formation" than popularized depictions of Korean adoption processes as "smooth, peaceful, and progressive."[26] The remainder of this chapter examines how such works attend to transnational adoption within the broader history of militarized violence and colonialism in Korea. Transnational adoption, in other words, is not an isolated or insular establishment, but a racialized, gendered development affiliated with other militarized repercussions and formations in and beyond the peninsula.

kate-hers RHEE and Out-of-Control Feelings

Both RHEE and Kaisen reject notions of a monolithic adoptee artist identity or coherent adoptee cultural archive, a critical perspective I share as well. However, analyzing these two artists' works through the lens of an adoptee counterpublic usefully identifies interlocking conditions that propel adoptee returns to South Korea. More specifically, the adoptee counterpublic clarifies the related motivations connecting seemingly disjointed diasporic cultural works.[27] This contextualization is especially useful in considering the prevalent ways in which the South Korean and U.S. states continue to describe overseas adoption as a natural outgrowth of national development and an international gesture of love and goodwill on the part of "receiving" countries.[28]

In her public performance *Sex Education for Finding Face in the 21st Century*, RHEE troubles these assumptions by enacting undisciplined, dissonant sentiments. In contrast to the tender feelings of love, gratitude, and altruism associated with Korean transnational adoption and American militarized intervention, RHEE's performance concentrates on shock, fear, and curiosity. As her improvisational stage, RHEE uses the glimmering city of Seoul—the headquarters for colonial, administrative, and military rule for at least two hundred years in Korea, and the South Korean state's current capital and commercial hub. She conceptualizes her own body as a returning commodity redirected to South Korea following her involuntary removal nearly two and a half decades earlier. A diasporic artist currently based in Berlin, RHEE was born in Seoul but adopted by a white working-class family in the United States in 1978 and subsequently raised in a racially segregated suburb of Detroit. The artist's visit to South Korea in 2002 marks one of her earliest returns to the country following her overseas adoption.

In *Sex Education*, RHEE mobilizes site-specific performance as a mode of social critique in South Korea. She dramatically laughs, shakes, and gesticulates at unassuming tourists and shoppers enjoying a leisurely afternoon in the Seoul district of Myeong-dong.[29] A place historically associated with South Korean light industry factories and gendered labor, including clothing and manufacturing sweatshops, Myeong-dong is now an international tourist hot spot, as well as an eating and shopping core of Seoul. In a uniform commonly worn by high school students—including a white, short-sleeved collared blouse paired with a knee-length navy skirt—RHEE resembles the South Korean teenagers frequenting Myeong-dong for an afterschool hangout session. Her frenetic movements and noticeably bloated abdomen, however, distinguish her from the crowd while hinting at a potential pregnancy. Alluding to the lack of accessible contraception and sex education in South Korea's school system and the escalating rate of teen pregnancy during the country's era of rapid development (1960–1980), *Sex Education* attracts a growing circle of onlookers. In the video documentation of the performance, surrounding spectators are heard asking in Korean, "What is this?" "Scary!" and "She's crazy!" For nearly thirty minutes, RHEE convulses in public until two startled Seoul Metropolitan Police Officers confront the artist and intervene in what they describe as an "out-of-control" performance.

In several ways, *Sex Education* emblematizes RHEE's oeuvre as a mul-

Still image from *Sex Education for Finding Face in the 21st Century,* 2002. (Courtesy of kate-hers RHEE.)

timedia performance artist who interrogates the political and social codes dictating normative neoliberal life, with its breakneck speed, commodity production, and flexible capital. Trained in time and performance art at the School of the Art Institute of Chicago, as well as in video and drawing at the University of California, Irvine, RHEE cites the "experiment on the body" (specifically, her own body) as the primary medium of her performances.[30] Inspired by performance art's capacity to enact physical, psychic, and affective transformation through its use of time, RHEE's energetic acts depend on interactions between the audience and artist to the extent that spectatorship becomes the heart of her works-in-action. Through this mode of address, the artist's body materializes as a primal site of scopophiliac consumption. RHEE consistently places herself in contexts in which her racialized and sexualized body is easily looked at, recorded, and monitored, whether in the public streets of Seoul and national television (*Missing Persons Project* [2005]) or on the Internet (*Double Eyelid Tape Tutorial for Monolids of Steel* [2015]). Although she is susceptible to surveillance and public scrutiny, RHEE reappropriates the audience's voyeuristic gaze to parody its violent tendencies and unsettle its hierarchal structure. Locking eyes with her audience and refusing to look away even as spectators turn their glances elsewhere from embarrassment or fear, RHEE's antagonistic performances produce a chain of return looks that confront an array of social taboos that exist along the edge of public discourse.

While RHEE uses a variation of aesthetic strategies to enact these disruptive moves, *Sex Education* draws on a deluge of excessive feelings that cannot be contained within the contours of the human body. In so doing, it provokes different lines of reactions and questioning among her audiences. In a more pressing manner, RHEE's effusive feelings are mobilized as social feelers that tap the damaging consequences of American militarized intervention and South Korean nation building, including the transnational adoption industry. Hence, instead of conceptualizing RHEE's performance as emanating from an effeminized or wounded self, I converse with Sara Ahmed, José Esteban Muñoz, and Sianne Ngai to redefine excessive feelings as a public mode of relationality. Here the affective registers an accumulation of dynamic exchanges and experiences that remain unarticulated or uncommunicated within the public sphere.[31] In the case of *Sex Education,* I draw on RHEE's excessive emotions as a performative tactic that conjures a militarized genealogy of racialized, gendered, and sexualized subjectivities long disavowed by the national public, including adoptees and their birth mothers.

In considering the important role played by excessive feelings as a symbolic form of adoptee returns in *Sex Education,* I find Muñoz's engagement of the affective especially provocative. Reworking object-relations theory originating from Kleinian psychoanalysis, Muñoz describes affect as a form of displaced attentiveness through which subjects extend toward and experience the other.[32] Grappling with a depressive stance he theorizes as "down . . . and brown feelings," or a schematic of emotions that minoritarian subjects use as "receptors , . . to hear each other," Muñoz approaches different affects as expressive frequencies through which subalterns are seen, heard, and felt.[33] But while Muñoz is concerned with the empathic ways in which subalterns perceive and feel for one another, *Sex Education* does not generate moments of warm or fuzzy connectivity with RHEE's social surroundings. Instead, the so-called negative sentiments of alienation, loneliness, and madness conjured throughout the performance mimic the dominant feelings associated with non-normative subjects rejected by the South Korean state and relegated to the periphery of public life.

In the performance, RHEE's body is in almost constant, frenetic motion as she alternates between fits of high-pitched laughter and moments of clammed-up, trembling stupor. Knees buckling and chest heaving, RHEE remains speechless but intermittently rubs her distended abdomen while motioning at the audience. Encircled by a glowing aura of neon lights, digital screens animated with advertisements, and a flowing currency of purchased commodities, RHEE's sensational outbursts trigger a chain of actions and reactions: while her laughter stokes curiosity and fear among spectators, she, too, draws on these responses to induce an extension of uneasy transactions. As moments of silence overtake the audience, RHEE's shrieking laughter becomes even louder, and her jerky movements become more pronounced.

In response, spectators are unable to tear their eyes away from her. Passing bystanders, including young students dressed in attire that resembles RHEE's uniform, stop dead in their tracks, whisper to one another, and gaze with widened eyes, even as they attempt to look away. Others briefly leave the public square, only to return to the spectacular performance. Reveling in an air of confusion that hovers between disgust and voyeuristic fascination, RHEE laughs until she is dragged away by the police.

The dynamic (re)encounters between RHEE and the audience move toward a conceptual engagement. That is, the circuit of feelings activated between RHEE and spectators are not final destinations in and of themselves; nor are they purely emotive responses. Instead, they are provocations that compel the audience, though to differing degrees, to problematize what is seen, heard, and touched.[34] Such inquiries are evident in the audiovisual documentation of *Sex Education,* captured by a colleague who filmed RHEE's performance from a short distance. In the video documentation, audience members ask the camera operator several questions, including, "Is this really a performance?" and "What kind of performance is this?" Another says, "Disturbing!" Attracted to *and* repelled by the sight of RHEE, spectators, as the artist suggests, are encouraged to "confront their own telling interpretations" of the public performance.[35] Using multiple media technologies, including the Internet, public events, and film festivals, to circulate and redistribute her work, RHEE produces a plurality of access points beyond the isolated moment of the live performative act. As a multimedia production, *Sex Education* is mediatized into a nine-minute experimental video posted on the artist's website.[36] In the video short, documentation footage from the performance is remixed with interchangeable shots of a laughing, crying, and stoic RHEE standing alone in a bare room.

As RHEE explained to me during a conversation in 2016, the audiovisual documentation and the experimental short are not so much evidential traces of an ephemeral performance as they are material extensions and imaginative iterations of *Sex Education*.[37] In addition to the experimental short's availability on RHEE's website, the film continues to be shared and screened at versatile spaces throughout North America, Asia, and Europe, including venues beyond the adoptee counterpublic, such as the "Shoot Yourself: Artists in Their Own Light" Fusebox Festival in Austin, Texas (2014). This open-ended mnemonic lifecycle of *Sex Education* points to what Christopher Bedford refers to as the "viral ontology" of performance and memory, or performance's capacity to morph and multiply so that it "yields a body of critical [memory] work that extends the primary act . . . into the indefinite future through reproduction."[38] The merging of past, present, and future in *Sex Education* suggests that the central "object," or definitive endpoint, of the performance is not necessarily RHEE's body but the radiating line of affective responses, reactions, and questions from future audiences situated across divergent spaces and temporalities.

Yet even as I underscore the relevance of spectatorship in my own engagement with *Sex Education,* I argue that the profound implications of RHEE's performance should not and cannot be restricted to the realm of audience comprehension. After all, RHEE's performance registers a sense of failure insofar as bemused spectators readily interpret the artist as a "crazy" delinquent roaming the streets of Myeong-dong. These miscues signal a politics of refusal that deviates far from the naturalized temporal logics governing the returns of transnational adoptees to South Korea. Within this narrative rendering of chrononormative time, adoptees are portrayed in two primary ways: as temporary returnees who tirelessly search for their birth families before leaving again for their adoptive homes, or as diasporic members of the *dongpo* (Korean transnational community) committed to remaining in South Korea as productive contributors to the national citizenry.

In the latter option, adoptee returnees are expected to become fluent in Korean, educate themselves on the cultural and social etiquettes of South Korea, and potentially date or even marry South Korean citizens. The failure to assimilate as productive income earners and law-abiding citizens trigger unflattering portrayals that depict "aberrant" adoptees as criminal outsiders, as recently observed in two highly publicized cases of overseas adoptees deported by the U.S. government to South Korea: Adam Crapser in 2017 and Philip Clay in 2012. (Crapser remains in South Korea, while Clay committed suicide in Seoul in May 2017 after five years of residing in the country.)[39] Although these scenarios of leaving or staying are quite different, they both depend on an illusionary optics of disappearance: adoptees are expected to extract themselves from the country voluntarily or unassumingly meld into a seemingly homogeneous population. Through her confrontational public performance, which hints at leisure or "unproductive" time and even perceived mental illness, RHEE blatantly fails to meet these assumptive requirements.

In a more general sense, the suggestion of failure in *Sex Education* points to Jennifer Doyle's observation about the need to critique the incessant "patrolling border between art and politics."[40] This pushback, as Doyle argues, brings focus back to audiences who "actively seek [the artwork] out, who follow the artist's career and give themselves over to the work's processes."[41] Hence, as a cultural critic and "follower" of RHEE's cultural work, I move away from a conventional rubric that equates the political value of performance to the prerequisites of transparency and reception. Instead, I gravitate toward a more complex understanding of the performance based on its own terms and conditions. For RHEE, these terms not only are informed by her desire to challenge the comfortable or apathetic viewing experiences of her audiences. They also reflect her capacity to pull together an incongruent assemblage of militarized bodies out of time and out of space with the chrononormativity of national history.[42] Specifically, RHEE juxtaposes her own hypervisible and disobedient body with the insuppressible returns of transnational adoptees, birth mothers, and gendered laborers in twenty-first-century South Korea.

In the most obvious sense, RHEE's insistence that the public contend with her corporeality is a damning critique of popular sentiments directed at single motherhood, teen pregnancy, and citizens' spotty access to reproductive healthcare in South Korea. Until April 2019, abortion was illegal in South Korea (with a few notable exceptions), and the availability of contraception remains uneven across the country.[43] Through the public act of finding rather than losing face, RHEE figuratively mirrors civic attitudes toward unwed teen pregnancy, including shame, disappointment, and embarrassment. But perhaps in a more urgent manner, *Sex Education* situates the phenomenon of teen pregnancy within a sustained arc of South Korean militarized development, especially given the state's practices of gendered surveillance and population control that include emigration, forced sterilization, and overseas adoption. By orchestrating the performance in a busy shopping district filled to the brim with upscale beauty shops, fashionable boutiques, electronic shops, music stores, and restaurants frequented by international tourists, RHEE conjoins the figure of the "anonymous pregnant girl" with the apparatuses of transnational adoption, gendered labor, and commodity production and exportation.

As noted earlier in this chapter, transnational adoption became part of South Korea's overarching development agenda between 1960 and 1980, a precipitous moment that overlapped with government policies of accelerated economic planning within a militarized context, or what Seungsook Moon refers to as the forging of South Korean militarized modernity.[44] Between 1960 and 1987, under consecutive military regimes led by Park Chung-hee and Chun Doo-Hwan, the South Korean state adopted an unfettered economic development model committed to actualizing a "bright" future, where the state would be ideally positioned to restitch the two Koreas through the sheer virtue of its financial prowess, military power, and political alliance with the United States. Under the scope of sequential five-year plans between 1962 and 1981, the South Korean government also built a national labor force dependent on heteronormative logics: cisgender men were drafted for military service and heavy industrial labor, while cisgender women were encouraged to become housewives or were deployed in unskilled factory work and military sex work in urban metropoles.⁴⁵ The institutionalization of these ideals, policies, and practices produced a militarized citizenry in which the labor of non-normative bodies, such as biracial children and working-class single women, was deemed mandatory for, yet socially disposable to, the South Korean national polity.⁴⁶

With the mass recruitment of young women predominantly from the countryside for light manufacturing work in the clothing, electronics, and furniture industries in urban centers such as Seoul, the rate of unwed pregnancy soared among female factory workers.⁴⁷ Stigmatized by families with little to no recourse provided by the state, thousands of women placed their newborns in orphanages and with welfare agencies, commonly assuming that the separation from their children would be only temporary. The statistics provided by the South Korean government are staggering: according to the Ministry for Health, Welfare, and Family Affairs, a total of 48,247 children were adopted between 1971 and 1980, with 17,627 belonging to single unwed mothers. Between 1981 and 1990, almost 66,000 children were adopted, with nearly two-thirds, or 47,153 children, belonging to single mothers age twenty-two or younger.⁴⁸ These numbers demonstrate how young women recruited for factory labor gave birth to the vast majority of Korean children given up for overseas adoption between 1970 and the early 1980s. Even as these birth mothers were disparaged by the public, their labor—literally, their participation in grueling factory work and the process of giving birth to future adoptees—contributed to the maturation of a sophisticated capitalist infrastructure.⁴⁹ Facilitated through four state-approved agencies, intercountry adoption in 2010 generated revenues of up to $35 million in fees for the South Korean state. In contrast, in the same year the South Korean state offered approximately 50,000 won (roughly $48 dollars) per month to "qualified" single mothers who chose to care for their child.⁵⁰

Painfully aware of the connective tissue linking teen pregnancy and transnational adoption to the nation's developmental paradigm, RHEE resituates her returning body, a human export rerouted back to South Korea, in relation to a flowing circuit of Samsung electronics, high-end apparel, and digital technology. The performance of overflowing affects within the tourist confines of Myeong-dong signals how overseas adoption developed alongside, rather than separately from, the production of South Korean popular commodities now feverishly consumed by an international audience. In an even more insidious sense, RHEE's failure to remain quiet or subdued in public space is a rejoinder to the principles of self-restraint, deference, and diligence deemed necessary for South Korea's militarized modernity. Employing tactics such as arbitrary imprisonment, corporal punishment, surveillance, sexual violence, and torture, the South Korean military government constructed a highly disciplined workforce responsible for building one of the largest market economies in the world.

Forged within this cauldron of militarized violence are *surplus* populaces whose labor is mobilized for national productivity and the securing of a viable citizenry, even as their bodies are marginalized or removed altogether from the domestic population. Excess or surplus labor, as Roderick Ferguson and Jin-kyung Lee remind us, is an ordinary product of capitalist accumulation that congeals with the intensification of capital.[51] Yet as a form of redundancy that exceeds the limits of political citizenship determined by the state, surplus bodies are unnecessary for the continued maintenance of the national economy precisely because they are "superfluous to capital's average requirements for its own valorization."[52] Simply put, the gendered labor and projected value of birth mothers (e.g., the children they bear) and overseas adoptees (e.g., their affiliation with the West and the monetization of their adoptions) are extractable from their material bodies. Even as adoptee returnees are configured as "valued" forms of human capital, which assumes a total collapsing between the self and capital, their actual presence in South Korea produces affective undercurrents of ambivalence, curiosity, and, at times, noticeable discomfort and disdain. These affective traces resonate with adoptees' longtime status as minoritarian bodies distinguished by physical, linguistic, and cultural differences in South Korea and the United States.[53]

Sex Education exemplifies the central problematic of adoptee returnees as expendable excesses *and* human capital through the hypervisible appearance of RHEE's misbehaving body within the consumerist-driven confines of Myeong-dong. The obstinacy of her body registers a foreclosure in the sense that RHEE's out-of-control feelings do not culminate in a cathartic and comforting release. Instead, the explosive discharge of unrelenting emotions hangs thickly in the air, intimating the unbearable costs of militarized economic development and the bureaucratic, biopolitical reproduction of militarized violence within the everyday realm. RHEE's adamant refusal to fade away into the vast sea of shoppers, however, exposes a contradictory positionality. While RHEE traces the causal beginnings of adoptee deracination to the damaging politics of war, displacement, and national economic development, her unruly performance of return resituates transnational adoptees as agents of cultural critique. That is, *Sex Education* performs an alternative historiography that resists identification with an existing genealogy of inalterable pain, suffering, and disappearance. In effect, RHEE's socially deviant feelings tear apart the sentimental logic of Korean transnational adoption as a benevolent humanitarian intervention and point to how adoptee returns precipitate diasporic excesses that the state cannot hide, appease, or resolve.

Jane Jin Kaisen and *The Woman, the Orphan, and the Tiger*

Similar to RHEE's *Sex Education for Finding Face in the 21st Century,* Jane Jin Kaisen's *The Woman, the Orphan, and the Tiger* considers how accumulated forms of racial, gendered, and sexual violence linked to militarized colonial warfare underpin the contemporary making of the South Korean state and the Korean diaspora.[54] A feature-length (72 minute) experimental film, *The Woman* also explores the return of transnational adoptees and other diasporic figures to South Korea through a composite of black-and-white archival film, varied media sources, oral testimonies, scouting footage, and staged performances. While cultural critics and scholars frequently refer to *The Woman* as a documentary, especially since the film draws on aesthetic conventions popularly associated with documentarian practice, Kaisen's work departs from the more traditional iterations of this genre in several noticeable ways. Missing, for instance, are a singular authoritative voice or "talking head," a chronological storyline, and citations for archival sources embedded in the film. What condenses in their place are entangled vocal textures, broken narrations in multiple languages, and perceptual discordance between imagery and acoustics. As a result, these discursive elements complicate the ways in which the documentary film is normatively encountered as an indexical practice committed to truthful or objective portrayals of reality.[55]

In a less obvious sense, Kaisen fixates on the indexical capacity of the official documentary image, only to disrupt that capacity; she thus references the questionable documentation practices associated with Korean transnational adoption. Through the metastructure of the film, *The Woman* quietly comments on the practice of identity forgery and the "missing" status of paperwork that have long plagued social welfare agencies facilitating transnational adoption in South Korea.[56] As Anaïs shares in *Twinsters,* her discovery of a twin sister after twenty-five years of separation was even more shocking, given that the certified paperwork from her adoption agency confirmed that she was an only child: "For me, it was impossible that she [Sam] could be my twin. . . . I knew that I didn't have a twin because it was written all over my papers that I was an only child." Thus, in productive conversation with RHEE's performance, Kaisen's film is less concerned with the faithful preservation of truth claims than in destabilizing state categories of proper national identity vis-à-vis adoptee returns.

In part, *The Woman*'s examination of the material, discursive, and epistemological underpinnings of recognizable transnational adoptee identity links back to Kaisen's own diasporic trajectory as a transnational adoptee raised in Denmark. In writing about her oeuvre in an unpublished essay in 2016, Kaisen describes how her constructed subjectivity informs her aesthetic praxis insofar as her works explore identity formation within the discursive context of social and historical representation.[57] A multimedia visual artist born to a family from Jeju Island; adopted by a working-class family in Århus, Denmark; and trained in the visual arts at the Royal Danish Academy of Arts, the University of Copenhagen, and the University of California, Los Angeles, Kaisen explains how the diasporic transfer from Korea to Denmark to the United States via "an axis from global south to the west" culminated in prominent erasures—not of an authentic self but of a given name, social context, and language(s) replaced by other cultural, social, and linguistic markers.[58] This south-to-west migration is brokered by a liberal process of racial assimilation that integrates adoptees into a Danish, Protestant, and predominantly white society internationally celebrated for its steadfast commitment to gender equality and human rights. However, Denmark's practice of restricting asylum seekers from Muslim-identified countries and its embracing of ultra-right political parties such as the Danish People's Party underscore the white-supremacist sentiments that structure Danish policies toward adoptees, immigrants of color, and refugees. Kaisen describes the enduring sense of fragmentation induced by the state's asymmetrical application of social equality ideals. Whereas the absorption of Korean overseas adoptees into an all-American milieu depends on a nullification of race through the state's recognition and appropriation of difference, Denmark's assimilation of bodies of color hinges on a discourse of racelessness consolidated through the mastering of the Danish language and cultural codes and the erasure of "non-Danish" qualities.[59] Ultimately, however, total assimilation for citizens of color, including transnational adoptees, is impossible because their bodies retain visible traces perceived by the Danish state as undeniable proof of ontological difference.[60]

Hence, in close proximity to but not quite of the Scandinavian, American, or South Korean populace, Kaisen and other diasporic adoptees raised in Western Europe are perceived as illegible forms of racial difference across these heterogeneous spaces: the unassimilable trace that is Kaisen's body signifies an incongruent position within national populaces organized around the principles of racial and ethnic purity, as well as familial lineages determined by blood and citizenship. This "almost the same but not quite" sentiment produces a state akin to W. E. B. Du Bois's concept of "double consciousness" and Frantz Fanon's description of a schizophrenic condition produced by the colonial gaze: one is taught to constantly look at oneself through a prevailing optics that privileges whiteness, heterosexuality, and perceived ethnic purity as universal and naturalized norms.[61] As we shall see, the unassimilable body and its association with diasporic returns emerge as a strategy of cultural critique in *The Woman, the Orphan, and the Tiger*.

Within the context of the adoptee counterpublic, Kaisen's exploration of transnational identitarian (re)construction and her nuanced exploration of racial, gender, and sexual dynamisms beyond a U.S.-ROK binary is crucial because it demonstrates the far-reaching global impact of American military intervention. Kaisen and other Korean adoptees raised in Scandinavia, including the poet Maja Langvad (Denmark) and the scholar Tobias Hübinette (Sweden), surmise that two factors in particular explain the disproportionate number of Korean children adopted by Scandinavian families.[62] One is the region's comprehensive welfare systems that diminished the available "supply" of domestic adoptees. Two is its steadfast alliance with the United Nations Command (UNC) during the Korean armed conflict.[63] While refusing to provide military forces during the war, Sweden, Denmark, and Norway each contributed medical workers and supplies to support South Korean and UNC efforts in the peninsula. During a research trip to Seoul in July 2013, in fact, I passed by several war commemoration posters plastered on the walls of the Samgakji subway station near the Yongsan Garrison.[64] In these rather large and colorful posters, white Norwegian aid workers are uniformly portrayed as diligent hands tending to and healing wounded yet smiling Korean women and children.

Consequently, even as *The Woman* addresses nonbiological social kinships formed vis-à-vis transnational adoption, the film cautions against romanticized idealizations of homogeneous communities in which a singular adoption identity simply replaces racial and ethnic sameness. Langvad, who is featured in the film as its only Danish-speaker, directly confronts these discrepancies by describing her sense of dislocation among adoptee returnees in South Korea: "There is a kind of displacement in being adopted to Europe. I am very aware of that and see myself in a Western, but most often, American context here [in Korea]." And while featuring a scattering of discrepant memories of search and return narrated by Korean transnational adoptees, *The Woman* delves into diffused yet interrelated forms of racial and sexual violence pivotal to the militarized modernity of South Korea. For Kaisen, this militarized arc encompasses Korean "comfort women" forcibly recruited as sex slaves by the Japanese Imperial Army during the Asia-Pacific War; the biracial children of American soldiers and Korean women; the *zainichi* (ethnic Korean) community in Japan; and multiethnic, multiracial sex workers associated with the U.S. military stationed throughout South Korea. In the process of locating adoptee returns within these nested histories, *The Woman* exposes a broad meshwork of economic apparatuses, historical conditions, and social norms that underlie and are reproduced by the extraction

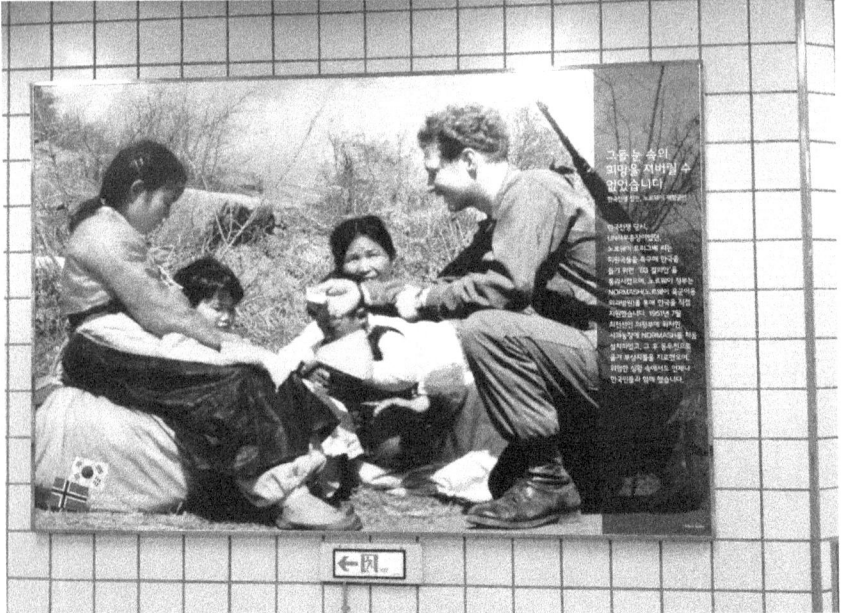

Poster depicting Scandinavian humanitarian workers during the Korean War, Samgakji subway station, Seoul.
(Photograph by the author.)

of children from the Korean Peninsula. Transnational adoption, then, is not an isolated or discrete formation but an enduring institution derived from an accrual of militarized and colonial conditions in contemporary South Korea.

To mediate reencounters with these connections, Kaisen deploys a method of critical juxtaposition, or the "bringing together," of disparate histories, spaces, temporalities, and bodies to foreground the relational binds, rather than essentialized commensurabilities, that connect varied cohorts of women to one another.[65] The film's beginning includes heavily edited footage from the Women's International War Crimes Tribunal on Japan's Military Sexual Slavery, a people's tribunal convened for five days in Tokyo in December 2000 to determine the Japanese state's criminal liability for the perpetration of sexual violence against "comfort women" between 1930 and 1945. Rendered in slow motion, the opening frame portrays an elderly survivor moving toward a podium with an anguished expression on her face. While her mouth opens and quivers, sounds from the tribunal are muted and an indecipherable cacophony of voices in English and Danish overwhelm the screen.

The strategic pairing of the moving image of the "comfort woman" with the vocality of multiple cohorts of women, including transnational adoptees and military sex workers, intimates how South Korean nation building depends on the rendering of racialized gendered subjects as expendable sacrifices necessary for national security. The South Korean government's consistent record of diplomacy and economic development policies substantiate this calculus of disposability. During the tribunal, officiating members critiqued the passage of the ROK-Japan Normalization Treaty in 1965, a bilateral agreement that normalized diplomatic relations between South Korea and Japan. As part of the exchange, the Japanese state provided more than $800 million in economic aid, while both countries agreed that the contract would settle all colonial grievances, including violent sexual crimes committed against "comfort women."[66] Japan's lucrative financial aid further leveraged South Korea's booming economic development between the 1960s and 1980s, the same period that witnessed the exponential growth of the country's transnational adoption industry. That in the process "comfort women" were expunged from international juridical records was apparently considered a sacrifice worth making.

Another sequence of shots shows black-and-white archival moving imagery of American soldiers interacting with Korean women, which is paired with contemporary footage of two Korean babies resting in an orphanage. Jane Jeong Trenka—a Korean adoptee, published writer, and one of the film's core narrators—offers the following commentary:

> *One step away from a Korean American woman married to a white man*
> *One more or the same step away from a Korean military wife with a soldier husband*
> *Another step away from a war bride*
> *Another step war booty*
> *Step, camptown prostitute*
> *Step, comfort woman*
> *Step, comfort child.*

Conjuring a tree of social kinship constituted by branching steps, Trenka comments on how war brides, "comfort women," and overseas adoptees are interlinked through a continuity of militarized policies and colonial and sexual violence rather than through racial, ethnic, and national identity.

Insisting on the associations that situate overseas adoptees within a larger social, historical, and economic context, *The Woman* considers different modes of manufacturing, circulation, and transportation that carry Korean orphans-cum-adoptees and other "domestic returns" from South Korea to a transnational nexus of sites. In some instances, these very adoptees are rerouted back to South Korea as "tourists," "visitors," or "returnees." In a scene captured within the first third of the film, Kaisen's camera documents a long tracking shot at Incheon International Airport near Seoul. In general, the film's sustained focus on the airport as a crucial site of interrogation is informative, given the airport's contemporary affiliations with technologies of racial interrogation, surveillance, and multitemporality: while the airport depends on and reproduces a sense of linear and continuous time (e.g., the exigency of scheduled departure and arrival times), its policed, bounded, and heavily monitored space gives way to unsettling experiences of interrupted, routinized, and stalled time. Within this context, Kaisen gestures to the ways in which one's long search for "family" and "roots" does not always end at intended points of arrival or destination. Indeed, as the camera captures rows of nearly empty seats within the airport's interior, Jennifer Kwon Dobbs, another narrator of the film, reconsiders the differentiated meanings of "search" as this term applies to narratives of adoptee displacement and return. Mapping a trail of militarized spaces and human bodies that appear during return trips to South Korea, Dobbs's commentary refers to how adoptees' "process[es] of search" unexpectedly lead to "pathways" or revelations that are as disturbing as they are revealing. During their stays in South Korea, transnational adoptees come face to face with an underground web of maternity homes, privatized orphanages, and isolated concentrations of "young women pregnant and at the end of their third terms."

Others, during their return, witness the dominance of American presence in South Korea by confronting a trail of hastily built camptowns, red-light districts, and military campuses scattered across agricultural zones, such as Camp Red Cloud near the border city of Uijeongbu. In one scene filmed in Uijeongbu, the camera captures a familiar portrayal of childhood with one striking exception: as frolicking children enjoy a seemingly carefree afternoon in a grassy playground replete with a shiny swing set, U.S. military helicopters hover above, producing sonic pollution that reverberates throughout the skyscape. Consequently, instead of finding family or ethnic roots, these uneasy returns reveal a massive "production structure" reinforced by a scaffolding of human bodies, militarized sexual labor, and economic resources mobilized toward a "singular migration" that is Korean transnational adoption.

The film's implied connections between transnational adoption and biopolitical modes of production, however, are not limited to the South Korean interior but radiate beyond national borders to engender a militarized diasporic geography. In one such scene, contemporary news footage from an adoptee-related event at Minnesota's Mall of America, the second-largest shopping complex in the United States, is displayed. (Minnesota is home to the largest Korean transnational adoptee population in the country.) As Dobbs tersely states, the footage depicts a "four-day extravaganza" in which members from a Korean adoptee organization invited by the mall embody "Korean-ness" through the modeling of *hanbok,* the narration of Korean folk tales, and the performance of poongmul for a predominantly white, middle-class audience. For Dobbs, the voyeuristic gaze directed at these racialized bodies within a "neoliberal utopic space" located in the metaphorical heartland of U.S. empire directly links notions of racial and ethnic authenticity to purchasing power, capitalistic consumption, and the desire for ownership. Aware of how not only corporate industries but also the South Korean and U.S. states recalibrate adoptees from perpetual outsiders to Korean cultural experts within the dizzying consumerist space of the all-American mall, Dobbs exclaims, "Wow . . . our bodies are being utilized, still, in order to proliferate the very economics that made possible the production of our bodies . . . as adoptees!"

While *The Woman* insists on this persisting cycle of displacement and rerouting that renders adoptees desired commodities, the film also suggests an array of subversive potentialities that crystallize during these return trips to South Korea. Near the beginning of the film, while Incheon International Airport travelers are transported via a moving walkway, Grace Cho narrates her conflicting, push-pull feelings toward Korea. Despite her sentiments of unease during visits to the country, Cho nevertheless returns again and again to South Korea. In many ways, this enduring sense of anxiety is informed by the hypervisibility of Cho's racialized and gendered body and the intrusive ways she is recognized as fundamentally "other" in Korea. As the daughter of a Korean woman and a white American soldier once stationed in South Korea, Cho experiences herself as "awkward" and "different from other Koreans." Given the diffused repercussions of U.S. military presence on the peninsula since 1945, including sexual intimacy between Korean women and American soldiers, Cho describes how the public's identification of her body as "mixed-race" registers unspoken assumptions about who she is and where she comes from. For Cho, return trips to South Korea reify and reproduce the embodied "reverberations of [this militarized] history."

Pointing to these negative inferences of her "different" body, Cho explains how her perceptible presence in South Korea ironically upends the dominant narrative of American militarized conquest, paternalistic tutelage, and deracination. Cho's consistent returns to the country stubbornly remind other Koreans of her existence and her refusal to be extracted from public memory, challenging the country's protracted history of transnational adoption, removal of multiracial children, and public shaming of Korean women romantically associated with American soldiers. Taking fleshed form, Cho's body resignifies biracialism as a diasporic mode of feminist critique that, on the one hand, acknowledges the violent ramifications of American militarized presence, and on the other, punctures heteronormative discourses of ethnic purity so pivotal to national belonging in South Korea. In other moments throughout *The Woman,* the mixed-race population tucked away within the hidden seams of South Korean society is visualized by the presence of multiethnic sex workers who exist outside the Korean ethnic collectivity altogether. Kaisen's attention to these racialized bodies does not merely catalogue the problematic discourses pertaining to South Korea's so-called transition from a poor "aid recipient" to a wealthy "donor" nation. It also fractures the fictionalized narrative of South Korean racial and ethnic homogeneity, given that more than 90 percent of contemporary sex workers in the country self-identify as Filipinx or Eastern European.[67]

The symbolic mobilization of racial impurity as a strategy of cultural intervention points to an earlier observation regarding Kaisen's conceptualization of the returning diasporic body as an antagonistic presence within the national interior. While this formulation of the unassimilable body might be described along the lines of historical damage and injury, I reassemble the related notions of racial excess, national "outsideness," and identitarian fragmentation into a critical mode of remembering that refutes the state's attempts to forget "deviant" diasporic subjectivities. More precisely, the inscrutability of militarized diasporic bodies produced by the Korean War registers an incommensurability that is outside of and in excess to the state's protocols of extraction and removal, or conversely, racial assimilation and incorporation. As material forms of return and refusal, Korean diasporic bodies produce different ways of knowing and modes of becoming that challenge dominant presumptions of national belonging and citizenry in South Korea. Subsequently, Kaisen suggests that diasporic returns rupture the recognizable stories we are told and tell ourselves about the "self, community . . . and representation."[68] Given the differences that constitute the still emergent, always shifting Korean adoptee counterpublic, the types of transnational sites of alternative sociality discussed in this chapter are politicized platforms produced by and negotiated among adoptees. These heterogeneous spaces and formations do not replicate or supplant biological bonds; nor do they produce a homogeneous adoptee community. Instead, they problematize the twin projects of South Korean national development and American exceptionalism, while also refusing to be solely defined by or delimited to these dominant discourses.

The potential affinities and diasporic excesses associated with the adoptee counterpublic are especially evident in the concluding scenes of *The Woman.* In the last few minutes of the film, a small group of transnational adoptees gather at the famed War Memorial of Korea. This museum and outdoor exhibition area in Seoul honors soldiers and other male actors affiliated with the founding of the modern South Korean state; its impressive military tanks and massive replications of guns and other displayed weaponry are designed to "enhance [the] warrior spirit defending this great country [South Korea]."[69] Filming amid a changing crowd of passing tourists and children, Kaisen and other adoptees, including Langvad, Dobbs, and Trenka, participate in what initially appears to be a lighthearted gathering. Playfully working with and handling a colorful assortment of large, hand-made papier-mâché puppets, including a tiger, a green-colored puppet dressed in military fatigues, a small baby figurine, and a puppet with bright red circles on its cheeks, Kaisen and the other puppeteers prepare for a public performance.

As the sequence jump-cuts between the War Memorial and the giggling performers, the buoyant tone of the film abruptly changes when the handheld camera captures the gathered women interchangeably beating the figurines with long sticks before eviscerating and setting fire to one of the puppets in a muddy knoll near the War Memorial. Captured through a sequence of close-up shots, the burning effigy resembles a blushing bride-to-be, as hinted by the puppet's *yeonji gonji* (a Korean wedding custom in which the virginal female bride wears round patches of blood-red makeup). The War Memorial is an especially poignant space for the site-specific performance, given that the burned figurine symbolizes a constellation of South Korean ethnocentric virtues and gendered practices. Rather than representing the literal body of the birth mother or an abstraction of the Jungian mother archetype, the effigy symbolizes nationalistic virtues, including fidelity to the (South) Korean "motherland," heterosexual marriage, future fecundity, and (female) sexual purity. Following this explosive scene of symbolic birth and violent destruction, the film comes full circle by ending as it began: while slow-motion footage depicting curious children at the War Memorial appears on-screen, a discordant cacophony of voices inundates and overwhelms the frame.

Situated within the broader aims of the film, I suggest, this eruptive scene of national birth and staged death reinforces two observations. For one, the ritualistic performance centered on the bride puppet makes painfully obvious a circuitous logic of militarized violence sutured to diasporic returns: the violence enacted against the feminized figurine is performed by adoptee returnees, or racialized gendered subjects resituated within the militarized confines of the hypermasculine South Korean nation-state. In turn, this adoptee performance symbolizes a contemporary ecology of human bodies, spaces, and subjectivities repeatedly reproduced by the presence of the American military in South Korea. Second, and in direct dialogue with RHEE's disruptive performance in *Sex Education,* the performative encounter among the puppeteers demonstrates how diasporic returnees conceptualize "excessive" or "negative" feelings, such as anger and rage, as strategic

Still image from *The Woman, the Orphan, and the Tiger*, 2010.
(Courtesy of Jane Jin Kaisen.)

Still image from *The Woman, the Orphan, and the Tiger*, 2010.
(Courtesy of Jane Jin Kaisen.)

dynamisms that disavow the normative confines of the nuclear family, the ethnocentric nation-state, and American benevolence. Thus, the implied uses of "uncontrolled" and "bad" feelings are epistemological as much as they are embodied and visceral.

As Audre Lorde explains, the expression of anger is "loaded with information and energy" since it indexes a "grief of distortions" produced by disproportionate violence perpetrated against women of color for the sake of national security and militarized safety.⁷⁰ The performative crystallization of anger among adoptees at the War Memorial, then, does not merely signify an affective overload of accrued frustration and fury. Rather, the communal enactment of anger, "expressed and translated into action in the service" of a vision, re-creates an alternative collectivity exterior to and in tension with the atomic family unit and nation-family.⁷¹ Queering the naturalized masculine logics of the War Memorial, and charged through the frenetic flow of shared energy and intentions, the performers actualize a kinesthetic act of disidentification within and against the violence of Korean transnational adoption.⁷² Subsequently, the performance generates a social kinship that is circumstantial and contingent on mutual conditions of deracination, displacement, and return. As transient and stitched as such an improvisational "family" may be, the profound reencounter among diasporic adoptee returnees at the War Memorial engenders a radically different kind of relationality at odds with the ethnocentric structures of the Korean biological family and South Korean citizenship. Hence, not unlike RHEE's performance in *Sex Education*, Kaisen's *The Woman* exemplifies the ways in which adoptee returns materialize social alterities that exceed the singular histories of humanitarian intervention and irreversible colonial injury.

Coda

In this chapter, I mobilize the diasporic analytic of adoptee returns to identify how transnational adoption, a direct by-product of the Korean War, ensnares itself within the confines of political and economic life in contemporary South Korea. By drawing on RHEE's *Sex Education for Finding Face in the 21st Century* and Kaisen's *The Woman, the Orphan, and the Tiger* as the primary diasporic memory works of this chapter, I emphasize how the adoptee counterpublic contends with the devastating repercussions of the Korean overseas adoption enterprise, even while it provides opportunities to reencounter and explicitly name the industry's social, affective, and mnemonic excesses. Specifically, while RHEE's and Kaisen's works convey the potential rupture points of transnational adoption, they also use adoptee returns to forge alternative genealogies of history and social kinship that do not properly align with Americanized accounts of humanitarian intervention and South Korean national development. *Sex Education* and *The Woman, the Orphan, and the Tiger* therefore demonstrate how the South Korean state recalibrates the adoptee figure from an expendable subject existing on the fringe of normative citizenship to a returning subject incorporated into the country's political and economic infrastructure.

In closing, I return to the chapter's beginning to demonstrate how Korean adoptee returns, as a diasporic mode of mnemonic critique, also apply to the Netflix documentary *Twinsters*. While *Twinsters* largely focuses on the "positive" elements of transnational adoption and the fortuitous reunion between its sibling protagonists, it also details Anaïs's experiences of social isolation, anxiety, and loneliness as one of the few children of color raised in a predominantly white environment in France. In several monologues throughout the documentary, Anaïs repeatedly describes her feelings of out-of-placeness in conjunction with her forced removal from Korea and the involuntary separation from her twin sister. As Sam puts it, "[Anaïs] didn't choose to be adopted, she was sort of thrown into it. For her, it was traumatic. . . . [B]eing adopted was kind of a bad thing." Scattered in bits and pieces throughout the film, these troubling scenes build up to an emotional climax when the possibility of a bittersweet family reunion in South Korea is quashed. During a phone call with Ben Sommers, a social worker affiliated with the Spence-Chapin Services to Families and Children, Sam discovers that her biological mother has flatly denied that she ever gave birth to twin daughters. Sam and Anaïs's birth mother, in fact, never appears in the ninety-minute documentary.

During his explanation to Sam, Sommers attempts to situate this personal rejection within the broader social context of South Korea's welfare system. In particular, he emphasizes the extenuating circumstances faced by most unwed single mothers who must make the excruciating choice between raising their children with limited financial and social resources or giving them up for overseas adoption with the hope that they will have more secure and comfortable lives elsewhere. Offered as subtle cues rather than as explicit critiques of Korean transnational adoption, these scenes nevertheless exemplify how Sam's and Anaïs's own returns to South Korea signal an arc of racialized gendered excesses, as well as perpetual renunciations and refusals, that do not neatly fit into the chrononormative timeline of displacement, return, and happy family reunion.

4

Durational Memory

> What they have survived is an event to be endured,
> not a trauma to be healed. It is not part of their historical past,
> but of their durational present, and as such is both
> unforgotten and unforgettable.
>
> —Seong-nae Kim, "The Work of Memory"

In July 2013, I participated in a peace tour of South Korea organized by the Alliance of Scholars Concerned about Korea. The first of its kind, the four-day trip took place on the eve of the sixtieth anniversary of the Korean Armistice. With more than thirty scholars, filmmakers, activists, and artists from Korea and beyond, the tour included visits to the Demilitarized Zone (DMZ); the bullet-ridden bridge of No-Gun Ri, the site of a 1950 civilian massacre committed by the U.S. military; and Jeju Island, an oblong isle located just off the southwestern coast of South Korea. Reemerging as a popular destination for international tourists during the 1980s and recognized by the United Nations Educational, Scientific, and Cultural Organization as a World Heritage site in 2007, Jeju is described by the United Nations as a pristine ecosystem encompassing the "finest lava tube system of caves [found] anywhere." South Korea's official tourism organization depicts Jeju as an "island full of wonder."[1]

Yet, as was foregrounded throughout our trip, this idealized portrayal of Jeju as an "island full of wonder" myopically obscures a troubling history of multiple militarized colonialisms. A region culturally distinct from the Korean Peninsula, Jeju during the reign of the U.S. Army Military Government in Korea (USAMGIK) was openly characterized as a festering hotbed of leftist sentiments and communist activism.[2] Consequently, the island experienced a seven-year militarized campaign (1948–1955) staged by the U.S.-supported

South Korean Interim Government (SKIG) and its right-wing youth allies against guerrilla forces and the South Korean Labor Party. While statistics vary, most studies indicate that anywhere between fourteen thousand and eighty thousand civilians, or up to one-third of the island's population, were killed during this interval. A microcosm of the violent ferocity unleashed during the Korean armed conflict on the peninsula, the Jeju massacre remains within the periphery of a war that already exists along the edge of public memory. Today, Jeju inhabitants solemnly refer to the massacre as the "April Third Incident" or, simply, "4.3" (*sa-sam*), a reference to the date that marks the official beginning of the massacre, although a handful of earlier skirmishes also took place between the military state and leftist guerrilla forces.[3]

Recently, the devastating memories of 4.3 have taken on new meanings with the accelerated militarized buildup of Jeju Island. Under the auspices of the U.S. government, which maintains wartime control of the South Korean military, a new $970 million naval base was completed in 2016 in the coastal village of Gangjeong. Despite the anticommunist sentiments that affix the terrifying "past" of 4.3 to the island's remilitarization, these two events are casually treated by proponents of the U.S.–South Korean alliance as unrelated episodes. More often than not, 4.3 is discussed as an unavoidable military action that halted the spread of communism in Asia, while the new state-of-the-art naval base is perceived as both a tourist attraction *and* a security measure necessary to protecting American interests from China's economic power and North Korean aggression.[4] For island inhabitants, however, the remilitarization of Jeju not only signals the threat of rekindled warfare in Korea. It also constantly reminds that the past of 4.3 and the Korean War is anything but settled. Hence, acts of mourning for those who died during 4.3 are also critical memory practices associated with one's reencounter with the militarized present and a still undetermined future.

This extended description of Jeju's present-past foreshadows the vital questions pursued in this chapter—namely, what does it mean to remember, reckon with, and recount an atrocious event that is prolonged rather than isolated and discrete? Relatedly, what significances are attached to mourning and memory practices when the "vanished object" in question—in this case, the disappearance of a "unified" or "whole" Korea—is not dead and gone but suspended? Here the mentioning of mourning raises the specter of Sigmund Freud's theorizations of mourning and melancholia.[5] While Freud portrays mourning as a "healthy" mode of processing insofar as the grieving subject eventually accepts and lets go of loss, melancholia is a pathological stance, since the lamenting subject refuses to relinquish the lost object.[6] And yet in the case of Jeju Island and the Korean War, this dichotomous paradigm of mourning and melancholia does not wholly capture the political nuances, emotional complexities, and unique sense of temporal drag that condition an extended conflict. In other words, civilians' fettered attachments to the 4.3 Massacre is less about a pathological identification with a foregone past than it is about a congealed violence that infiltrates the everyday. As Seong-nae Kim, an anthropologist who has written extensively on the 4.3 Massacre, suggests, the violence that Jeju inhabitants endure is *not* an abstracted "trauma to be healed"; nor is it part of a "historical past" that needs to be let go. Rather, the continuing repercussions of war constitute a "durational present" that permeates daily life in "unforgotten and unforgettable" ways in Jeju. Thus, it seems necessary, even urgent, to flesh out the exigency of April 3 diasporic memory practices beyond Freud's dyadic paradigm of mourning and melancholia. In conversation with discussions in the previous two chapters, I mobilize the analytic of the diasporic to highlight dissonant memory practices that share an unsettling relationship with national formations such as Cold War political discourse and national citizenship. More specifically, the diasporic in this chapter signifies how cultural workers delink heterogeneous memory processes from "proper" national sites sanctioned by the U.S. and South Korean governments, ranging from the patrilineal ethnocentric family unit to the realm of (inter)national politics.

To contend with the entwined militarized formations of the 4.3 Massacre and Gangjeong naval base, I draw on two diasporic cultural productions that approach the contemporary "now" as an amplification of unforgotten, undead pasts. While Jane Jin Kaisen's multichannel video installation *Reiterations of Dissent* (2011/2016) and Dohee Lee's public performance *MAGO* (2014) are decisively distinct works, both cultural productions are anchored in robust rereadings of Cold War temporality.[7] Particularly, I am interested in how Kaisen and Lee reencounter Jeju's history through a framework I conceptualize as *durational memory*. Drawing from Seong-nae Kim's theorization of the durational present, which itself reconfigures Henri Bergson's critique of modern renderings of time, durational memories are intentional forms of remembering at odds with the chrononormativity of Cold War historicism.[8] Reconfiguring the present in relation to the persisting resonance of discordant pasts, durational memory destabilizes the naturalized schematic of successive time catalogued through the temporal logic of then and now. In the case of Jeju Island, linear time segues with the public discourse of national forgiveness, economic prosperity, and resolution. The merging of the past(s) with the present(s) in *Reiterations of Dissent* and *MAGO,* however, upends the spatialized dimensions of time as progressive and inevitable. Placing pressure on the "homogeneous and empty" characterization of modern time tracks how the Korean War's imagined ending hinges on a future incontrovertibility: Cold War storytelling presumes that the Korean conflict will end with the definitive victory of the capitalist "free world," enabled by the collapse of North Korea and its wholesale absorption into a global capitalist infrastructure.

Durational memory, in contrast, insists on a disarray of memories that deviate far from this dominant script. Imagining multiple, even strange and fantastic, temporalities, *Reiterations of Dissent* and *MAGO* generate a complex of subversive memories that refuse to be appeased by state-mediated processes of beautified nation building, forgiveness, and exoneration. Pointing to the limitations of Cold War political discourse, *Reiterations of Dissent* and *MAGO* emphasize three pressing qualities of durational memory. First, these diasporic cultural productions register how the present constitutes competing versions of the past(s) that contradict or are unfathomable to nationalist renderings of time. Second, through the conjuring of heterogeneous pasts, durational memories suggest alternative paradigms of experienced time—or, more precisely, the *durational*—that exceed the contours of Cold War temporality. The durational, as Bergson states, diverges from the mechanization of modern time, which measures temporality through a cyclical range of invariable units, including seconds, minutes, and hours, that then accrue into days, months, and years.[9] This understanding of mechanized time links to modernizing notions of political and social progress that justify a colonial power's occupation of other sovereign spaces, such as the United States' intervention in Korea. The durational therefore marks the conspicuous disjuncture between chrononormative temporality and "immiscible times," or what Bliss Cua Lim theorizes as "multiple times that never quite dissolve into the code of modern time consciousness."[10] As further elaborated in this chapter, Kaisen and Lee conceptualize durational memory and "immiscible times" through the aesthetic strategy of remediation.[11] While remediation traditionally refers to how "newer" media (i.e., digital media) incorporate and remix "older" media (e.g., analog footage), Kaisen and Lee both deploy this praxis to indicate how multiple temporalities overlap with, meld, and fold into one another. Contextualized this way, the Gangjeong naval base is a historical "remediation" of the 4.3 Massacre.

Third, Kaisen's and Lee's reenactments of durational memory accentuate the significance of audiences' participatory engagement. Note that I resist defining durational memory along the idealized terms of audience "activism"; after all, artwork and performances are always already situated in power-laden spaces regulated by socioeconomic, gendered, and spatial norms. But a willful assertion of the participatory, however imperfect or incomplete, anticipates transient moments of opening necessary for the imagining of decolonized presents and futures. As Judith Butler reminds us, the use of expressive culture to mediate public assemblies underscores the conditions that motivate and impel social action, even as it highlights the enduring dynamisms of power that potentially undermine those very intentions.[12] Hence, attentive to the problematic associations commonly affiliated with reductive notions of "public engagement" and "audience," I locate *Reiterations of Dissent* and *MAGO* as diasporic cultural productions that foster decolonizing modes of historical remembering unaccounted for by Cold War temporal logics.

The chapter builds on this conceptualization of durational memory in the following manner. The next section discusses Kaisen's *Reiterations of Dissent* through a historical contextualization of the 4.3 Massacre and the remilitarization of Jeju Island. In conversation with the discursive strategies mobilized in Kaisen's film *The Woman, the Orphan, and the Tiger* (see Chapter 3), *Reiterations of Dissent* highlights the highly constructed nature of nationalist historiography, as well as the durational memories that exist in relation to and against Cold War chrononormative time. Deploying what Kaisen describes as "dissident" translations of history, *Reiterations of Dissent* recalibrates Jeju's present through rebellious memories of pasts that defy U.S.–South Korean state discourses of reconciliation and forgiveness. Consequently, Kaisen configures durational memories as a beginning point and clearing ground for the long struggle against remilitarization, not only in Korea, but also in a disparate and vast region commonly naturalized as "Asia and the Pacific."

The final section of the chapter engages Dohee Lee's electrifying *MAGO*, a genre-bending multimedia performance that premiered in San Francisco in 2014. *MAGO* combines elements of Korean mythology, modern dance, electronica, and remediated filmic imagery to engulf its audience in an otherworldly environment. Reinterpreting a rich corpus of cosmologic symbols, mythology, and shamanic rituals, Lee approaches Jeju's remilitarization as a systemic protraction of the 4.3 Massacre. Yet by re-rendering the past as a synthesis between quotidian elements and fantastic symbols, Lee underscores how extant histories of the massacre cannot express the heterogeneous memories of Jeju civilians. By activating durational memories to create a communal mourning ritual, Lee portrays how Jeju inhabitants have endured the brutal force of multiple empires through alternative paradigms of historical narration and becoming. Conversing with Lim's understanding of the fantastic, *MAGO*'s "out-of-this-world" imagery attests to how a decolonized future remains foreclosed in the confines of a here and now that is faithful to Cold War historiography.

Dissident Translations and
Reiterations of Dissent

Originally showcased as part of Kaisen's solo exhibition "Dissident Translations" in 2011 in Åarhus, *Reiterations of Dissent* pulls together a haphazard array of moving images, including U.S. military films, contemporary footage from transnational media outlets, and personal documentation shot by Kaisen in Jeju. Encompassing eight monitors evenly distributed across a semicircle, *Reiterations of Dissent* remediates these moving images into eight looped film shorts, each displayed on a different screen. In these shorts, Kaisen juxtaposes two significant events related to Jeju: the atrocities committed during the 4.3 Massacre and the recently constructed Gangjeong naval base.[13]

The ten-minute film short "Retake: Mayday" remediates black-and-white archival footage first shot by the U.S. Army Signal Corps, an agency responsible for overseeing communication systems in the American military. The military film, catalogued as "Mayday" at the U.S. National Archives, captures a chain of arson fires and fatal attacks that took place in Jeju's Ora Village. Depicting scenes of burning houses, civilians interviewed by military officers, and limp corpses strewn across a rocky plain, this found footage narrates the events as a malicious communist rebellion heroically halted by the South Korean military with support from the United States. Yet Dong-man Kim, a Korean documentary-film maker and one of the intervening voices of "Retake: Mayday," states that these "Americanized" images are meticulously framed to produce the optical illusion of the United States acting as a humanitarian arbiter of justice: "[The film] was created just like a movie set by a particular director . . . the scenes of battle, the burning of the village, and the urgent chase." The depicted fires, in fact, were executed by a cadre of extreme right-wing members of the Northwest Youth League, a paramilitary group trained by the U.S.-backed SKIG.[14]

Reiterations of Dissent subverts this historicization by decentering the state as the a priori voice of historical memory and exposing audiences to multiple narratives of the 4.3 Massacre. Pulling apart and piecing the film back together in heavily revised form, "Retake: Mayday" remediates the military footage with recent testimonies and other audiovisual sources provided by massacre survivors, activists, and filmmakers such as Dong-man Kim. In part, the video installation's attention to the manufacturing of South Korea's official version of 4.3 is amplified by Kaisen's references to the meta-qualities of filmmaking. One sequence shows Dong-man Kim in an editing room with two small television monitors. The left-hand monitor depicts a still frame from the Ora fires film featuring South Korean soldiers "protecting" villagers from guerrilla attacks (or so the narrative goes), while the right-hand

Installation view of *Reiterations of Dissent*, ARTSPECTRUM, Leeum Samsung Museum of Art, Seoul, 2016. (Courtesy of Jane Jin Kaisen. Photograph by Hyunsoo Kim.)

screen displays more recent imagery of exhumed skeletal remains belonging to civilians murdered by SKIG officers and right-wing youth. Producing a split-screen effect, this polarized arrangement hints at how *Reiterations of Dissent* evokes wildly different versions of 4.3 through the juxtaposition of dissonant narrations and temporalities.

In several ways, "Retake: Mayday" exemplifies how Kaisen conceptualizes durational memory in the *Reiterations of Dissent* installation. As discussed at length in Chapter 3, Kaisen's overarching oeuvre concerns a range of diasporic subjects who contend with the (inter)national politics of Cold War historiography in Western Europe, South Korea, and the United States. A transnational adoptee raised in Denmark, Kaisen describes how her aesthetic sensibilities contemplate queer modes of sociality and remembering at odds with heteronormative categories, including political citizenship and the biological family. While *Reiterations of Dissent* departs from *The Woman, the Orphan, and the Tiger* in its chosen medium and subject matter, Kaisen's diasporic commitment to the untamable memories of war in excess of national history is evidenced in this multichannel installation, as well.

To start, we might refer back to the title of the artist's 2011 solo exhibition, which includes *Reiterations of Dissent*, to highlight Kaisen's reinterpretation, or "dissident translation," of Korean War historiography. Here the relationship between dissident translation and durational memory deserves some unpacking. For Kaisen, dominant Cold War historiography "translates" the Korean War through the grammar and syntax of familiar phrases, such as American liberation, the free world, and democratic progress.[15] In turn, these semiotic signs depict American military intervention as an altruistic event that "freed" Koreans from the jaws of Japanese colonialism and communism while supporting South Korea's transformation from a country that suffered from "crushing poverty to one of the world's most dynamic economies."[16] This nationalist script subsequently locates 4.3 within a distant past while conveniently occluding recalcitrant memories that do not fit into or align with this historical narrative. In contradistinction, a dissident translation rerenders the contemporary moment through the aperture of persevering pasts that disrupt linear temporality. Specifically, the concept of dissident translation or "translating otherwise" privileges the multifaceted memories of subjects who, more often than not, "embody marginal positions" or reside within transborder spaces, literally and figuratively, as they are frequently crossing or located between national spaces.[17] Self-identifying as a militarized migrant forcibly "transported, accepted, and denied" through overseas adoption, Kaisen approaches translating otherwise as a diasporic mode of memory exploration that maps the difficult historical terrain of violent migration nullified by "Eurocentric understandings of knowledge, memory, subjectivity, and perception."[18]

Consequently, Cold War historiography is provincialized as a *single* interpretation rather than as an objective fact. Reaching far beyond the boundaries of "textual interpretation and mediation from one language to another," a dissident translation, as Kaisen conceives of the term, is a "political act," a "condition," and the "state of being in translation."[19] In conversation with postcolonial feminist theorists such as Trinh T. Minh-ha and Tejaswini Niranjana, who engage translation as a practice of disruption rather than of continuity, Kaisen's oeuvre identifies the untranslatable traces between state history and localized knowledges that tell us otherwise.[20] As a discursive tool that generates durational memory, dissident translations are therefore diasporic rereadings of continuing pasts that engender multiple interpretations of the here and now.

Aesthetically, Kaisen's concept of dissident translations closely aligns with her incisive critiques of visuality and her troubling of the recognizable. In particular, Kaisen problematizes the assumed relationality between progressive time and the documentarian rendering of truthful, transparent history through two related methods. First, her works rupture a coherent visual narrative through contradictory images and temporalities that occupy a single plane of vision (e.g., the television screen). Second, her oeuvre translates vision as a multisensorial process constituted by the sonic, kinesthetic, and tactile. Thus, by multiplying the ways in which the audience reencounters the recognizable visualization of history, *Reiterations of Dissent* questions the terms and relations that underlie representation. While Kaisen carefully acknowledges the damaging power of the image maker's gaze (in this case, the U.S. and South Korean states' omnipresent gaze), her multimedia works emphasize the agentive role(s) played by transnational audiences in the decoding of hegemonic imagery and national history.

To demonstrate the relationality between dissident translation and durational memory, I turn to the structural elements of *Reiterations of Dissent* and Kaisen's use of the multichannel video installation. An art form historically linked to space, corporeality, and the body, video/film installation initially gained traction during the 1960s when artists, including Nam June Paik, experimented with a variety of mediums. Multichannel installation encompasses performance, photography, film, animation, and virtual art, at times being described as a "moving" practice without a methodological essence.[21] The absence of a unified core of principles has produced diverse works that not only depend on the visual but also tap the sensorial and kinesthetic. The audience-observer might approach a three-dimensional, multichannel installation from a number of perspectives: viewing it from afar, walking around it, or standing close to it. This menu of perceptual possibilities shifts the audience's orientation to produce divergent knowledges.[22] Consequently, *Reiterations of Dissent* mimics the contested process of historiographical construction: the installation's screens force the audience to acknowledge the divergent dimensions of narrative making because any single standpoint permits only partial views. The audience must choose which screen to look at initially and which monitor(s) to ignore or encounter at a later moment. Each monitor reaffirms, contradicts, or detracts from the visual and sonic elements that surface across other screens, simulating the entwined processes of memory making and forgetting.[23] In this way, multichannel installation works against the logic of the classical film diegesis, since the multiple screens do not fuse into a coherent sum total but, rather, shatter the very possibility of a single coherent narrative.

Take, for instance, a pair of diametric scenes portrayed in "Lamentation of the Dead" and "The Politics of Naming," film shorts displayed on adjacent monitors in *Reiterations of Dissent*. Although both screens depict contemporary mourning rituals honoring those killed or disappeared during the 4.3 Massacre, they do so in very different ways. In "Lamentation of the Dead," a resplendently dressed *baksu* (male-identifying shaman) mediates the dead to quell their restless spirits. Performed at an unmarked execution site cloistered in the middle range of Mount Halla, the *gut* (shamanistic ceremony for the dead) is attended by only a handful of witnesses. Because of the pervasiveness of killings during the events of April 3, obscured massacre sites are commonplace throughout the island. The enclosed scene clashes blatantly with the nationally televised state ceremony depicted in "The Politics of Naming," organized each year since the early 2000s by the South Korean government. In the remediated clip, South Korean President Roh Moo-hyun in 2003 offers the first state acknowledgment of and apology for the killings. Yet Roh explicitly names the South Korean Labor Party and communist sympathizers as the primary culprits in the massacre. As hundreds of civilians gather at the national public cemetery, the South Korean national anthem plays softly in the background as a mourning crowd hums and lays wreathes and white flowers on grave sites.

Upon closer examination, President Roh's speech describes Jeju as a shining beacon of human rights and an island of beauty, peace, and leisure. Such portrayals overlap with the South Korean government's efforts to promote Jeju Island as an alluring vacation spot for domestic and international tourists. Popularly heralded as the "Hawai'i of South Korea" by South Korea's national tourism organization, Jeju is cosmetically transformed into a warm tropical island severed from the horrors of the past. Emulating what Vernadette Vicuña Gonzalez describes as the seamless merger between the military-industrial complex and the tourist economy, the South Korean Navy describes the Gangjeong naval base as an eco-friendly port that serves as "a new attraction for beautiful Jeju!"[24] Ironically, the suggested relation between Hawai'i and Jeju evokes an enduring present-past: the two islands share a modern history of colonial occupation and continue to serve as U.S. military outposts in the Pacific.

Within the context of state governance, Roh's apology overlaps with the official policy of "straightening up history" first adopted by President Kim Young-sam's administration in 1996. As indicated by Seong-nae Kim, the concept of "straightening up" refers to the state's attempt to purge and clean up South Korea's sordid past, consisting of sequential military dictatorships and human-rights violations. Yet if we draw on Sara Ahmed's feminist reworking of existential phenomenology, we might notice how the implied references of directionality and orientation in the policy of straightening up aligns with a selective set of heteronormative expectations characteristic of Cold War time.[25] For President Kim and President Roh, the straightening up of South Korean history suggests the "second building" of a virile nation-state committed to, as Seong-nae Kim observes, a "sacred theodicy of anticommunist national unification," a "moving forward" through a wedded alliance with the United States, and the cultivation of a vibrant national populace maintained through heteronormative reproductive relations, the gendered division of labor, and blood kinship.[26] The straightening up of South Korean history demonstrates how Cold War historiography is intimately bound to and sustained through the persistent force of chrononormativity.

The official state policy of straightening up simultaneously contradicts the lived realities of Jeju civilians and practices on the ground.[27] Nearly seventy years after the massacre, the remains of the most prominent resistance and guerrilla youth leaders remain suspended between a here and the afterlife, because they are prohibited from receiving burials in public cemeteries and excluded from state-sponsored commemorations. In the absence of government-organized burials, shamanistic *gut*s such as the one featured in "Lamentation of the Dead" become alternative requiems. Put differently, *Reiterations of Dissent* translates the *gut* as a durational memory practice that invokes the dead and reconstitutes execution sites as mnemonic spaces of resistance in the here and now. The installation reinterprets sites of state violence as dissonant spaces of "othered" narration and thus embodies durational memories denied by the U.S. and South Korean governments.[28] Even today, shamanistic rituals play an important role in public, political, and intellectual life in South Korea and throughout the Korean diaspora—although, as detailed in the subsequent discussion of *MAGO,* they, too, function within and against an overarching system of heteronormative relations and nationalist expectations.[29]

"The Politics of Naming" further discusses how the administrative practices of publicly recognizing the 4.3 Massacre in South Korea and the United States remain in constant flux. Despite the establishment of a truth commission in 1999, the formal stance of the U.S. and South Korean governments on 4.3 has depended on the administration in power in Seoul. While the camera offers a long shot of silvery tendrils of incense smoke uncoiling from a copper vessel placed at the center of the April 3rd Peace Memorial Park Altar, a narrator, via voiceover, offers the following description: "If you go to the memorial hall of the Jeju April 3 Incident, you can see a sign that says 'blank memorial stone' on it. The memorial stone has remained without anything carved on it. It means the people have not named the incident yet." The absence of a proper name provides sobering commentary on the South Korean and U.S. governments' wariness of recognizing the 4.3 atrocities as a military-sponsored cleansing. Indeed, as portrayed by the recent actions of conservative South Korean administrations led by Lee Myung-bak (2008–2013) and Park Geun-hye (2013–2017), the 4.3 Massacre is framed in history textbooks as a necessary counterinsurgency campaign deployed against communist enemies.[30] Hence, state discourse crafts the rampant killings as an unavoidable step taken on the hard road to recovery, emancipation, and liberation from North Korean communist influence.³¹ Linked to the humanist tropes of freedom, progress, and rescue, state-sanctioned violence is galvanized as an essential mechanism of economic prosperity and national security.

Yet Kaisen's use of multiple temporalities in *Reiterations of Dissent* underscores how the narrative of national progress is stymied by the refusal of Jeju inhabitants to forget or move on from the 4.3 Massacre. Civilians, in fact, define the massacre as fundamental to their sense of everyday space and time in Jeju. To demonstrate this, I turn to the film short "Ghosts." In the beginning of the footage, an overhead camera provides an extreme wide shot of Jeju's majestic geography, replete with the snow-capped mountaintop of Halla, a luminous crater lake, and a screeching crow fluttering in the distance. The frame then jumps unexpectedly to a second sequence of medium-shot scenes, depicting a windswept forest tucked away in a mountain cavity captured by a shaky portable camera. The sudden change in scale moves the audience from aerial observation to a more intimate location that transforms the camera lens into the observer's eye. The forest scene is stitched to the aerial frame through a single ominous figure: a black crow, which, by the next sequence of shots, has multiplied into a rapturous flock. Amplified by the quivering treatment of the camera, the frenetic movement of crows in the forest materialize in different tempos, ranging from slow motion to normal time, back to slow motion. Characteristic of *Reiterations of Dissent* as a whole, the rendering of plural time attends to the different temporalities that dwell in and constitute daily life in Jeju. Through this multiplicity, Jeju is reinscribed as a *heterotopic* space in which different temporalities exist and unfold within bounded sites.³² During the height of the 4.3 Massacre, between 1948 and 1950, the cavernous tunnels, forests, and open meadows of Mount Halla were particularly macabre sites, as the SKIG military and the Northwest Youth League executed massive numbers of villagers, suspected communist sympathizers, and family members of leftists.³³

In another scene, the camera closely tracks a bucolic field carpeted with swaying strands of golden grass and large porous rocks—the same terrain that decades earlier bore the bodies of murdered civilians. A solemn voice pierces the screen: "When I was little, I saw those things, and my heart felt sad. During the Korean War, the slaughter of 4.3 continued because war itself is killing. Thus, we never talked about 4.3. In my childhood, I did not hear much about 4.3. I just heard adults who gathered around in their spare time, or on someone's sacrifice day, whispering about the 4.3 victims." This narration produces a profound sense of disassociation, not only between what is seen (a rustic landscape) and heard (a description of gruesome body parts) but also among discrepant forms of knowledge negotiated by civilians. Although the speaker readily points to the regime of silence imposed on 4.3 survivors ("We never talked about 4.3. . . . I did not hear much about 4.3"), he also provides discrepant memories that disrupt such silence ("When I was little I saw those things. . . . [T]he slaughter of 4.3 continued. . . . I . . . heard adults . . . whispering"). The conflicting impressions make perceptible the pressure points that impinge on the speaker. On the one hand, the narrator, now an adult, is able to speak of the secrets he was forbidden to know as a child. On the other hand, decades of enforced silence have produced excruciating tensions that are difficult to discard. In an attempt to recount the horrors he witnessed as a child, the narrator makes audible durational memories that refuse to desist.

The rampant killings alluded to in "Ghosts" take hypervisible form in the film short "Island of Endless Rebellion," which remediates archival footage that portrays dozens of bloated corpses left to disintegrate in Jeju's open air. These disturbing images dovetail with more recently shot footage that depicts archeologists recovering nearly four hundred skeletal remains during a massive excavation at Jeju International Airport in 2007.[34] While the workers gingerly disinter matted hair, teeth, and femur bones from the freshly dug site, the camera captures the faces of anguished family members and elderly survivors as they hover anxiously over the excavation site. The delicate act of exhuming bone shards from beneath the earth's surface and the sudden exposure of those shards generate a discombobulating tension between silence and disclosure. Actively suppressed by the U.S. and South Korean governments for nearly half a century, a formal investigation into the 4.3 atrocities was finally launched in the late 1990s due to escalating pressure from survivors, pro-democracy groups, journalists, and engaged academics. Despite these efforts to make this violence perceptible in relation to the island's remilitarization, the 4.3 Massacre remains an incidental event in South Korean history. Survivors, bystanders, and witnesses still live side by side with former paramilitary officers and participants who perpetrated or benefited from these atrocities. *Reiterations of Dissent*'s documentation of the exhumation process registers this core contradiction: while the South Korean government frames 4.3 as part of a reconciled past, the recovered remains of those disposed by SKIG and right-wing youth repudiate such idealized claims.

Against this backdrop of violent amnesia, the oppositional imagery of *Reiterations of Dissent* aims to translate otherwise. In "History of Endless Rebellion," vocal protests related to the 1948 presidential elections in Korea are remixed and remediated. During the presidential elections held in Korea on May 10, 1948, Jeju emerged as the only region in the country to overwhelmingly resist plans for separate elections held in the North and South, with more than 80 percent of the island population voting against such plans.

Jeju civilians also organized a demonstration on March 1, 1947, protesting the presence of the USAMGIK. Some historians cite this demonstration as the actual beginning of 4.3, since the South Korean police opened fire on the crowd, killing six and critically injuring several others.[35] While several narrators in "History of Endless Rebellion" describe the 4.3 Massacre as a "continuation of [Jeju's] traditional resistance," archival imagery captures a lively group of protesters carrying a banner etched with the words "Immediate Withdrawal of U.S. and Soviet Armies" in English and Korean. The protest against *both* American and Soviet occupation underscore civilians' recognition of Korea as a strategic geopolitical location within Cold War polemics and their desire to distance themselves from this bipolar world order. Many Jeju residents assign responsibility for the violence of 4.3 to the United States, as redacted government documents reveal how the American government materially supported and maintained vigilant tabs on the atrocities committed during the 4.3 Massacre.[36] Taking stock of the U.S. military's presence in Jeju Island before, during, and after 4.3, the narrators of "History of Endless Rebellion" explicitly name the American government as the primary perpetrator of crimes: "[The 4.3 Massacre] was before the establishment of South Korea. It occurred under the American occupation forces."

Considering Jeju's durational past, *Reiterations of Dissent*'s pairing of the 4.3 atrocities with the Gangjeong naval base symbolizes how U.S. geopolitical interests still inform "peacetime" military buildup. Although 4.3 and the Gangjeong naval base are distinct historical formations, they are materially connected through American global interests secured through the continued division of Korea. Following the U.S. military's return of the Camp McNabb military base to Jeju's local government in 2006, Gangjeong Village was almost immediately selected by the South Korean state to house a new naval base complex in 2007.[37] As the Korean/American activist Christine Ahn attests, the proposed base is a repercussion of bipolarized perceptions, since continued militarism is associated with the U.S. state's desire to eradicate communism from the Korean Peninsula and to counter China's economic growth.[38] Although the Gangjeong naval base is under the official aegis of the South Korean state, the site's designation as a U.S. cooperative security location, or a facility that is "not technically 'American' . . . but gives [the U.S. state] political cover in localities," places Gangjeong squarely in the hands of the U.S. Armed Forces.[39] Under the current iteration of the Mutual Defense Treaty and Status of Forces Agreement between the United States and South Korea, the U.S. state is able to mobilize South Korean military facilities at its own discretion.[40] Subsequently, the high stakes of American involvement in Gangjeong are evident. According to Ellen O'Kane Tauscher, the former U.S. undersecretary of state for arms control and international security affairs, the

Still image from *Reiterations of Dissent*, ARTSPECTRUM, Leeum Samsung Museum of Art, Seoul.
(Courtesy of Jane Jin Kaisen. Photograph by Hyunsoo Kim.)

Gangjeong naval base responds to the U.S. request that the South Korean military create an integrated regional missile defense system as a means to maximize "allies' . . . strategic flexibility."[41] Currently, the base is outfitted with an Aegis ballistic missile defense system, including twenty warships, submarines, and an American-designed missile-intercepting system.

Reiterations of Dissent uses archival imagery and more recent televised footage to identify the continuities rather than breaks that affix the 4.3 Massacre to the Gangjeong base. The final scenes of "History of Endless Rebellion" depicts SKIG armed vehicles barreling through Jeju's narrow streets, the burning of *hanok*-style homes, and Jeju civilians frantically fleeing from their villages. Bookending these remediated black-and-white clips are contemporary moving images of corporate Daewoo bulldozers tearing into Gangjeong's shoreline and slow-motion film of international solidarity activists and Jeju civilians such as Gangjeong's Mayor Kang Dong-Kyun angrily clashing with South Korean police. In these scenes, a voiceover pithily clarifies the linkages among the United States, the 4.3 Massacre, and the remilitarization of the island: "Standing at a distance, the United States subjugated without getting blood on their hands at all, that was 4.3. The naval base is a continuation of this." The camera's lingering on and zooming in to Mayor Kang's expressive face highlights the prominent role that he and other Jeju civilians have played in critiquing military outposts across the Pacific.

The militarization of Gangjeong Village, in other words, not only revives memories of 4.3 but also evokes Jeju's—and, to a greater extent, Korea's—

"geopolitical curse" within the history of U.S. militarized imperialism in the North Pacific.[42] Jeju and Korea occupy vital locations within the global security system, as exemplified by the United States' "pivot" toward Asia and the state's rechanneling of economic and military resources into this vast geographical space. This so-called pivot has translated into new military outfits constructed throughout Asia, including the integration of a Terminal High Altitude Area Defense system (THAAD) in the South Korean city of Seongju in 2017. For former Secretary of State Hilary Rodham Clinton, the U.S. government's (re)turn toward Asia and the Pacific expresses a commitment to construct a "more mature security and economic architecture." In turn, this process contributes to American prosperity since U.S. investments in the area, as observed by Clinton, will "pay dividends for continued American leadership."[43] Designated as oceanic sacrifice zones, island spaces such as Jeju, the Philippines, the Ryukyu Islands (Okinawa), Guam, Hawai'i, and Puerto Rico have endured the devastating imprint and toll of American militarization, including the seizure of indigenous lands, the destruction of local ecological systems, the housing of military bases, and the installment of live-fire training sites.

This heightened focus on the reenergized militarization of the Pacific and Oceania has mobilized Jeju civilians, fostered unexpected political alliances and transnational affinities in and beyond Korea, and generated a wave of organized resistance, including direct actions, letter-writing campaigns to the U.S. and South Korean governments, hunger strikes, and coordinated solidarity protests in Jeju.[44] Exemplified by the "Save Jeju Now" campaign, Jeju civilians work closely with activists from the United States, Guam, Hawai'i, the Ryukyu Islands, and the Philippines to contest the presence of the U.S. military across a chain of islands.[45] These shared experiences of war, (settler) colonialism, and displacement cultivate an affinity-based understanding of security. Deploying "the scales of the (civilian) body" as a set of metrics, affinity-based security safeguards life and the natural environment; procures basic needs, including food, shelter, education, and health; and preserves cultural identifications.[46] As Mayor Kang stated at the Moana Nui Conference in 2013 in Berkeley, Jeju civilians have learned from the past sixty years of occupation that "peace should be kept by peaceful means."[47] Affinity-based security therefore prioritizes *demilitarization* over militarization, *indispensability* over expendability, and *peace* over war.[48]

Reiterations of Dissent points to how the imparted lessons of the enduring past must be reappraised as framing principles that inspire current social movements for Korean decolonization.[49] That is, rather than relegating the past to the anteriority of history, Jeju civilians confront the 4.3 Massacre as an ethical foundation that informs contemporary solidarity efforts to organize and resist. As David Scott points out, the possibility of a different future is anchored in the ability to articulate the relationality between pasts and presents so that subjects might partake in a "permanent critique of our historical era."[50] For *Reiterations of Dissent*'s multiple narrators, this historical materialist approach resonates in meaningful ways. As one narrator puts it in "History of Endless Rebellion," the mantra "Jeju Island as Peace Island" is used as part of everyday vernacular in Gangjeong. Through this mundane act, Jeju civilians address the 4.3 Massacre as an unresolved event that will remain until the Korean War is finished. As a narrator poignantly observes in *Reiterations of Dissent*: "To truly pacify those who were killed under false accusation and to console the spirit of the deceased there should be no more war on the island. Longing for those things, we chose the name 'Peace Island.'" Despite the strategic usurping of "Peace Island" for entrepreneurial purposes in South Korea, Gangjeong villagers' reappropriation and constant re-sounding of this phrase underscores how durational memories of the 4.3 Massacre motivate transnational antimilitarism efforts in Jeju and Korea.

MAGO and Communal Mourning Practices

In *Reiterations of Dissent,* Kaisen remembers difficult pasts to reengage, or "translate otherwise," the contemporaneous conditions of Cold War historiography. In turn, these historical reencounters or durational memories motivate social actions oriented toward a demilitarized Korea. Dohee Lee, too, is concerned with how memories of dissonant pasts associated with Jeju Island push against the absolutist renderings of Cold War historiography. Lee shares an intimate relationship with the island: she was born in Jeju and raised there until she was seven. A long-time resident of the San Francisco Bay area, she describes the visceral shock and the sense of déjà vu she felt when she first learned of plans for the new naval base in Gangjeong.[51] In her multi-genre, "six-chapter" performance *MAGO,* Lee resituates Jeju's past and present as they relate to the island's position as a negotiating chip within the political stage of global security interests. Yet in perceptible ways, *MAGO* departs from Kaisen's video installation insofar as Lee mobilizes supernatural figures to mediate violent memories of living pasts denied by the U.S. and South Korean nation-states. Lee conceptualizes the 4.3 Massacre alongside a readaptation of Korean cosmologic symbols, mythological figures, speaking animal oracles, and shamanistic rituals. Her syncretizing of the ordinary and extraordinary dovetails with her critique that the experiences of Jeju civilians remain unheard in the "real" world.[52]

MAGO's performance of durational memories and Lee's use of unhuman forms to narrate human pasts overlap with Bliss Cua Lim's engagement with the fantastic. In her observations regarding immiscible times, Lim explains how fantastic formations such as deities are too often disparaged as an "anachronistic vestige of primitive, superstitious thought."[53] However, precisely because of their incongruity with secular notions of modern historical time, these elements illuminate the rationalizing terms that delineate the so-called real from the unreal. The stubborn persistence of the supernatural, or "othered," ways of being also points to how different sensibilities of history and temporality refuse to be readily ingested by or incorporated into chronological time.

Lim's articulation of the fantastic as a mode of temporal critique reflects Lee's understanding of the mythological and folkloric. As Lee explains, the poignant resonance of local mythologies and the folkloric in present-day Jeju registers a continuum of resistance that precedes American militarized presence.[54] Once an independent kingdom referred to as Tamna (or Tamla), with an indigenously distinct culture, Jeju was absorbed into the Goryeo Dynasty in the twelfth century and became a vassal of the Chosŏn Dynasty in the fourteenth century.[55] While Chosŏn rulers imposed dominant ideological systems, including Confucianism, on Jeju civilians, these structures did not wholly eradicate or supplant indigenous social, political, and spiritual belief structures; rather, they were "indigenized" by islanders and selectively adapted to local beliefs, practices, and conditions.[56] Today, islanders still refer to their strong relationships with land and water, as well as their local dialects and mythologies, as distinct cultural elements that distinguish Jeju from the rest of Korea.[57] Following several generations of political tension and open conflicts between Jeju and Korean monarchial rule, Jeju and Korea were both colonized by Japan in 1910. After the Japanese empire collapsed in 1945, the USAMGIK and the SKIG occupied Jeju Island. Exposed to and ruled by multiple intersecting forms of colonialism (i.e., China, Korea, Japan, and the United States), Jeju today remains part of the South Korean national polity, albeit as a semiautonomous region.[58]

Within this prolonged context of colonial conquest and reoccupation, mythologies and the folkloric for Lee are *not* whimsical cultural traditions or totalizing gestures removed from the everyday. Rather, civilians summon ancestral figures and mythological deities as symbolic restorers of health, healing, and justice.[59] Lee titled her performance after one such figure: Mago is a female deity associated with the divine acts of creation, healing, and protection in Jeju and Korea. Islanders interpret mythologies that repeatedly sound across time and space as transmitted expressions of survival rearticulated through a highly stylized mode of narration and storytelling. Therefore, Lee's readapted use of otherworldly figures such as folkloric deities, shamans, and speaking animals throughout her oeuvre indexes how fantastic remediations of unremembered pasts frame persistence and resistance in relation to and beyond the contemporary present. Lee observes, "Many people [tend to] view myths as 'fake' stories, but they revolve around people who've tried hard to change society.... These mythologies carry everything: changing cultures, environment and ecosystems, ideological belief systems."[60] As we shall see, Lee's readaptation of cultural mythologies and shamanic rituals in *MAGO* also breaks with a complex of social norms and state policies that determine proper mourning and memory practices in Jeju and South Korea.

For José Esteban Muñoz, this imaginative rerendering of divergent pasts suggests a deep longing for a different world beyond "romances of the negative and toiling in the present."[61] While such conceptualizations are seemingly antithetical to the quotidian, Muñoz argues that magical thinking is "relational to historically situated struggles" because it hints at other ways in which we might (en)counter and know the present-day.[62] Thus, the collapse between the everyday and the fantastic calls forth expressive symbols, stories of survival, and memory practices that move beyond a present day shaped by a dooming sense of foreclosure or permanent postponement. In a similar sense, I suggest that *MAGO*'s reencountering of pasts through a reconfiguration of mythic and folkloric symbols provides opportunities to envision, live, and actualize beyond a "totalizing rendering of reality."[63] As a mode of durational memory and an alternative method of historical narration, folkloric mythology exists alongside and against national reckonings of proper historical time.

MAGO melds the fantastic and the mundane by pairing the goddess Mago and the shamanic with mundane figures familiar to those who reside in Jeju. In the opening chapter, performed in the Yerba Buena Center's entrance lobby, Lee appears as Mago, wearing a *hahoetal* mask (an adornment affiliated with Korean shamanic rituals) and delicate layers of translucent white paper. Associated with worldly creation and the abundance of oceanic life, Mago drags long tentacles of tapering seaweed-cloth behind her. She moves slowly as her mouth vocalizes indecipherable sounds that are digitally remixed with a cacophony of breaths and guttural pronunciations. In juxtaposing these incongruent sonic echoes with sustained moments of silence, Lee's performance produces an immersive soundscape that both intrigues and baffles. After a fifteen-minute span, Lee transitions into the second chapter. She sheds the outermost layers of her clothing, as if she is molting loosened and dead skin. Gesticulating frenetically as she erupts into a sequence of rhythmic breathing practices, Lee eventually leads audience members into the center's auditorium, where they are seated in cascading rows surrounding the main stage.

Throughout the performance, three large screens wrap around the stage: two horizontal cloth screens flank the background, while a vertical screen is

Still image from *MAGO,* Yerba Buena Center for the Arts, San Francisco, 2014. (Courtesy of Dohee Lee. Photograph by Pak Han.)

lodged in between. At times, the blue-, red-, and black-tinged glows from the rich scenery illuminate and absorb into Lee's porous skin, producing an aqueous melding between artist and projected imagery. At other times, the audiovisual elements of the screens provide a sensuous backdrop that enhances Lee's embodied presence on stage. For instance, throughout the ninety-minute performance, the screen moves from medium shots of Jeju's dewy forests and subaquatic perspectives of ocean life to evacuated aerials of bombed-out landscapes. In each of these scenarios, the contiguity of Lee's body with the haptic "skin" of the screen suggests an intimate meshing between human and nonhuman. This fusion might hint at several effects: the transformation of Asian women's bodies into prosthetic extensions of machinery via global migratory labor or, relatedly, the techno-Orientalist configuration of Asian bodies into "technologically advanced" yet "intellectually primitive" objects. But my description of *MAGO*'s human/nonhuman hybridization suggests a very different possibility. Specifically, I describe how the interfacing between Lee's body and the screen enhances the otherworldly, "supra-human" quality of her performance.[64] Indeed, not unlike kate-hers RHEE's improvised performance discussed in Chapter 3, Lee's magnetic presence onstage provokes a range of responses and reactions from her audience. And yet, while RHEE produces an unsettling look that forecloses the public's voyeuristic and hypersexualized gaze, Lee's ethereal embodiment suggests an *open* mode of audience reencounters. The remainder of this chapter focuses on how Lee's hypervisible body mediates decolonizing exchanges with the audience to identify, track, and unravel militarized colonial knowledges.

In the third chapter, "Waterways," Lee alternatively sits and stands at center stage as she sings about Jeju's enduring relationship with land and water, and the natural ecology of the island. Alluding to Mago's presence, each of the three voluminous screens displays filmic imagery of Jeju's coastline dotted with local fishermen. Eventually, the scene transitions into documentary footage of an underwater realm, with the caption "Sea of Jeju" appearing on the right-hand screen. Portraying wavering tentacles of coral and seaweed, and tiny slivers of fish, the teeming oceanscape reflects the submerged perspectives of the *jamnyeo* ("diving woman"), Jeju's celebrated lineage of female sea divers. Today, the *jamnyeo* are frequently referred to as the *haenyeo*, a more common term coined during the Japanese colonial period and later popularized by the Jeju tourism industry.[65] The stage is inundated with blue-tinged hues of the ocean while Lee undergoes another metamorphosis. She now wears clothing resembling the ritual attire of the *mudang* (female-identifying shaman): gauzy white garments, a head adornment worn by grieving subjects during funeral rituals in Korea, and *hangul*-filled scrolls draped across her chest. Lee performs a *gut*, or shamanistic ceremony, for ancestors to console and communicate with the dead. In particular, she dedicates the ritual to those killed during the 4.3 Massacre, including youth guerrilla fighters and children. As Lee enunciates the deceased's names in a steady tone, *soombrisori* (high-pitched whistles) made by the *jamnyeo* fill the airy auditorium. Intermittently, Lee stops and lifts her head to look at and acknowledge the felt presence of the audience; in return, audience members nod while others whisper the names of the dead.

The synthesis of Mago, the *jamnyeo*, and the *mudang* registers Lee's reconfiguration of patriarchal mourning rituals enacted for those killed under violent circumstances in Jeju. Similarly to Kaisen's *Reiterations of Dissent*, *MAGO* translates shamanic rituals, or "localized" lamentation work, as a durational memory practice that addresses the unresolved deaths of the 4.3 Massacre in the here and now. Lee's remediation of undead memories through textured references to Mago, the *jamnyeo,* and *mudang* is notable for other reasons. Since the Chosŏn Confucian Dynasty (1392–1910), the work of mourning in Jeju has been associated with patrilineal genealogies of kinship and social status determined by perceived gender, class, and age.[66] The disappeared, in fact, are not held in equal esteem among the living.[67] For instance, deceased members removed from reproductive lineages of patrilineal kinship, including young people under fifteen and unmarried women without children, are not provided with formal ancestral ceremonies. Rather, secret ceremonies known as the *kamaegi morun sikgye* are held within the gendered confines of the home, since mourning is delegated to "women in the family and kinship community."[68] Beyond such private ceremonies, these selective cohorts of the deceased are considered aberrant figures who occupy a status outside the normative bounds of blood family and ancestral worship.

More recently, state policies have regulated the practice of mourning for and remembering the dead in Jeju. These policies determine the rule of familial genealogy, or *chokbo* (*jokbo*), in conjunction with kinship through bloodline.[69] Due to the sheer number of children and young people killed during the 4.3 Massacre, posthumous adoption of the deceased by friends, acquaintances, and others unrelated by blood is a culturally sanctioned practice in Jeju because it provides the dead with social bonds beyond the biological family. However, since the South Korean state's implementation of the Jeju Special Law of Restitution for the Victims of the April 3rd Incident in 2000, genealogical caregivers are not legally acknowledged and cannot benefit from the law's provisions, such as medical care and financial reimbursement provided to the family of the dead. As mentioned in the discussion of *Reiterations of Dissent*, guerrilla youth leaders are explicitly excluded from public ceremonies and cannot be buried in state-regulated cemeteries.

Lee's reconfigured mourning ritual in *MAGO* therefore breaks with these conventions in several ways. In the most obvious sense, the linking of durational memory with mediating figures such as Mago and the *jamnyeo* points to an underlying desire to rupture the privileging of patriarchal figures and patrilineal lines of kinship within contemporary mourning rituals. In part, Lee reroutes the status of Jeju's forgotten dead in relation to and through "deviant" gendered figures such as the *jamnyeo*. While South Korean popular media and the tourism industry now tout Jeju's sea divers as feminist iconoclasts and heroines, the *jamnyeo* historically have occupied an outsider status in Jeju society as undervalued laborers belonging to the lower socioeconomic strata.[70] As peripheral figures who are often the primary breadwinners in their families, the *jamnyeo* negotiate and at times diverge from Confucian gendered roles, which traditionally ascribe Korean women to the domestic realm of the household.

Yet in a more urgent manner, I suggest, Lee's deployment of fantastic figures symbolizes a wholly different conceptual approach to 4.3 mourning practices beyond the gendered circuit of spatial and temporal norms. In particular, the evocation of supranational deities such as Mago demands a different epistemological orientation around historiography and time. As Helen Hye-Sook Hwang observes, mythological figures in Jeju and South Korea are sociocultural elements that predate or exist outside national formation.[71] Hence, such deities challenge the singularity of South Korean modernity firmly built on "patriarchal (read Confucian) rules in East Asia" and American anticommunist benevolence.[72] Within the narrow confines of this modern historical context, the South Korean nation-state is characterized by a naturalized division of gendered labor and intellectual capacities, with cisgender men identified as public and political figures and cisgender women identified as the domestic linchpins of the home and reproducers of the national populace.[73] As mentioned earlier in this chapter, we might also reference Cold War historiography's investments in heterosexual reproduction, the gendered alliance between South Korea and the United States, and a "moving forward" that discards the past as concluded and closed episodes. These gendered principles are not purely discursive or abstract framings; rather, they underpin social and material practices of remembering and mourning in Jeju.

Hence, Lee's calling forth the names of the "non-normative" dead alongside "non-normative" figures such as Mago hints at a desire for a divergent spatiotemporal mourning paradigm. Through its interweaving of reconfigured mythical symbols and everyday figures, *MAGO* resituates those killed during the 4.3 Massacre within "othered" spaces and spheres delinked from the borders of the nation-state, patrilineal blood kinship, and traditional mourning time and space. Lee's revised performances of *MAGO* across an arrangement of performance venues, academic conferences, artists' gatherings, and antimilitarization events in North America (the United States and Canada), Asia (Japan, Korea, Jeju Island), and the Internet provide opportunities for the living and disappeared to co-inhabit diasporic and virtual spaces that exceed domesticated social codes that traditionally bind mourners to the deceased in Jeju.[74] Resonating in some ways with Diana Taylor's theorization of the mnemonic practice of "DNA," or the ethical performance of *social* (rather than national or ethnocentric) bonds among gathered participants, Lee's re-sounding of names in *MAGO* reassures the "deviant" dead that they "are neither forgotten nor 'surrogated'" and that "no one else will take their place."[75]

In part, Lee's insistence on enumerating the dead within a performative space depends on her conceptualization of the audience as members of and contributors to a communal ritual practice. Indeed, Lee invites her audience to become observing participants rather than passive spectators or consumers of the performance. For Lee, the communal mourning ritual departs from a set of prescribed rites performed in a perfunctory or mechanized manner. Rather, the communal ritual is a contingent, open-ended mode of communication that takes place in and through the performance space. Within this context, Lee identifies herself as the primary mediator of emergent and, at times, skeptical and contentious interactions with her surroundings. In return, Lee addresses her audience as varied participants in the performance, whether or not they perceive themselves in that way. As Lee notes, this distinct approach to performance does not appeal to all audience members; in fact, it triggers contrarian and pessimistic reactions. However, these "negative" responses push Lee to contend critically with the discursive possibilities and limitations of her artistic praxis while also dispelling idealized notions of a homogeneous participating audience. Differentiated audiences, in other words, constitute a key component of Lee's aesthetic praxis as a multimedia performance artist.

This fluctuating relationality between the artist and audience resonates with Frazer Ward's rigorous reassessment of performance in relation to public participation. Refusing to overgeneralize the audience as a "like-minded group" of "innocent bystanders," Ward nevertheless is interested in the subjective conditions that underpin the making of a temporary "we" (or multiple "we's") through the performative act.[76] For instance, within the confines of social and economic conditions, audience members decide whether to attend a particular performance, engage the artist if invited to participate, stay or leave during the event, or contemplate the performance's political and affective impact following its live iteration. While underscoring the artist's role in determining the conditions of spectatorship and reception, Ward refers to these qualities as the "ultimately ethical dimensions" of performance.[77] Here the ethics of performance are less about the idealized relationships, sentimental values, or overlapping intentions shared by artist and audience than about the potential ways in which different performances generate dynamic opportunities to confront a working set of critical questions and assumptions.

These ethical dimensions of performance touch on an earlier observation about durational memory. For both Kaisen and Lee, durational memory remediates the present to directly confront the living past(s) of the Korean War. Rearticulating divergent pasts as part of a here and now, durational memory provides a discursive framework for articulating the relationship between the present and the still undetermined future. Along this vein, a communal mourning ritual for Lee provides a zone of emergent (re)encounters that does more than illuminate how unrelenting violence persists in everyday life. The dialogical moments forged between artist and audience, at their most fruitful, engender unanticipated pathways for dialectical inquiry and mutual moments of historical reexamination. In turn, Lee encourages her audiences to consider their differing knowledges of and relationships to militarized violence in and beyond Korea.

The participatory potentials of durational memories are most evident in the last few chapters of *MAGO,* in which Lee squarely situates Jeju's remilitarization within the context of the 4.3 Massacre and the continuation of the Korean War. In the fourth chapter, "Journey," Lee remediates a minute-long segment of black-and-white military archival footage that appears on all three stage screens. The film features a huddle of young and elderly civilians arrested by American and SKIG soldiers, a young refugee with shell shock, and a lifeless Korean civilian killed during a bombing raid. Resembling the cinematic technique of flashback, the remediated footage is looped for several minutes to amplify how the present, as Maureen Turim states, "returns to" and "dissolves to an image in the past."[78] Yet the juxtaposition of this filmic flashback with the embodied presence of a quivering Lee who remains at center stage during the filmic sequence intimates a different order of temporalities: perhaps it is the *past* that remains in and dissolves into an image of the *present*. At the end of the segment, Lee underscores this reversal by speaking directly to the audience, addressing them with the following repeated phrase: "Sixty years and it still continues. Sixty years and it still continues."

In the penultimate chapter, "Invited Ritual: Crow," Lee engages the audience even more pronouncedly. During the act, Lee impersonates the Jeju black crow, an animal associated on the island with obscured memories and misfortune. Surrounded by imagery of crows sitting on the sprawling branches of leafless trees, Lee walks across the stage at a frenzied pace, with tufts of black feathers framing her face. As I discussed in my analysis of *Reiterations of Dissent,* the crow is commonly interpreted by civilians as the only creature to have witnessed the flurry of mass executions that decimated the island populace during the 4.3 Massacre. Lee's personification of the crow registers other significations, as well. Within Korean mythology, fantastic renditions of crows, such as the *samjok-o* (three-legged crow), are affiliated with the omniscient power of the sun, trickster propensities, and prophetic powers. Within this folkloric context, crows assume divinatory powers, as they are able to visualize the past and foretell the future. *MAGO* readapts this mythological rendering so that the crow symbolizes a concrete link to the undead past, the continuing present, and the unrealized future: for Lee, the crow as witness represents the restless spirits of those murdered on the island, even as the animal oracle converses with the audience about the unfortunate conditions of the present and the open-ended potentials of the future.

At the beginning of "Invited Ritual: Crow," representations of Jeju's unrequited spirits take material form as a choir of other performers, donning eerie white masks, encircle Lee onstage. Punctuated by moments of silence, Lee's address to the audience begins by repeating two questions: "What did you see? What did you hear?" Shifting her gaze across the expanse of the auditorium, Lee continues to press the audience. "What did you see? What did you hear?"

Circumambulating the stage and approaching audience members seated in the two front rows, Lee continues to ask until a chorus of echoing answers is heard across the auditorium: "colonialism," "bombs on my grandmother's

Still image from "Invited Ritual: Crow," *MAGO*,
Yerba Buena Center for the Arts, San Francisco, 2014.
(Courtesy of Dohee Lee. Photograph by Pak Han.)

house in Iraq," "police brutality [in the United States]," "airstrikes in Gaza." As Lee pursues the questioning, a layering of responses fills and overwhelms the space. Toward the end of this nearly seven-minute segment, the simultaneous answers become indistinguishable, enmeshed. For Lee, this reciprocated practice of listening and response within the performance space fosters a horizontal sense of social relationality distinct from identitarian formations anchored in the biological, national, and ethnocentric. Within this participatory exchange, Lee draws on Jeju as a specific example of militarized violence; in response, audience members identify different forms of racialized, gendered, and sexual violence that they know of or have witnessed. Upon closer examination, the geographical spaces recounted by audience members in this rendition of *MAGO*—from the United States to Iraq and Palestine—gestures to a form of subversive knowledge as these evocations expose how dispersed acts of militarized warfare are not at all isolated or exceptional. Rather, Lee's performance underlines how militarized violence disproportionately affects racialized and gendered communities deemed disposable, non-essential, or superfluous to the project of international global security. As a result, dense concentrations of loss and death generate a diasporic matrix of necropolitical spaces shaped by the structural violence of American military intervention and colonial occupation.

Through this actualization of durational memory, the audience's shared examples illuminate how Jeju's durable past depends on America's extensive history of domestic racial terror and international warfare consolidated through military security outposts and "black sites" scattered across the United States, the Americas, the Middle East, and Asia.[79] The responses from the audience therefore suture domestic racial violence committed "right here" in the United States to the militarized violence committed "over there" in Korea and elsewhere. For Lee, these vocalized connections impel her interlocutors to resituate militarization within a global geography of war, imperialism, and occupation that radiates across a concatenation of seemingly disjointed sites:

> It's not just Jeju. It's these other places, too. Different countries [such as the United States] have immense power to take away life and land. They do what they want to do. So people in the performance realized that they and I were not only addressing [Korea's history], but we were also talking about the present moment and how colonialism lives in so many places. We experience, see, and hear all of these things, but sometimes we don't talk about it; we don't make the connections. So by asking people, "What did you hear? Can you tell me what you saw?" I didn't want to lecture to people, but I wanted them to listen and speak to one another.

By narrating Jeju's multiple histories of militarized colonialism through a reconfiguration of cultural myths and symbols, Lee renders perceptible the sedimentation of slow violence beyond paradigms of national and progressive time. Ultimately, these variable references to militarized presence in Jeju do not rectify or resolve the devastation wrought by the Korean War and other U.S.-initiated wars across different sites. Instead, *MAGO* attempts to reorient the audience toward a decolonial disruption of Cold War historiography. More specifically, Lee's conjuring of alternative historical framings and fantastic approaches to (un)knowing Jeju's fraught history is a decolonizing tactic, because *MAGO* pulls apart established narratives of national progress anchored in militarized violence and insecurity. *MAGO*, however, does not merely intervene in dominant narrations of Cold War history. As a facilitator of durational memories, *MAGO* engenders a transnational geography of diasporic affinities shaped by distinct yet interrelated experiences of militarized colonial violence and American occupation.

Marked by an extended moment of silence, Lee draws "Invited Ritual: Crow" to a close with a final overture to her audience: "Open your eyes. Open your ears."

Coda

This chapter conceptualizes durational memory within the context of the Korean War and Jeju's extended history of militarization and multiple colonialisms. Focusing on how memories of heterogeneous pasts underpin the here and now, it examines how *Reiterations of Dissent* and *MAGO* actualize divergent temporalities that push against the linearity of Cold War historicism. While Kaisen's and Lee's works deploy different aesthetic tactics to craft durational memory, both of their diasporic memory productions rely on notions of participatory engagement in their conjuring of enduring pasts. That is, if Cold War national memories approach chrononormative time as a predetermined movement toward the inevitable, durational memories accentuate the open-ended, pluralistic elements of diasporic revisionary historiography. For Kaisen and Lee, durational memory is a vacillating (un)remembering process that overlaps with varying notions of the "audience," whether this term refers to actual bodies within a performance space or a "sense of community as a horizon of experience that is anything but empirical."[80]

To close, I return to a vignette offered at the opening of this chapter regarding my visit to Jeju Island with a group of scholars, activists, and artists in 2013. During our day-and-a-half excursion to the island, we visited Gangjeong Village, the site of South Korea's new naval base, and Jeju City, home to the April 3rd Peace Memorial Park that houses a monument dedicated to those killed during the 4.3 Massacre. The monument, a rectangular concrete stone placed inside a beautiful domed hall, remains unadorned, unnamed. As on-site docents explained, the monument has no official inscription because the historical definition shifts in accordance with the ebb and flow of U.S. and South Korean political governance. In the past twenty years alone, 4.3 has been described as a "counterinsurgency campaign" and "communist rebellion," as well as a "people's uprising" and "civilian massacre."

While some residents have pressed for an inscribed title, the memorial's staff are hesitant, given the divergent memories of the 4.3 Massacre. Several trip participants also remarked that such a definitive act would block or stymie critical remembering. When I privately asked one of these participants what she understood as "critical remembering," she described a process in which the past is redefined as a crucial component of the present. For this participant, the official naming of the memorial stone as a tragic remnant of the past would sever the ties between the 4.3 Massacre and Jeju's current process of remilitarization. Commenting on the "power contingencies of memory," this participant referred to how the unnamed stone constantly reminds of the "inconvenient" memories purposefully expunged and dis(re)-membered by South Korean and U.S. national history. To me, the unnamed

Unnamed 4.3 monument stone, April 3rd Peace Memorial Park, Jeju City, Korea, July 2013. (Photograph by the author.)

stone also serves as a sobering reminder that the Korean War remains unended, unfinished.

My colleague's poignant descriptions remind me how the unnamed stone embodies the potential, even hopeful, dynamisms of durational memory. The monument's adamant *refusal* to be named does not signify an erased past; nor does it symbolize a universalized history that transcends all moments in time. Rather, by insisting on the animated relationality of past(s), present(s) and future(s), the stone's "blankness" underscores how the politicized terrain of remembering underscores a future (or futures) that is not yet determined. Within the highly contested realm of remembering and forgetting the Korean War, durational memory foregrounds how a reorientation of the past(s) in conjunction with the present can induce, as Scott suggests, "a politics for a possible future."[81] Thus, even while they direct us to pasts that have long been rejected and denied by the state, durational memories foreground the unknowing, contingent, and anticipatory qualities of the present and future.

An Opening

Wreckoning

*A sunlit hike
along the coastline*

*rift of the Pacific
rearranging
our view.*

*Spring rush—
wild fennel, sage,
rosemary. Bankside
cypresses.*

*All right then,
back to Oakland, horizon
circling the sunset*

*the sun suspended
like a lit balloon.*

5,593 miles from Pyongyang.

Where my grandfather spent time.

*Where my family
might have lived*

*had it not been
for division.*

Where.

*Cotton shirts wet
from summer
sweat.*

Not unlike
New York in August, but without
garbage's soiled scent.

The Taedong River,
emerald and shadows.

Short-horned grasshoppers
wedding air, distracting

couples who are stretching
their legs, lingering

near water—last days
of summer.

Twilight. A bridge. Reminding
me of a summer

where I haunted
bridges, seeking summer walks
cooled by evening.

Not unlike tonight.

Headlights' beams
catching bow waves.

People
coming back home

after a day
in the office, factory, the fields.

"Reunification Road"

122 miles between Seoul and Pyongyang.

Google tells me that in a plane moving 560 miles per hour
the trip would take 22 minutes.

Walking, five to six days.

I've stood on this road before.

*A dust-turn path boarded
by the sky.*

The demilitarized zone.

Aerial view: roofs of sky blue houses resembling arrows.

Cameras keep watch.

*American, British, German and Australian tourists
pay to have a close-up view from
the South Korean side.*

*"Unification Hill (Odusan Unification Observatory): A venue for
education on security matters, Unification Hill is situated where the
Hangang River and the Imjingang River meet. At Odusan
Unification Observatory, you can also [pay to] observe the daily lives of
North Koreans."*

*I have walked through
these grounds.*

A soldier tells me,

*This is bruised land, scarred land,
but our land. In each*

*blue house, a blue line
is drawn across the carpet, not unlike*

*the division created
by my second-grade teacher*

*designating the classroom's "noisy" zone
from the "quiet" zone.*

This time, if I cross, I will be shot.

How much a body can
and cannot change things.

A body crossing this blue line
staying flesh.

I am not a Phoenix breathing fire
to blaze the land

into cinder, ash, craters.

But, after seventy years of separation,
a crossing body

that does not transform, destroy, decimate
might feel like an indictment?

A waste.

A lie deformed into many truths.

Nation-states
are born from blue tape

governing lives,
separating families, silencing
the familial to echoes.

Sleeping in phosphorescent
blue light.

How scatological logistics
transform a room into

a site of an unending war.

—Cristiana Kyung-hye Baik, March 2018

To Locate

A lie deformed into many truths.

The following is an excerpt from a *Jimmy Kimmel Live* episode filmed at the Hollywood Walk of Fame in Los Angeles, California, in 2017:

Question: Do you believe the United States should take military action against North Korea?
Answer from pedestrian: I would say yes, for sure.

Question: And where exactly is North Korea?
Answer from pedestrian: What, on the map? I don't know. I'm horrible at geography.

As the broadcaster asks these questions, hearty laughter from the audience is audible. Throughout the four-minute segment, several pedestrians and onlookers provide similar answers.

At the end of it all, no one is able to identify the location of North Korea or the Korean Peninsula on the color-coded map.

To Know with Certainty

Where my family
might have lived

had it not been
for division.

Where.

What do you know about North Korea? is the question I posed to ——, ——, ——.

Before hearing their answers, I anticipated the responses.

Axis of Evil
Human rights violator
Torturer
Deluded
Brainwashed
Communist
Poverty
Famine
Defectors
Black Hole
Third World

But how do you know this to be true? is the second question I posed.

People stare with blank expressions.

Turn on the news.

Respected news outlets such as the New York Times *report these things on a weekly basis.*

North Koreans, they want things that everyone wants—it's not their fault they live under a dictator.

To See, to Master

Aerial view: roofs of sky blue houses resembling arrows.

Cameras keep watch.

American, British, German and Australian tourists pay to have a close-up view from the South Korean side.

> A View From Above

In a 2006 press briefing to the U.S. Central Intelligence Agency, Donald Rumsfeld (U.S. secretary of defense from 2001 until 2006) referenced a satellite image of Korea that depicts the peninsula's light footprint in a truthful manner. While the southern half of the peninsula is mapped by crisscrossing arteries of white veins and bright circular bulbs that signify dense concentrations of electricity and light, the northern half is almost all shadow, almost completely dark.

In response, Rumsfeld states that this is his favorite photograph of all time, excluding the photographs of his wife and family: "It says it all. That's the south of the Demilitarized Zone, the same as north, same resources north and south, and the big difference is in the south it's a free political system and a free economic system."[1]

Today, the accumulation of captured wavelengths correlates with one's liberation, happiness, and freedom.

In conjunction with these perceptions, an arrangement of other considerations.

A General Sketch

Sleeping in phosphorescent
blue light.

U.S. Defense Strategies from Above (Aerial Views Are Imperative):
Air Pressure
Saturation Bombing
Precision Bombing
Scorched-Earth Policy
Enclose, Close Off, Suffocate
Napalm Dust
A Belt of Radioactive Cobalt
Destruction Radius

A General Sketch (*continued*)

I am not a Phoenix breathing fire
to blaze the land

into cinder, ash, craters

Calculations (estimates)
      635,000 tons of American bombs dropped in the north
      32,557 tons of United Nations–endorsed napalm dropped in the north

Results
      3,000,0000 civilians killed, the majority concentrated in the north (my family and the families of friends are nestled somewhere in these numbers)
      8,700 factories destroyed in the north
      5,000 schools destroyed in the north
      1,000 hospitals destroyed in the north
      600,000 buildings destroyed in the north (in 1953, only two buildings remained standing in the capital city)

A journalist was recorded as saying: *Every city is a collection of chimneys.* These strikes continue through diplomacy, including U.S.- and UN-approved food and trade sanctions.

Questions for Numbers

What do numbers remember?

Do numbers relay the true essence of American violence and the force it took for the United States to nearly obliterate a sovereign nation that it considered (still considers) a pesky thorn on its capitalist side?

Would vocalizing these numbers, out loud, challenge U.S. media coverage of North Korea?

If numbers are not convincing enough, how else might we craft a counter-history that is more factual, more believable to Americans?

Questions (*continued*)

Do statistics embody the fleshed traces of the pain, fear, panic, chaos, anger, madness produced by war?

Do numbers correspond with the sheer determination it takes to rebuild a society left in ruins, even under the promise of future bombs?

Do numbers help us to see more clearly? If so, what is it that we're seeing?

Is it possible to reduce the dead to statistics? (I hold myself accountable to this question.)

What must one do to ensure that they will never be vulnerable again to American military strikes?

An Earnest Attempt to Search

122 miles between Seoul and Pyongyang.

Google tells me that in a plane moving 560 miles per hour the trip would take 22 minutes.

When I searched for "North Korea" on Google, the search engine's PageRank (PR) algorithm generated 3,710,000 results in .71 seconds. The generated links are a composite index and a constantly evolving snapshot of the keyword's "vital pulse" in the realm of virtual information. The progressive order of websites that appear on Google is determined by the following factors:

1. The frequency and location of a keyword on a web page.
2. The length of time the websites have existed.
3. The number of "touches" or links associated with each site.

The sites that appear first on the search list are considered the most relevant, the most important. Here in the United States, Google searches are determined by the PR algorithm—a calculation designed by Lawrence Edward Page (a corporate executive, Internet entrepreneur, and multibillionaire) for maximum returns.

On April 13, 2018, the top-generated links are as follows:

"UN Appeals for Aid to North Korea as Donations Drop" (*Wall Street Journal*)
"They Escaped from North Korea: Personal Stories and Mementos of Defectors" (*ABC News*)
"Pompeo says he can imagine a ground invasion of North Korea" (*Axios*)
"North Korea" (*Wikipedia*)
"Trump's Syria Threats Why North Korea Wants Nuclear Weapons" (CNN.com)
"North Korea Revealed" (Reuters.com)
"North Korea Fast Facts" (CNN.com)

Last Impressions

To feel in solidarity with him or to build with him or to like what he does, it is not necessary for me to grasp him. It is not necessary to try to become the other (to become other) or to "make" him in my image.[2]

174 | AN OPENING

A space in outstretched time

AN OPENING | 175

Waiting

Fields

Heartbeat

(Un)detected

Missing

*governing lives,
separating families, silencing
the familial to echoes.*

*Sleeping in phosphorescent
blue light.*

*How scatological logistics
transform a room into*

a site of an unending war.

> I am trying to fold race into geopolitics and geopolitics into poetry. Hence, geopolitical poetics. It involves disobeying history, severing its ties to power.
>
> —Don Mee Choi, *Hardly War*[3]

In *Reencounters: On the Korean War and Diasporic Memory Critique,* I consider the enduring effects and affective antagonisms of the Korean War. Mobilizing diasporic cultural works as aesthetic mediations of memory, this book attunes to a persisting cycle of militarized repercussions indicative of rather than exceptional to the everyday. Drawing on reencounters as a core concept, each chapter examines the routinized elements of daily life, only to foreground their insidious origins. This book demonstrates how Korean militarized migrations are repackaged as American immigration history; how the silences of war congeal into the hardened marrow of familial bonds; how war's human returns become integral to the inner workings of national economies; and how the politics of national forgiveness collapses martial and leisure economies. In so doing, the book examines the terms and conditions of recognition that reconfigure war's manifestations as part of the contemporary moment.

This sense of the Korean War's protraction indicates how the U.S. state recalibrates the enduring conflict as a just and justifiable intervention necessary to maintaining global security and a "free" democratic world order. In effect, Cold War political discourse scripts the Korean War through a teleological lens, underscoring how the conflict will finally end with the North Korean state's demise. And yet the uneasy deferment of such a foreseeable ending troubles this self-evident truth. Specifically, diasporic memory works amplify the temporal disjuncture between the normative expectations of "homogeneous and empty" history and the embodied realities of the Korean War's status as a suspended struggle. Mired within this interval, Koreans and Korean diasporic subjects live in a zone of perpetual waiting and uncertainty.

To be sure, my emphasis on the Korean War's endurance does not aim to attenuate or anesthetize the bruising blow of "slow" militarized violence, which touches lives in distinct yet interrelated ways. Spanning from sharp pains associated with decades-long familial separations to the potential threat of nuclear annihilation on the Korean Peninsula, war reorients us toward its ever diversified forms in the twenty-first century. Reencounters with the effects of war intimate how brute forms of violence are conditioned by governmental apparatuses that permit populaces to live—or, conversely, to gradually perish—day by day. As Caren Kaplan notes, the "time and space of contemporary war" is characterized by an inalterable structuring that implicates all of us in the machinery of militarized conflict, albeit in different ways and through different means.[4]

While tracing the blurred boundaries between wartime and peacetime, this book offers no easy (re)solution as to how or when the Korean War will end or whether the U.S. military will end its occupation of the peninsula. However, by suggesting the everyday as a potent terrain in which to return to, reassess, and remember otherwise, the book pushes against the twin logics of inevitability and foreclosure so crucial to Cold War temporality and political discourse. Taking hold of the Korean War's diverse ramifications, I have described how diasporic subjects and spaces treated as disposable excesses by the U.S. and South Korean states resist wholesale absorption or assimilation into national historiographies. Enacting unruly memories, these diasporic excesses, in fact, accentuate the untenable conditions of militarized colonial infrastructures and transnational solidarities that refuse to be limited to the imagined Korean nation-homeland. In part, reencountering the Korean War encompasses a willingness to untether ourselves from enduring tales we have long been taught to know and trust within formal educational contexts, our given families, and social networks. In turn, the evocation of radically different memories orients us toward demilitarized presents and futures that are seemingly impossible or out of reach in the here and now.

Thus, it seems appropriate to conclude this book with my own diasporic memory practices of the Korean War and to partake in a mnemonic praxis of untethering. Strangely enough, the focus of my closing occupies both a central and peripheral place in this book: "North Korea." Here I reference the country in quotations, because the North Korea to which the American public has been exposed for nearly seventy years is a comedic object refracted through the polarized lens of Americanized Cold War discourse. Forever demonized by the U.S. government as the sole culprit of the Korean War and a heartless violator of human rights, North Korea is also a common punchline on late-night television shows, in slick studio films, and in documentary exposés. Given Americans' limited access to the Democratic People's Republic of Korea, North Korea occupies a perplexing place within the U.S. social imaginary: a lack of contact, for Americans, has somehow devolved into an incessant desire to definitively know, see, and touch. Indeed, the familiar narrative of North Korea as an impoverished place headed by a cruel demagogue who murders his own family members is anchored by an Orientalizing fascination for the incomprehensible other. In effect, the desire to know, catalogue, and study the inaccessible other crystallizes through hypersensationalized tabloid-like discourse and imagery that satiates the hunger for transparency and evidential truth.

In this vexed field of ideological representations, one-dimensional caricatures and complex realities become muddled to the degree that the former substitutes for the latter. In the fictional feature-length film *The Interview*

(2014), Kim Jong-un, played by the Korean/American actor Randall Park, becomes the only living national politician to hold the dubious honor of being assassinated on the silver screen. One might also recall Margaret Cho's farcical portrayals of Kim Jong-un and Kim Jong-il on *30 Rock,* as well as her appearance on the 2015 Golden Globes as the robotic DPRK Army General "Cho Yung Ja." In these contexts, America's disdain for North Korea mutates into good and innocent American humor, as North Koreans are doubly cast as dangerous deviants *and* "normal humans" who want to consume global commodities that Americans freely enjoy. This oppositional construction of North Koreans—as monstrous and evil, as well as ordinary and "just like us"—becomes a proxy for and supplants the gray zones of complex subjecthood that can never be fully documented through the extractive methods of racialized documentation and visual capture.

But even in my attempts to problematize these troubling portrayals of North Korea in the United States and much of the West, I have struggled to articulate what it means to remember, reassess, and reencounter North Korea without seeking to elucidate, uncover, and ultimately contain. In part, this difficulty stems from my uncertainty about what I know and do not know about North Korea. Undoubtedly, I resist U.S. ideological portrayals of the North Korean state and, more generally, the Korean War. This book has sought to complicate Cold War ideological portrayals and discourse by offering alternative considerations, perceptions, and memories of the Korean conflict. Yet as a feminist ethnic studies scholar trained and situated in the United States—and as someone who cannot possibly speak for others who inhabit a very different position from my own—I am anxious that my observations, no matter how carefully framed or researched, will unintentionally contribute to existing power differentials and bolster one-sided perspectives of an "authentic" North Korea in the United States. And while any critical memory of the Korean War must destabilize the United States' deeply skewed portrayals of North Korea, I also distance myself from utopian narratives that reduce this place to an anti-imperialist society unblemished by state violence.

What, then, do I recognize and know about North Korea? What is it that I seek to question and unknow? Does questioning simply imply a countermove that replaces a hegemonic narrative with a more truthful version of history, or does it entail a different epistemological project altogether? My ties to this very real and very imagined place align with what Cristiana Kyunghye Baik notes in "Wreckoning": North Korea *is where my grandfather spent time* and *Where my family / might have lived / had it not been / for division.* Given these ties, how do I make sense of a global history that is also my history without subsuming this reality to the confines of personal biography, familial sameness, and cultural authenticity? *What else* is potentiated by this mnemonic praxis of questioning?

In considering these inquiries, I find Édouard Glissant's contemplation of opacity in *Poetics of Relation* a generative provocation. For Glissant, the "right to opacity" does not seek to mark, decipher, and "reduce things to the Transparent."[5] On the contrary, opacity acknowledges the problematics of epistemology and knowledge formation, and how complex subjecthood and differences point to an "irreducible singularity."[6] Framed this way, to question is not simply antithetical to the enmeshed projects of knowing and containing. Instead, questioning holds us accountable to the shape-shifting conditions of power that determine who and what we recognize in our daily lives.[7] As a mode of refusal, the act of questioning considers how the desire to make transparent and categorize is too often sutured to projects of knowledge that justify conquest, enclosure, and occupation. By extension, questioning asks us to acknowledge that even in our most deliberate attempts to problematize the status quo, our maneuvers to debunk, challenge, and clarify are always already partial, subjective, and incomplete. In other words, there are limitations as to what we can access and definitively know.[8] But it is precisely this partiality, this incompleteness, that animates interstices of opening and moments of connectivity through relational difference: to unknow permits us to "feel a solidarity" without seeking to "become the other" or "'make [others] in my image."[9] Only then may we begin to understand that "it is impossible to reduce anyone, no matter who, to a truth that he would not have generated on his own."[10]

Mobilizing Glissant's essay as a starting point and my sister's poem as a guide, the preceding pages contain passing observations, data and statistics, images, and borrowed poetry stanzas reassembled in my continuing attempts to question and unknow North Korea, at least in the ways that the United States perceives this place. In place of a more traditional conclusion that encompasses a comprehensive compilation of the book's key findings, this essay-in-progress materializes as an open-ended sequence of memory practices that formulates questioning *as* a critical form of remembering. Indeed, questioning is pivotal to what the poet Don Mee Choi calls a "geopolitical poetics," or cultural forms of expression that potentiate discordant memories in tension with dominant historiography. In part, these vexed acts of remembering otherwise interrogate the "humorous," the "familiar," and the "ordinary" by underscoring the accumulative violence that condition these very terms. These discursive processes of questioning, however, are not conclusive or finite; nor do they aim to supplant existing narratives with more truthful representations of "real life" in North Korea. Rather, the aforementioned pages ask us to reconsider dominant perceptions by resensitizing us to the "limits of every method" and untethering our knowledges, even if a little bit, from the official "law of facts" that govern the everyday.[11] In a narrower sense, these diasporic memory practices provide an imperfect means for me to reencounter a place that feels so different and distant, yet so proximate and close to my diasporic personhood. They attempt to make sense of unrealized relationships, an arc of militarized migrations, and an unwritten history of familial dispossessions and disappearances that can never be rectified, reclaimed, or made transparent. In other words, they allow me to remember through and with opacity.

Notes

A Note on Methodology

1. I use the pronoun "their" in the place of "him" or "her" because several interlocutors do not conform to or are critical of a binary gender system.

2. Nadine Naber, *Arab America: Gender, Cultural Politics and Activism* (New York: New York University Press, 2012), 22.

The Delicious Taste of Army Base Stew: An Introduction

1. *BooDaeChiGae* was included in *Still Present Pasts* (2003–present), a traveling exhibit organized by Korean/American academics, activists, and cultural workers. For more information on Yoo's *BooDaeChiGae* and the *Still Present Pasts* exhibition, see the project's website at http://stillpresentpasts.org/boodaechigae. See also Grace M. Cho, "Performing an Ethics of Entanglement in *Still Present Pasts:* Korean Americans and the 'Forgotten War,'" *Women and Performance* 16, no. 2 (2006): 303–317; Ramsay Liem, "History, Trauma, and Identity: The Legacy of the Korean War for Korean Americans," *Ambrosia Journal* 29, no. 3 (2003–2004): 111–129. For a compelling study of *budae jjigae* in relation to the "forgetfulness" of the Korean War and nostalgic feelings of "postwar" conditions, see Nicolyn Woodcock, "Tasting the 'Forgotten War': Korean/American Memory and Military Base Stew," *Journal of Asian American Studies* 21, no. 1 (February 2018): 135–156.

2. Cho, "Performing an Ethics of Entanglement in *Still Present Pasts*."

3. Grace M. Cho, "Eating Military Base Stew," in *Gender, Sexuality, and Intimacy: A Contemporary Reader*, ed. Jodi O'Brien and Arlene Stein (Los Angeles: Sage, 2014), 321–324.

4. It is important to emphasize that South Korea was *not* an official signatory of the Korean armistice, as South Korean President Rhee Syngman advocated for the continuation of warfare until Korea was unified under ROK (Republic of Korea or South Korea) rule.

The United States was recognized as the de facto leader of the United Nations Coalitional Forces in South Korea: ibid. See also Ji-Yeon Yuh, "Cooking American, Eating Korean," in *Beyond the Shadow of Campton: Korean Military Brides in America*, by Ji-Yeon Yuh (New York: New York University Press, 2004), 126–153.

 5. Offered as a comment on the *Still Present Pasts* website, http://stillpresentpasts.org/boodaechigae.

 6. Mary Dudziak, *War Time: An Idea, Its History, Its Consequences* (Oxford: Oxford University Press, 2012).

 7. See Dorinne Kondo, *World-Making: Race, Performance, and the Work of Creativity* (Durham, NC: Duke University Press, 2019), 31–33.

 8. Kondo, *World-Making*, 32.

 9. "Division system" is a term that Nak-Chung Paik coined to describe the all-encompassing effects of prolonged division in the Korean Peninsula and the broader system of Cold War power relations that affect every facet of political, social, and cultural life in Korea: see Nak-Chung Paik, *The Division System in Crisis: Essays on Contemporary Korea*, trans. Kim Myung-hwa, Sol June-Kyu, Song Seung-cheol, and Ryu Young-joo (Berkeley: University of California Press, 2011).

 10. Lisa Yoneyama, *Cold War Ruins: Transpacific Critique of American Justice and Japanese War Crimes* (Durham, NC: Duke University Press, 2016). By underscoring the state's power in (inter)national negotiations for peace, I do not mean to minimize critical social movements mobilized by civilians of the past six decades, particularly in South Korea—for instance, the *Minjung* (People's) movement during the 1980s and the vociferous Candlelight Movement protests that led to the eventual impeachment and removal of President Park Geun-hye in 2016–2017. Indeed, I discuss the importance of such people-led movements throughout this book. Rather, this book critiques the stance of the nation-state as the ultimate mediator of formal justice (since the state is also the primary enforcer of violence) and compels readers to grapple with the possibilities and limitations associated with (inter)national politics.

 11. Raymond Williams, *Keywords: A Vocabulary of Culture and Society*, new ed. (Oxford: Oxford University Press, 2014), 49.

 12. Sarita See, *The Decolonized Eye: Filipino American Art and Performance* (Minneapolis: University of Minnesota Press, 2009); Mimi Thi Nguyen, *The Gift of Freedom: War, Debt, and Other Refugee Passages* (Durham, NC: Duke University Press, 2012); Cathy Schlund-Vials, *War, Genocide, and Justice: Cambodian Memory Work* (Minneapolis: University of Minnesota Press, 2012).

 13. See, *The Decolonized Eye*, xviii.

 14. Macarena Gómez-Barris, *The Extractive Zone: Social Ecologies and Decolonial Perspectives* (Durham, NC: Duke University Press, 2017).

 15. Because the interdisciplinary literature on aesthetics is quite extensive and draws from multiple (inter)disciplines and fields (including sociology, art history and practice, decolonial studies, film and media studies, and cultural theory), I focus explicitly on the conceptualization of aesthetics in conjunction with perception, the sensorium, and the political (rather than strictly delimiting aesthetics to the "philosophy" of art, cultural production, and beauty). For instance, while their theoretical works are quite distinct, Jill Bennett and Sylvia Wynter mobilize aesthetics as a working analytic that challenges the normative arrangement of power, knowledge (and knowledge production), and social relations within the realm of the everyday: see Jill Bennett, *Practical Aesthetics: Events, Affects, and Art after 9/11* (London: I. B. Tauris, 2012); Sylvia Wynter, "Rethinking 'Aesthetics': Notes towards a Deciphering Practice," in *Ex-Iles: Essays on Caribbean Cinema*, ed. Mbye Cham (Trenton, NJ: Africa World Press, 1992), 237–279.

16. Wynter, "Rethinking 'Aesthetics.'"
17. Judith Butler, *Frames of War: When Is Life Grievable?* (New York: Verso, 2009), 2.
18. Joseph Tanke, "What Is the Aesthetic Regime?" *Parrhesia* 12 (2011): 77–88, esp. 78.
19. Bennett, *Practical Aesthetics*, 13.
20. Ibid., 14.
21. Ibid.
22. Ibid., 11–12.
23. Ibid., 4.
24. Ibid., 13.
25. Ibid., 43.
26. See Yoneyama, *Cold War Ruins*; Jodi Kim, *Ends of Empire: Asian American Critique and the Cold War* (Minneapolis: University of Minnesota Press, 2010); Heonik Kwon, *The Other Cold War* (New York: Columbia University Press, 2010).
27. As of September 2018, Japan had yet to finalize postwar settlement and normalization treaties with both Russia and North Korea: see Yoneyama, *Cold War Ruins*, 5.
28. Dipesh Chakrabarty refers to this as the "historical transition" period, a transitive moment in which "third-world histories" are written through the "overriding (if often implicit)" themes of "development, modernization, and capitalism": Dipesh Chakrabarty, *Provincializing Europe: Postcolonial Thought and Historical Difference* (Princeton, NJ: Princeton University Press, 2000), 31. For astute critiques of the racialization, gendering, and sexualization of the U.S. War on Terror, see Jasbir Puar, *Terrorist Assemblages: Homonationalism in Queer Times* (Durham, NC: Duke University Press, 2007).
29. Nguyen, *The Gift of Freedom*.
30. Inderpal Grewal, *Saving the Security State: Exceptional Citizens in Twenty-First Century America* (Durham, NC: Duke University Press, 2017), 5–6.
31. Chandan Reddy, *Freedom with Violence: Race, Sexuality, and the U.S. State* (Durham, NC: Duke University Press, 2011).
32. Bennett, *Practical Aesthetics*, 45.
33. Walter Benjamin, "Theses on the Philosophy of History" in *Essays and Reflections*, ed. Hannah Arendt, trans. Harry Zohn (New York: Schocken, 1968), 253–264.
34. Lisa Yoneyama, *Hiroshima Traces: Time, Space, and the Dialectics of Memory* (Berkeley: University of California Press, 1999), 29–30.
35. Here I gesture to the notion of "performativity" in Judith Butler, *Gender Trouble*, 3d ed. (New York: Routledge, 2008), 185. While Butler deploys this concept to address the social construction of gender (and more specifically, the illusion of gender as a fixed biological entity), performativity as a methodological approach is useful in tracking the repetition, reification, and normalization of Cold War political discourse as it relates to racialized, gendered, and sexualized norms.
36. Lauren Berlant, *Cruel Optimism* (Durham, NC: Duke University Press, 2011), 10. I am grateful to Sunny Xiang for her careful reading of my manuscript and her suggestion of explicitly engaging Berlant's conceptualization of "crisis ordinariness."
37. Yoko Taguchi and Marisol de la Cadena, "An Interview with Marisol de la Cadena," *NatureCulture*, February 2017, https://www.natcult.net/interviews/an-interview-with-marisol-de-la-cadena.
38. See Marianne Hirsh, *Family Frames: Photography, Narrative and Postmemory* (New York: Columbia University Press, 1997). The idea of transgenerational hauntings was first offered in the collaborative work of Maria Torok and Nicolas Abraham: Maria Torok and Nicolas Abraham, *The Shell and the Kernel: Renewals of Psychoanalysis*, vol. 1 [Chicago: University of Chicago Press, 1994]). The notion of spectral elements, which resist em-

pirical modes of documentation, refers to the influential scholarship of Avery Gordon: see Avery Gordon, *Ghostly Matters: Haunting and the Sociological Imagination* (Minneapolis: University of Minnesota Press, 1997). For a partial bibliography on recent Asian/American and ethnic studies works that address the Korean War and memory through postmemory, intergenerational trauma, and hauntings, see Grace M. Cho, *Haunting the Korean Diaspora: Shame, Secrecy and the Forgotten War* (London: University of Minnesota Press, 2008); Cho, "Performing an Ethics of Entanglement in *Still Present Pasts*"; Daniel Kim, "'Bled in, Letter by Letter': Translation, Postmemory, and the Subject of Korean War: History in Susan Choi's *The Foreign Student*," *American Literary History* 21, no. 3 (October 2009): 550–583; Seo-Young Chu, *Do Metaphors Dream of Literal Sleep? A Science-Fictional Theory of Representation* (Cambridge, MA: Harvard University Press, 2010); Youngmin Choe, "Postmemory, DMZ in South Korean Cinema, 1999–2003," *Journal of Korean Studies* 18, no. 2 (Fall 2013): 315–336; Jung Joon Lee, "No End to the Image War: Photography and the Contentious Memories of the Korean War," *Journal of Korean Studies* 18, no. 2 (Fall 2013): 337–370; Joseph Darda, "The Literary Afterlife of the Korean War," *American Literature* 87, no. 1 (2015): 79–105; Sandra So Hee Chi Kim, "Suji Kwock Kim's 'Generation' and the Ethics of Diasporic Postmemory," *positions: asia critique* 4, no. 3 (2016): 635–667.

39. Cho, *Haunting the Korean Diaspora*, 29.

40. As discussed throughout this book, "comfort women" (*jugan ianfu* in Japanese) is a euphemism used for more than 150,000 colonized subjects (mostly Korean women) forced into sexual servitude by the Japanese Imperial Army during the Asia-Pacific War(s). To this day, the Japanese government evades accountability and responsibility for the atrocities committed against these women. For an illuminating interdisciplinary study of "comfort women" and the prolonged history of multipronged activism against the Japanese, South Korean, and U.S. nation-states, see Elizabeth Son, *Embodied Reckonings: "Comfort Women," Performance and Transpacific Redress* (Ann Arbor: University of Michigan Press, 2018).

41. Kim, "'Bled in, Letter by Letter.'"

42. Ruth Leys, *Trauma: A Genealogy* (Chicago: University of Chicago Press, 2000), 6.

43. Butler, *Frames of War*, 5.

44. While *kyopo* (or *gyopo*) has generally shifted from a derogatory term to a popular moniker applied to Korean diasporans or "overseas" Koreans visiting the Korean Peninsula, it retains negative connotations. For instance, *kyopo* is often used to refer to non-Korean-speaking diasporic subjects visiting South Korea as tourists.

45. Simone Browne, *Dark Matters: On the Surveillance of Blackness* (Durham, NC: Duke University Press, 2015), 9.

46. For critiques of the suturing of memory studies to trauma studies, see Leys, *Trauma*; Andreas Huyssen, *Present Pasts: Urban Palimpsests and the Politics of Memory* (Stanford, CA: Stanford University Press, 2003).

47. For a genealogy of texts that address memory through the lens of trauma, see Giorgio Agamben, *Homo Sacer: Sovereign Power and Bare Life* (Stanford, CA: Stanford University Press, 1998); Cathy Caruth, *Unclaimed Experience: Trauma, Narrative, and History*, 20th ed. (Baltimore: Johns Hopkins University Press, 2016); Shoshana Felman and Dori Laub, *Testimony: Crises of Witnessing in Literature, Psychoanalysis and History* (New York: Routledge, 1991); Marianne Hirsch, *Family Frames: Photography, Narrative and Postmemory* (Cambridge, MA: Harvard University Press, 1997); Primo Levi, *Survival Auschwitz* (New York: Touchstone, 1996).

48. Hirsch, *Family Frames*, 19.

49. Ibid., 20. Here Hirsch draws on Roland Barthes's observations on photography and death in *Camera Lucida: Reflections on Photograph* (New York: Hill and Wang, 1980).

50. Hirsch, *Family Frames*, 22.

51. Donald Trump offered these remarks at the seventy-second session of the United Nations General Assembly Meeting on September 19, 2017. For a complete transcription of his remarks, see the White House government website, https://www.whitehouse.gov/briefings-statements/remarks-president-trump-72nd-session-united-nations-general-assembly.

52. Catherine Lutz, "Making War at Home in the United States: Militarization and the Current Crisis," *American Anthropologist* 104, no. 3 (September 2002): 732–735.

53. Charles S. Young, "POWs: The Hidden Reasons for Forgetting Korea," in *The Korean War at Sixty: New Approaches to the Study of the Korean War*, ed. Steven Casey (London: Routledge, 2012), 155–171. See also Christine Hong, "Introduction: The Unending Korean War," *positions: asia critique* 23, no. 4 (2015): 597–617. I use "military-industrial complex" to mean the interlinking of the military sector with governance, academic knowledge production, social life, and the global economy.

54. For a particularly incisive engagement of the overlaps between militarized life and civilian life through the analytic of logistics, see Deborah Cowen, *The Deadly Life of Logistics: Mapping Violence in Global Trade* (Minneapolis: University of Minnesota Press, 2014). Monica Kim, *The Interrogation Rooms of the Korean War: The Untold History* (Princeton, NJ: Princeton University Press, 2019), smartly addresses the history and consolidation of a militarized surveillance regime with the onset of the Korean War.

55. Ann Laura Stoler, *Duress: Imperial Durabilities in Our Times* (Durham, NC: Duke University Press, 2016), 5.

56. Christine Hong, prepared remarks, Oral History Roundtable Discussion, University of California, Riverside, February 18, 2015. During her brief talk, Hong emphasized that her observations about the historiographical turns of the Korean War are informed by the commentary of Youngju Ryu of the University of Michigan, Ann Arbor, at The (Unending) Korean War Conference held at New York University in April 2011.

57. For critiques of Cold War historiography and the Korean War, see Bruce Cumings, *The Origins of the Korean War*, 2 vols. (Princeton, NJ: Princeton University Press, 1981); Chalmers Johnson, *Blowback: The Costs and Consequences of American Empire* (New York: Holt, 2004); Kuan-Hsing Chen, *Asia as Method: Toward Deimperialization* (Durham, NC: Duke University Press, 2010); Christine Hong, "Manufacturing Dissidence: Arts and Letters of North Korea's 'Second Culture,'" *positions: asia critique* 23, no. 4 (2015): 743–784; Yoneyama, *Cold War Ruins*.

58. Leonard Rifas, "Korean War Comic Books and the Militarization of U.S. Masculinity," *positions: asia critique* 23, no. 4 (2015): 619–631.

59. Namhee Lee, *The Making of Minjung: Democracy, and the Politics of Presentation* (Ithaca, NY: Cornell University Press, 2007), 7.

60. Chunghee Sarah Soh, *The Comfort Women: Sexual Violence and Postcolonial Memory in Korea and Japan* (Chicago: University of Chicago Press, 2008); Chungmoo Choi, "The Discourse of Decolonization and Popular Memory: South Korea," *positions: asia critique* 1, no. 1 (Spring 1993): 77–102.

61. Cumings, *The Origins of the Korean War*.

62. Even after South Korea was established in 1948 and fighting between the two Koreas temporarily halted in 1953, elements of Japanese colonial governance remained firmly intact (e.g., centralized policing and surveillance practices, family law, and the legal-juridical system). Simultaneously, the sexual economy of the U.S. military and USAMGIK's instrumentalization of women's bodies for the procurement of national safety were founded on an elaborate infrastructure of public health policies and administrative channels already estab-

lished by the Japanese colonial government in Korea: see Ki-young Shin, "The Politics of the Family Law Reform Movement in Contemporary Korea: A Contentious Space for Gender and the Nation," *Journal of Korean Studies* 11, no. 1 (Fall 2006): 96; Dong-choon Kim, *The Unending Korean War: A Social History*, trans. Kim Sung-Ok (Larkspur, CA: Tamal Vista, 2009), 30; Johnson, *Blowback*; Cumings, *The Origins of the Korean War*, vol. 2. See also Seungsook Moon, *Militarized Modernity and Gendered Citizenship in South Korea* (Durham, NC: Duke University Press, 2005); Na-Young Lee, "The Construction of Military Prostitution in South Korea during the U.S. Military Rule, 1945–1948," *Feminist Studies* 33, no. 3 (Fall 2007): 453–481; Katherine Moon, *Sex among Allies: Military Prostitution in U.S.-Korea Relations* (New York: Columbia University Press, 1997).

63. Naoki Sakai, "Trans-Pacific Studies and the U.S.-Japan Complicity," in *The Transpacific Imagination: Rethinking Boundary, Culture, and Society*, ed. Naoki Sakai and Hyun Joo Yoo (Singapore: World Scientific Publishing, 2012), 279–216. See also Setsu Shigematsu and Keith Camacho, "Introduction: Militarized Currents, Decolonizing Futures," in *Militarized Currents: Toward a Decolonized Future in Asia and the Pacific*, ed. Setsu Shigematsu and Keith Camacho (Minneapolis: University of Minneapolis Press, 2010), xv–xlviii, esp. xvi. The transpacific alliance continues to take contemporary forms through global capitalist alliances such as the Trans-Pacific Partnership (TPP). For a brief yet nuanced reading of the TPP's relationship to accrued histories of colonialism, militarization, and neoliberalism, see Arnie Saiki, "TPP at the End of the Line: A Briefing on Economic Cooperation and Capacity Building," *American Quarterly* 69, no. 3 (September 2017): 501–512.

64. Yoneyama, *Cold War Ruins*.

65. See Christine Hong and Henry Em, "Coda: A Conversation with Kim Dong-Choon," *positions: asia critique* 23, no. 4 (Fall 2015): 837–849; Mark Selden and Dong-choon Kim, "South Korea's Embattled Truth and Reconciliation Commission," *Asia-Pacific Journal: Japan Focus* 8, issue 9, no. 4 (March 1, 2010), http://apjjf.org/-Mark-Selden/3313/article.html. See also Kim, *The Unending Korean War*. As Kim emphasizes, the South Korean Truth and Reconciliation Commission, established by South Korean President Noh Moo-hyun's administration (2003–2008), ended its investigation in December 2005 and published a four-volume, three-thousand-page report that documents massacres and other atrocities that the Japanese colonial regime (1910–1945) and subsequent South Korean authoritarian regimes (1948–1993) committed on both sides of the peninsula. The report is marred by amnesiac conditions: for instance, it does not address crimes that the U.S. military committed; nor does it document the South Korean police regime's and the U.S. military's normalized use of sexual violence, including rape. But the report was one of the first public efforts to systematically probe and scrutinize the militarized violence affecting the everyday lives of Koreans during and after the armed conflict.

66. For a complete transcript of the June 15 2000 North-South Joint Declaration, see http://londonkoreanlinks.net/2000/06/15/north-south-joint-declaration.

67. Nan Kim, *Memory, Reconciliation, and Reunions in South Korea: Crossing the Divide* (New York: Lexington, 2016).

68. Yoneyama, *Cold War Ruins*.

69. For a critique of the establishment of the United Nations, the Declaration of Human Rights, and transitional justice, see Randall Williams, *The Divided World: Human Rights and Its Violence* (Minneapolis: University of Minnesota Press, 2010).

70. See Cumings, *The Origins of the Korean War*; Martin Hart-Landsberg, *Korea: Division, Reunification, and U.S. Foreign Policy* (New York: Monthly Review, 1998).

71. Yoneyama, *Cold War Ruins*, 12. As Yoneyama emphasizes, Jacques Derrida conceives of true justice as a form of "alterity" and "aporia" to existing mechanisms of law, rule, and

order, since these instrumentalized apparatuses tend to maintain, reproduce, and amplify violent injustices. Derrida's own concept of justice, in relation to aporia, is based on the critical scholarship of Emmanuel Levinas: see Jacques Derrida, "Force of Law: The 'Mystical Foundation of Authority,'" in *Deconstruction and the Possibility of Justice*, ed. Drucilla Cornell, Michel Rosenfeld, and David Gray Carlson (New York: Routledge, 1992), 3–67.

72. Yoneyama, *Cold War Ruins*, 7.

73. See *The Decolonized Eye*, xxix.

74. Ibid., xxx.

75. See Laura Hyun Yi Kang, *Compositional Subjects: Enfiguring Asian/American Women* (Durham, NC: Duke University Press, 2002). 3.

76. See, e.g., William Safran's influential "Diasporas in Modern Societies: Myths of Homeland and Return," *Diaspora* 1, no. 1 (Spring 1991): 83–99.

77. See Grace Kyungwon Hong, *The Ruptures of American Capital: Women of Color Feminism and the Culture of Immigrant Labor* (Minneapolis: University of Minnesota Press, 2006).

78. The work that Hong references here is Cherríe Moraga's preface in Cherríe Moraga and Gloria Anzaldúa, *This Bridge Called My Back: Writings by Radical Women of Color* (Latham, NY: Kitchen Table/Women of Color Press, 1981).

79. Hong, *The Ruptures of American Capital*, vii.

80. Ibid., ix.

81. Ibid.

82. Ibid., xvii. Here Hong refers to Kimberlé Crenshaw's theorization of intersectionality, which addresses identification through the intersection or intertwinement of race, gender, sexuality, class, and ableism (the idea of interlocking dynamisms underlying identification, however, is discussed in earlier works, including the Combahee River Collective's Statement published in 1977): see Kimberlé Crenshaw, "Mapping the Margins: Intersectionality, Identity Politics, and Violence against Women of Color," *Stanford Law Review* 43, no. 6 (July 1991): 1241–1299.

83. Fatima El-Tayeb, *European Others: Queering Ethnicity in Postnational Europe* (Minneapolis: University of Minnesota Press, 2011), xxxv. For other critical queer-of-color texts that engage diaspora beyond the notion of ethnic, national, and familial origins, see Gayatri Gopinath, *Impossible Desires: Queer Diaspora and South Asian Public Cultures* (Durham, NC: Duke University Press, 2005); David Eng, *The Feeling of Kinship: Queer Liberalism and the Racialization of Intimacy* (Durham, NC: Duke University Press, 2010).

84. El-Tayeb, *European Others*, xxxiii.

85. Ibid., xxxv.

86. Kwon, *The Other Cold War*, 8.

87. Hyun Oh Park, *The Capitalist Unconscious: From Korean Unification to Transnational Korea* (New York: Columbia University Press, 2016), 183.

88. For a full Korean-to-English translation of President Park Geun-hye's "Dresden Declaration" of March 2014, see http://cogitasia.com/president-park-geun-hyes-dresden-declaration.

89. Postcolonial scholars use the concept of "decolonization" to reference social movements for national sovereignty organized by and among African and Asian subjects colonized by waning European powers after 1945 (especially after the Bandung Conference of 1955). My use is more expansive and exceeds the confined realm of *national* politics. Indeed, in conversation with theorists such as Sylvia Wynter, Catherine Walsh, and Walter Mignolo, I approach decolonization as a radically different process that accentuates how the very concept of the progressive and enlightened "modern nation-state" is a by-product of colonial power. Although these scholars deploy "decoloniality" rather than "decolonization" to signal

this key difference, I have opted to use "decolonization" throughout this book, because this term is explicitly used by critical scholars (for example, Nak-Chung Paik, Chungmoo Choi, and Kuan-Hsing Chen) who address colonial violence within the geopolitical context of Asia. For general theorizations of decoloniality and decolonization, see Sylvia Wynter, "The Ceremony Must Be Found: After Humanism," *boundary 2* 12, no. 3 (Spring–Fall 1984), 19–70; Walter Mignolo, *The Darker Side of Western Modernity: Global Futures, Decolonial Options* (Durham, NC: Duke University Press, 2011). For discourses of decolonization specific to the histories of Asia and Korea, see Chen, *Asia as Method*; Paik, *The Division System in Crisis*; Choi, "The Discourse of Decolonization and Popular Memory."

90. Ji-Yeon Yuh, "Moved by War: Migration, Diaspora, and the Korean War," *Journal of Asian American Studies* 8, no. 3 (October 2005): 278.

91. Yen Le Espiritu, *Body Counts: The Vietnam War and Militarized Refugees* (Berkeley: University of California Press, 2014); Schlund-Vials, *War, Genocide, and Justice;* Nguyen, *The Gift of Freedom*; Ma Vang, "The Refugee Soldier: A Critique of Recognition and Citizenship in the Hmong Veterans' Naturalization Act," *positions: asia critique* 20, no. 3 (2012): 685–712; Eric Tang, *Unsettled: Cambodian Refugees in the New York City Hyperghetto* (Philadelphia: Temple University Press, 2015); Viet Nguyen, *Nothing Ever Dies: Vietnam and the Memory of War* (Cambridge, MA: Harvard University Press, 2016).

92. Elizabeth Freeman, *Time Binds: Queer Temporalities, Queer Histories* (Durham, NC: Duke University Press, 2010).

Chapter 1

1. For commentary on the racialized, gendered, and sexualized history of "naturalized" American nationality in relation to Asian/Americans, see Susan Koshy, *Sexual Naturalization: Asian American and Miscegenation* (Stanford, CA: Stanford University Press, 2005). For commentary on the racialized and sexualized dimensions of American citizenship in the context of Korean migration after World War II, see SooJin Pate, *From Orphan to Adoptee: U.S. Empire and Genealogies of Korean Adoption* (Minneapolis: University of Minnesota Press, 2014).

2. For (im)migration histories specific to Koreans, see Won Moo Hurh and K. C. Kim, *Korean Immigrants in America: A Structural Analysis of Ethnic Confinement and Adhesive Adaptation* (Teaneck, NJ: Fairleigh Dickinson University Press, 1984); Nancy Abelmann and John Lie, *Blue Dreams: Korean Americans and the Los Angeles Riots* (Cambridge, MA: Harvard University Press, 1997); Won Moo Hurh, *The Korean Americans* (Westport, CT: Greenwood, 1998); Pyong Gap Min, *Preserving Ethnicity through Religion in America: Korean Protestants and Indian Hindus in New York City* (New York: New York University Press, 2010). It is particularly striking how this body of literature theorizes Korean (im)migration to the United States in three sequential "waves": 1903–1905, 1951–1964, and 1965 to the present.

3. Ji-Yeon Yuh, "Moved by War: Migration, Diaspora, and the Korean War," *Journal of Asian American Studies* 8, no. 3 (October 2005): 278. For instance, the sociologist Pyong Gap Min states that Koreans have "become immigrants . . . using two mechanisms: [heterosexual] family reunification and occupational immigration": see Pyong Gap Min, "Koreans' Immigration to the U.S.: History and Contemporary Trends," Research Report no. 3, January 27, 2011, Research Center for Korean Community, Queens College of the City University of New York, 25.

4. Elizabeth Freeman, *Time Binds: Queer Temporalities, Queer Histories* (Durham, NC: Duke University Press, 2010).

5. According to the Convention Relating to the Status of Refugees (1951), the United Nations defines a refugee as someone who is forced to flee his or her country because of

persecution, war, or violence. A refugee has a well-founded fear of persecution for reasons related to "race, religion, nationality, political opinion or membership in a particular social group." While this definition has been expanded since 1951, it continues to serve as a blueprint for refugee policy across the globe, including in the United States. Yet, as emphasized throughout this chapter, the emergent definition of the refugee is a historical formation linked to Cold War polemics, anticommunist sentiments (e.g., most refugee seekers to the United States historically have been defined as those escaping from communist regimes), and the privileging of European migrants. For a closer analysis of the development of refugee policy, see Laura Barnett, "Global Governance and the Evolution of the International Refugee Regime," *International Journal of Refugee Law*, 14, nos. 2–3 (April 2002): 238–262; Carl J. Bon Tempo, *Americans at the Gate: The United States and Refugees during the Cold War* (Princeton, NJ: Princeton University Press, 2015); Randall Williams, *The Divided World: Human Rights and Its Violence* (Minneapolis: University of Minnesota Press, 2010).

6. Yuh, "Moved by War," 280–281.

7. Ann Laura Stoler, "Introduction: 'The Rot Remains': From Ruins to Ruination," in *Imperial Debris: On Ruins and Ruination*, ed. Ann Laura Stoler (Durham, NC: Duke University Press, 2008), 9.

8. Chandan Reddy, *Freedom with Violence: Race, Sexuality, and the U.S. State* (Durham, NC: Duke University Press, 2011), 165. Nayan Shah's scholarship also emphasizes the relationship between legislation and law, racialized and sexualized subjectivity, and historical agency: see Nayan Shah, *Stranger Intimacy: Contesting Race, Sexuality and the Law in the North American West* (Berkeley: University of California Press, 2011).

9. Legacies of the Korean War is a growing archive of oral histories organized by a group of critical scholars in Korean/American studies, including Namhee Lee, Christine Hong, and Ramsay Liem. Segments of the interviews, as well as complete transcripts, are available to the public on the website, http://legaciesofthekoreanwar.org. As Ramsay Liem and Deann Borshay Liem shared via e-mail in May 2017, the project team is still developing comprehensive protocols to share complete audiovisual recordings of interviews with the broader public.

10. See Eleana J. Kim, *Adopted Territory: Transnational Korean Adoptees and the Politics of Belonging* (Durham, NC: Duke University Press, 2010).

11. For a historical contextualization of the U.S. military's arrival in and occupation of Korea following World War II, see Bruce Cumings, *Origins of the Korean War*, 2 vols. (Princeton, NJ: Princeton University Press, 1981), vol. 1; Martin Hart-Landsberg, *Korea: Division, Reunification, and U.S. Foreign Policy* (New York: Monthly Review, 1998); Dongchoon Kim, *The Unending Korean War: A Social History*, trans. Sung-Ok Kim (Larkspur, CA: Tamal Vista, 2009). For a contextualization of effects related to the U.S. military, the Korean War, and racial and sexual violence, see Katherine Moon, *Sex among Allies: Military Prostitution in U.S.-Korean Relations* (New York: Columbia University Press, 1997); Ji-Yeon Yuh, *Beyond the Shadow of Camptown: Korean Military Brides in America* (New York: New York University Press, 2004); Grace M. Cho, *Haunting the Korean Diaspora: Shame, Secrecy and the Forgotten War* (Minneapolis: University of Minnesota Press, 2008); Maria Höhn and Seungsook Moon, eds., *Over There: Living with the U.S. Military Empire from World War II to the Present* (Durham, NC: Duke University Press, 2010); Na-Young Lee, "The Construction of Military Prostitution in South Korea during the U.S. Military Rule, 1945–1948," *Feminist Studies* 33, no. 3 (Fall 2007): 453–481.

12. Lee, "The Construction of Military Prostitution in South Korea during the U.S. Military Rule," 453–454.

13. While the U.S. Department of Defense provided these numbers in 2016, it is important to note that the recent escalation in the Korean Peninsula has increased the

number of U.S. troops stationed in South Korea by at least twelve thousand (so the number of U.S. troops currently in the peninsula and Jeju Island is closer to thirty-five thousand): see Oliver Holmes, "What Is the U.S. Military's Presence near North Korea?" *The Guardian*, August 9, 2017, https://www.theguardian.com/us-news/2017/aug/09/what-is-the-us-militarys-presence-in-south-east-asia.

14. Lee, "The Construction of Military Prostitution in South Korea during the U.S. Military Rule"; Cynthia Enloe, *Maneuvers: The International Politics of Militarizing Women's Lives* (Berkeley: University of California Press, 2000); Mark Gillem, *America Town: Building the Outposts of Empire* (Minneapolis: University of Minnesota Press, 2007).

15. Lee, "The Construction of Military Prostitution in South Korea during the U.S. Military Rule," 454. It is also important to note that the demographics of military sex workers in South Korea have radically shifted in the past twenty or so years, since the vast majority (more than 90 percent) of sex workers in camptowns are now of Filipinx and Eastern European descent: see Hae Yeon Choo, *Decentering Citizenship: Gender, Labor, and Migrant Rights in South Korea* (Stanford, CA: Stanford University Press, 2016); Sealing Cheng, *On the Move for Love: Migrant Entertainers and the U.S. Military in South Korea* (Philadelphia: University of Pennsylvania Press, 2013).

16. Yuh, *Beyond the Shadow of Camptown*; Susie Woo, "A New American Comes 'Home': Korean War Adoptees and Cold War Sentiments of Race and Nation" (Ph.D. diss., Yale University, New Haven, CT, 2009).

17. In the article "Korean Refugee, Now Santa Ana Housewife" (*Los Angeles Times*, February 11, 1962, OC1), by Don Smith, Chang Sook Kim (also known as "Maria Cho") worked as a military language instructor in South Korea before her militarized migration to Monterey, California.

18. Hurh, *The Korean Americans*, 33; Woo, "A New American Comes 'Home,'" 9. As Hurh and Woo emphasize, statistics on the number of Korean military brides and adoptees who arrived in the United States before 1965 vary across different sources, since the U.S. government did not maintain disaggregated data specific to these subpopulations.

19. Yuh, "Moved by War," 278.

20. See Kim, *Adopted Territory*; Pate, *From Orphan to Adoptee*; Kim Park Nelson, *Invisible Asians: Korean American Adoptees, Asian American Experiences and Racial Exceptionalism* (New Brunswick, NJ: Rutgers University Press, 2016); Tobias Hübinette, "Comforting an Orphaned Nation: Representations of International Adoption and Adopted Koreans in Korea Popular Culture" (Ph.D. diss., Stockholm University, 2005).

21. Kim, *Adopted Territory*, 48.

22. Ibid., 60–61.

23. Rachel Winslow, "Immigration Law and Improvised Policy in the Making of International Adoption," *Journal of Policy History* 24, no. 2 (2012): 323–325. See also Kim, *Adopted Territory*; Woo, "A New American Comes 'Home'"; Elaine Tyler May, *Homeward Bound: American Families in the Cold War Era* (New York: Basic, 1988).

24. Hurh, *The Korean Americans*, 33; Woo, "A New American Comes 'Home,'" 9. As Yuh notes, "Korean women who arrived in the United States as the already married partners of American soldiers accounted for nearly 40 percent of all Korean immigration to the United States between 1962 and 1968: Yuh, "Moved by War," 279.

25. Winslow, "Immigration Law and Improvised Policy in the Making of International Adoption," 320.

26. Barnett, "Global Governance and the Evolution of the International Refugee Regime," 246. See also Tempo, *Americans at the Gate*; Yen Le Espiritu, *Body Counts: The Vietnam War and Militarized Refugees* (Oakland: University of California Press, 2014).

27. Barnett, "Global Governance and the Evolution of the International Refugee Regime," 249; Espiritu, *Body Counts*.

28. For instance, in 1943 the U.S. Congress passed the Magnuson Act, which rescinded the long-standing Chinese Exclusion Act of 1882, and in 1946 the Philippines gained independence from the United States while restrictions placed on South Asian immigration were rescinded.

29. The War Brides Act was followed by the Alien Fiancées and Fiancés Act (1946, Public Law 79-471), which provided additional temporary visas to women engaged to members of the U.S. military.

30. Kim, *Adopted Territory*, 53–55; Carl J. Bon Tempo, "'A Mystic Maze of Enforcement': The Refugee Relief Program," in Tempo, *Americans at the Gate*, 34–59.

31. See Christina Klein, *Cold War Orientalism: Asia in the Middlebrow Imagination, 1945–1961* (Berkeley: University of California Press, 2003); Nikhil Pal Singh, *Black Is a Country: Race and the Unfinished Struggle for Democracy* (Cambridge, MA: Harvard University Press, 2005); Jodi Melamed, *Represent and Destroy: Rationalizing Violence in the New Racial Capitalism* (Minneapolis: University of Minnesota Press, 2011).

32. Klein, *Cold War Orientalism*, 40.

33. Klein refers to this as a system of "global imaginary of integration." Ibid., 41.

34. Melamed, *Represent and Destroy*. See also Mae Ngai, *Impossible Subjects: Illegal Aliens and the Making of Modern America* (Princeton, NJ: Princeton University Press, 2004).

35. Winslow, "Immigration Law and Improvised Policy in the Making of International Adoption," 326.

36. Ibid.

37. There is a well-established body of literature that critiques the heteronormative and gendered relations between the United States and South Korea. In addition to the scholarship of Eleana J Kim, Hübinette, Nelson, Pate, Moon, Höhn and Moon, and Yuh, see Elaine Kim and Chungmoo Choi, eds., *Dangerous Women: Gender and Korean Nationalism* (New York: Routledge, 1998); Seungsook Moon, *Militarized Modernity and Gendered Citizenship in South Korea* (Durham, NC: Duke University Press, 2005); Jin-Kyung Lee, *Service Economies: Militarism, Sex Work and Migrant Labor in South Korea* (Minneapolis: University of Minnesota Press, 2010).

38. Smith, "Korean Refugee, Now Santa Ana Housewife," OC1.

39. "11 Asiatic War Brides Fly to New U.S. Homes," *Los Angeles Times*, November 22, 1951, 10.

40. Winslow, "Immigration Law and Improvised Policy in the Making of International Adoption," 326.

41. Tempo, *Americans at the Gate*, 43.

42. Woo, "A New American Comes 'Home,'" 187–188; Koshy, *Sexual Naturalization*, 10–12.

43. Koshy, *Sexual Naturalization*, 12. For incisive studies of the public portrayal of Asian women in American film and popular culture after World War II, see Gina Marchetti, *Romance and the "Yellow Peril"* (Berkeley: University of California Press, 1994); Celine Parreñas Shimizu, *The Hypersexuality of Race: Performing Asian/American Women on Screen and Scene* (Durham, NC: Duke University Press, 2007).

44. Woo, "A New American Comes 'Home,'" 236. For a cultural analysis of the impact of these Orientalizing tropes, see also Robert Lee, *Orientals: Asian Americans in Popular Culture* (Philadelphia: Temple University Press, 1999). Yet, as Koshy astutely points out, enduring notions of vice and prostitution continue to be associated with Asian women,

partially because of federal legislation that identified all "Asiatic females" as prostitutes or sex workers: Koshy, *Sexual Naturalization*, 10–12.

45. Ibid.

46. Nelson, *Invisible Asians*, 1.

47. For example, one of the earliest *New York Times* articles that Holt wrote about the adoption of Korean children (December 4, 1955) refers to adoptees interchangeably as not only "orphans" and "helpless by-product[s] of war" but also non-English-speaking children slowly settling into their "new life" in the United States as recent arrivals (in other words, as immigrants) and "Korean Americans."

48. Yuh, *Beyond the Shadow of Camptown*, loc. 689 (Kindle).

49. Ibid., loc. 849.

50. Ngai, *Impossible Subjects*.

51. For a recently published work that focuses on the politics of memory and reunification policies in Korea and beyond, see Nan Kim, *Memory, Reconciliation, and Reunions in South Korea: Crossing the Divide* (New York: Lexington Books, 2017). See also James A. Foley, *Korea's Divided Families: Fifty Years of Separation* (New York: Routledge, 2003).

52. An audiovisual segment of the interview and a partial transcript are available on the Legacies of the Korean War website, http://legaciesofthekoreanwar.org/story/eun-joung-lee. It is also important to note here that because Eun-Joung's mother has refused to discuss the war at length with Eun-Joung and her sisters, Eun-Joung focuses on her father's experiences with the war. A closer analysis of gendered dynamics and implications of the oral history is included in Chapter 2.

53. Ronald J. Grele, "Oral History as Evidence," in *History of Oral History: Foundations and Methodology*, ed. Thomas L. Charlton, Lois E. Myers, and Rebecca Sharpless (Lanham, MD: Altamira, 2007), 48.

54. Michel Foucault, *Power/Knowledge: Selected Interviews and Other Writings, 1972–1977* (New York: Pantheon, 1980), 81–82.

55. Japanese colonial rule deeply affected Park Chung-hee. Trained by the colonial military, Park was commissioned as a lieutenant in the Manchukuo Imperial Army. Admiring the organization and discipline of the Japanese military, Park also modeled his 1972 Yushin Constitution on the principles of the Meiji Restoration in Japan. For details, see Chung-in Moon and Byung-joon Jun, "Modernization Strategy: Ideas and Influences," in *The Park Chung Hee Era: The Transformation of South Korea*, ed. Byung-Kook Kim and Ezra F. Vogel (Cambridge, MA: Harvard University Press, 2011), 115–139.

56. Tomoji Ishi, "International Linkage and National Class Conflict: The Migration of Korean Nurses to the United States," *Amerasia* 14, no. 1 (1988): 23–50; Kazuko Suzuki, *Divided Fates: The State, Race, and Korean Immigrants' Adaptation in Japan and the United States* (Lanham, MD: Lexington, 2016); Moon, *Militarized Modernity and Gendered Citizenship in South Korea*.

57. Suzuki, *Divided Fates*.

58. Hurh, *The Korean Americans*, 33.

59. Hosu Kim, *Birth Mothers and Transnational Adoption Practice in South Korea* (New York: Palgrave Macmillan, 2016), 36. See also Byung Hoon Chun, "Adoption and Korea," *Child Welfare* 68, no. 2 (1989): 255–260; Kim, *Adopted Territory*.

60. Yuh, "Moved by War," 281.

61. Jodi Kim, *Ends of Empire: Asian American Critique and the Cold War* (Minneapolis: University of Minnesota Press, 2010), 197.

62. Stein Tonnesson, "Franklin Roosevelt, Trusteeship, and Indochina: A Reassessment," in *The First Vietnam War: Colonial Conflict and Cold War Crisis*, ed. Mark At-

wood Lawrence and Frederik Logevall (Cambridge, MA: Harvard University Press, 2007), 63–64.

63. Lee, *Service Economies*; Heonik Kwon, *Ghosts of War in Vietnam* (Cambridge: Cambridge University Press, 2008); Charles Armstrong, "America's Korea, Korea's Vietnam," *Critical Asian Studies* 33, no. 4 (2001): 527–540.

64. For budget details, see Choi Yongho, *The Vietnam War and South Korean Troops*, vol. 1 (Seoul: ROK Ministry of Defense, Institute for Military History Compilation, 2006). See also Lee, *Service Economies*.

65. Deann Borshay Liem (director of *Memory of Forgotten War*) and Korean/American scholar Ramsay Liem noted via personal communication that the number of Min Yong's sisters differs from source to source (a discrepancy that may stem from the confusion over which siblings were included in the new family registry created following Korean division). According to Ramsay Liem, Min Yong most likely had six siblings: his eldest brother, who was killed by the Northwest Youth League before he was able to enter North Korea; a brother who traveled to North Korea; a sister who traveled to North Korea as a nurse; two sisters who remained in South Korea; and a sister who immigrated to Japan.

66. For more details on the history of anticommunist surveillance and monitoring in South Korea, see Moon, *Militarized Modernity and Gendered Citizenship in South Korea*; Namhee Lee, *The Making of Minjung: Democracy, and the Politics of Presentation* (Ithaca, NY: Cornell University Press, 2007).

67. For excerpts from Jungran Shin's Legacies of the Korean War interview, in which Jungran was interviewed with her son, Sanghyuk "Sam" Shin, see http://legaciesofthekoreanwar.org/story/sanghyuk-shin-and-jungran-shin. During the interview, Sam describes his exposure to anticommunist propaganda and education in elementary school in South Korea during the 1970s and 1980s.

68. For a detailed analysis of the incubation and development of anticommunist governance in South Korea after 1950, see Moon, *Militarized Modernity and Gendered Citizenship in South Korea*; Lee, *The Making of Minjung*.

69. Namhee Lee, "The Korean War, Anticommunism, and the Korean American Community," 4, Legacies of the Korean War website, http://legaciesofthekoreanwar.org/wp-content/uploads/2015/08/Article-Namhee-Lee.pdf. The article is a shortened version of a chapter from Lee's *The Making of Minjung*.

70. Lee, "The Korean War, Anticommunism, and the Korean American Community," 7–8.

71. See Sang-hun Choe, "Six Ex-Officials in South Korea Are Sentenced for Blacklisting Artists," *New York Times*, July 27, 2017, https://www.nytimes.com/2017/07/27/world/asia/south-korea-park-aides-artists-blacklist.html?_r=0.

72. See Sang-hun Choe, "American Peace Activist Is Denied Entry to South Korea," *New York Times*, July 17, 2017, https://www.nytimes.com/2017/07/17/world/asia/south-korea-north-activist-christine-ahn-women-cross-dmz.html.

73. For an incisive critique of American immigration policy (particularly the Immigration and Nationality Acts of 1952 and 1965) made through a queer and feminist lens, see Margot Canaday, *The Straight State: Sexuality and Citizenship in Twentieth-Century America* (Princeton, NJ: Princeton University Press, 2011); Siobhan B. Somerville, "Sexual Aliens and the Racialized State: A Queer Reading of the 1952 U.S. Immigration and Nationality Act," in *Queer Migrations: Sexuality, U.S. Citizenship, and Border Crossings*, ed. Eithne Luibhéid and Lionel Cantú (Minneapolis: University of Minnesota Press, 2005), 75–91.

74. See Bruce Cumings, *Korea's Place in the Sun* (New York: W. W. Norton, 1997, 2005), 455; Sonia Ryang and John Lie, eds., *Diaspora without a Homeland: Being Korean*

in Japan (Los Angeles: University of California Press, 2009); Eun Sik Yang, "Korean Revolutionary Nationalism in America: Kim Kang and the Student Circle, 1937–1956," in *The Korean Peninsula in the Changing World Order*, ed. Eui-Young Yu and Terry R. Kandal (Los Angeles: California State University, Center for Korean-American Studies and Korean Studies, 1992), 173–198. See also the declassified FBI case of Diamond Kim, House Un-American Activities Committee Testimony, housed at the University of Southern California (USC) Korean American Digital Archive, http://digitallibrary.usc.edu/cdm/compound object/collection/p15799coll126/id/976/rec/8 (accessed June 5, 2015).

75. Nak-Chung Paik, *The Division System in Crisis: Essays on Contemporary Korea*, trans. Kim Myung-hwa, Sol June-Kyu, Song Seung-cheol, and Ryu Young-joo (Berkeley: University of California Press, 2011). While it pertains to the crystallization of polemical discourse among Korean diasporic subjects *before* the Korean War, Richard S. Kim, *The Question for Statehood: Korean Immigrant Nationalism and U.S. Sovereignty, 1905–45* (New York: Oxford University Press, 2011), provides an excellent historical context that traces the trajectory of communist/capitalist polemics among Koreans long before the end of World War II in 1945.

76. In a *Chicago Tribune* article published in February 1988, Ryan describes himself as a "peacemaker" who was fired by the FBI for "refusing an order as a matter of conscience." Ryan refused to surveil nonviolent activists protesting U.S. intervention policies in Central America. John Glover, FBI executive assistant director for administration at that time, confirmed that Ryan was the first FBI agent fired in two decades for refusing to conduct an ordered investigation: see "Act of Conscience Ends Career of 'Peacemaker' FBI Agent," *Chicago Tribune*, February 1, 1988.

77. Lee, "The Korean War, Anticommunism, and the Korean American Community," 19.

78. Victor Bascara, *Model Minority Imperialism* (Minneapolis: University of Minnesota Press, 2006), xxv.

79. Ibid.

80. Lisa Yoneyama, *Hiroshima Traces: Time, Space, and the Dialectics of Memory* (Berkeley: University of California Press, 1999), 88.

81. Ann Laura Stoler, *Duress: Imperial Durabilities in Our Times* (Durham, NC: Duke University Press, 2016).

82. Ibid., 12.

83. See Wayne Miller's Magnum Photos online profile, https://pro.magnumphotos.com/C.aspx?ERID=24KL534NBZ&VF=MAGO31_10_VForm&VP3=CMS3 (accessed May 5, 2016).

84. For a demographic profile of *Life*'s readership, see Erika Doss, ed., *Looking at "Life" Magazine* (Washington, DC: Smithsonian Institution Press, 2001).

Chapter 2

Epigraphs: Ramsay Liem, remarks at "The Making(s) of Memory Archives: Korean Americans and Oral History Praxis," roundtable discussion held at the University of California, Riverside, February 18, 2015; Ursula K. Le Guin, "The Operating Instructions," in *Words Are My Matter: Writings about Life and Books, 2000–2016* (Easthampton, MA: Small Beer, 2016), 6.

1. Melia Robinson, "A Deaf Artist Explains the Rules of 'Sound Etiquette'—and Why She's Kicking Them to the Curb," *Business Insider*, October 23, 2015, http://www.businessinsider.com/deaf-artist-christine-sun-kim-2015-10.

2. Shoshanna Felman and Dori Laub, *Testimony: Crises of Witnessing in Literature, Psychoanalysis and History* (New York: Routledge, 1991); Alan Wieder, "Testimony as Oral History: Lessons from South Africa," *Educational Researcher* 33, no. 6 (August–September

2004): 23–28; Paul Thompson, with Joanna Bornat, *The Voice of the Past: Oral History*, 4th ed. (Oxford: Oxford University Press, 2017); Donald A. Ritchie, *Doing Oral History*, 3d ed. (Oxford: Oxford University Press, 2015).

3. Cathy Caruth popularized the notion of trauma as "unclaimed" or deferred: see Cathy Caruth, *Unclaimed Experience: Trauma, Narrative, and History*, 20th ed. (Baltimore: Johns Hopkins University Press, 2016).

4. Dori Laub, "Bearing Witness, or the Vicissitudes of Listening," in Felman and Laub, *Testimony*, 57.

5. Luisa Passerini, "Memories between Silence and Oblivion," in *Contested Pasts: The Politics of Memory*, ed. Katharine Hodgkin and Susannah Radstone (New York: Routledge, 2003), 248.

6. Sherna Berger Gluck, "Advocacy Oral History: Palestinian Women in Resistance," in *Women's Words: The Feminist Practice of Oral History*, ed. Sherna Berger Gluck and Daphne Patai (London: Routledge, 1991), 205–219; Passerini, "Memories between Silence and Oblivion"; Sady Sullivan, "Public Homeplaces: Collaboration and Care in Oral History Project Design," in *Beyond Women's Words: Feminisms and the Practices of Oral History in the Twenty-First Century*, ed. Katrina Srigley, Stacey Zembrzycki, and Franca Iacovetta (London: Routledge, 2018), 252–260.

7. While I have my own questions regarding the privileging of terms such as "generational" in this project (etymologically, "generational" and "generation" refer to a line of descendants or offspring connected through blood kinship), it was important to me to use the terms and language provided by Hong and Kim. Throughout our interview and correspondence it also became clear that Hong and Kim mobilized "intergenerational" and "generational" as politically constructed terms (rather than essentialized categories signifying biological kin) that identify how and when participants first migrated to the United States (or to identify whether they were born and raised in the United States). I am grateful to Andrew Leong, who encouraged me to address the usage of such terminology in this project.

8. I am grateful for Joo Ok Kim's incisive reading of this chapter and her observations on the synergies between my engagement of aural history practice among Korean/Americans and Ma Vang's rigorous reading of Hmong women's narrations of U.S. militarized intervention in Laos and Southeast Asia. See Ma Vang, "Rechronicling Histories: Toward a Hmong Feminist Perspective," in *Claiming Place: On the Agency of Hmong Women*, ed. Chia Youyee Vang, Faith Nibbs, and Ma Vang (Minneapolis: University of Minnesota Press, 2016), 30–55 (for quoted phrases, see 28–29). See also Joo Ok Kim, "Declining Misery: Rural Florida's Hmong and Korean Farmers," *South* 29, no. 1 (Fall 2016): 25–37.

9. As a key term within oral history praxis, "intersubjectivity" emphasizes that emergent narratives can crystallize only through the dynamic relationships established between interlocutors, including the interviewer and interviewee (though the participatory composition of oral history may vary). "Intersubjectivity" also refers to an underlying sense of self-reflexivity among participants regarding the uneven power relations that shape the interview process and space. See Ronald Grele, *Envelope of Sound: The Art of Oral History*, 2d ed. (New York: Praeger, 1991); Robert Perks and Alistair Thomson, eds., *The Oral History Reader*, 3d ed. (New York: Routledge, 2015); Alessandro Portelli, *The Death of Luigi Trastulli and Other Stories: Form and Meaning in Oral History* (Albany: State University of New York Press, 1990); Ruth Behar, *Translated Woman: Crossing the Border with Esperanza's Story*, 10th anniversary ed. (Boston: Beacon, 2003); Mary Marshall Clark, "The September 11, 2001, Oral History Narrative and Memory Project: A First Report," *Journal of American History* 89, no. 2 (September 2002): 569–579.

10. Rebecca Schneider, *Performing Remains: Art and War in Times of Theatrical Reenactment* (New York: Routledge, 2011).

11. Toni Morrison, *Beloved* (New York: Vintage, 2004). See also Eve Oishi, "Screen Memories: Fakeness in Asian American Media Practice," in *F Is for Phony: Fake Documentary and Truth's Undoing*, ed. Alexandra Juhasz and Jesse Lerner (Minneapolis: University of Minnesota Press, 2006), 196–219. Here Oishi explicitly tackles the notion of rememory as it relates to Asian/American experiences (and specifically Japanese American experiences) of war, militarization, and migration.

12. Diana Taylor, *The Archive and the Repertoire: Performing Cultural Memory in the Americas* (Durham, NC: Duke University Press, 2003), 20.

13. This joint interview with Sukjong Hong and Danny Kim was conducted via Skype.

14. For more information on Nodutdol, see the organizational website, http://www.nodutdol.org/ (accessed March 2, 2017).

15. As Kim and Hong noted at the tail end of our interview, this is slowly changing, given that the Intergenerational project is reaching out to potential participants who are not members of or affiliated with Nodutdol.

16. The majority of interview sessions took place at Nodutdol's spacious office in Woodside, Queens.

17. A description of Hong's freestanding installation piece "My Mother Used to Tell Me" is available on the *Still Present Pasts* website, http://idesweb.bc.edu/stillpresentpasts/my-mother. In this contribution to the traveling exhibition—a multimedia installation that integrates propaganda fliers the U.S. military dropped in hollow missiles during the Korean armed conflict—Hong draws on the oral history of Kyung-hui Lee, an elderly survivor of the armed conflict, to examine the impact of psychological warfare on Koreans.

18. In many ways, the model that the Intergenerational project developed resonates with critical participatory-action research (CPAR): see Eve Tuck, "Re-visioning Action: Participatory Action Research and Indigenous Theories of Change," *Urban Review* 41 (2009): 47–65.

19. Kim's reference to a "people's history" of the Korean War alludes to Howard Zinn's classic *A People's History of the United States: 1492–Present* (New York: Harper Perennial Modern Classics, 1980), a critical revisionist history of the United States that troubles the nationalist glorification of American history by emphasizing the country's socially, economically, and racially exploitative structural underpinnings and systems.

20. The Intergenerational project's engagement with the discursive formation of oral history methodology and praxis in the United States is important in addressing the project's reformulation of oral history. Despite the ways in which oral history is commonly romanticized as a "radical" or "alternative" historical method in the United States, its beginnings within academia, specifically, tell a very different story. (Oral history, of course, has *multiple* beginnings beyond academic scholarship.) After World War II, Allan Nevins of Columbia University introduced and incorporated oral history as an academic practice that supplemented (rather than critiqued) primary sources in institutional archives (hence, oral history reproduced or reified "dominant" historiography). However, with the emergence of New Left academics in the United States after 1960, and influenced by the "cultural turn" of literary, historical, and social analysis during the 1970s and 1980s in the United States and in the United Kingdom, critical academics reappropriated oral history as a revisionary method that could disrupt the philosophical ideal of "neutral" or "objective" historical narration. For a brief history of oral history methodology in the United States, see Ronald Grele's illuminating "Oral History as Evidence," in *History of Oral History: Foundations and Methodology*, ed. Thomas L. Charlton, Lois E. Myers, and Rebecca Sharpless (Lanham, MD: Altamira, 2007), 33–34.

21. Here my reference to the "vernacular" is in conversation with Jacques Rancière and, in particular, his reconfiguration of the "vernacular" as a radical form of political engagement with the potential of disrupting the dominant social order (or what he refers to as the "police" order). Rather than conceiving the political in relation to state policies, official parties, and the law, Rancière offers a different understanding of the political as "the organization of powers, the distribution of places and roles, and the systems for legitimizing this distribution": Jacques Rancière, *Dis-agreement: Politics and Philosophy* (Minneapolis: University of Minnesota Press, 1999), 28.

22. Fred Moten and Stefano Harney, *The Undercommons: Fugitive Planning and Black Study* (Wivenhoe, UK: Minor Compositions, 2013), 113.

23. For engaging contemplations of the profitable "industry" of cultural memory production, see Marita Sturken, *Tourists of Memory: Memory, Kitsch, and Consumerism from Oklahoma City to Ground Zero* (Durham, NC: Duke University Press, 2007); Viet Thanh Nguyen, *Nothing Ever Dies: Vietnam and the Memory of War* (Cambridge, MA: Harvard University Press, 2017).

24. Grace K. Hong and Roderick Ferguson, "Introduction," in *Strange Affinities: The Gender and Sexual Politics of Comparative Racialization*, ed. Grace K. Hong and Roderick Ferguson (Durham, NC: Duke University Press, 2011), 9.

25. Again, it is important to emphasize that the oral/aural history paradigm that the Intergenerational project developed is still very much a work in progress.

26. Hong shared these individual steps in a PowerPoint presentation during "The Making(s) of the Memory Archive: Korean/Americans and the Practice of Oral History," a roundtable discussion I organized at the University of California, Riverside, on February 18, 2015. Hong and Kim also discussed these steps during our Skype interview.

27. Michael Frisch, *Shared Authority: Essays on the Craft and Meaning of Oral and Public History* (Albany: State University of New York Press, 1990). For a more recent cluster of essays and critical recalibrations of the notion of "shared authority" within oral history praxis (especially in relation to minoritarian contexts), see Perks and Thompson, *The Oral History Reader*; Anna Sheftel and Stacey Zembrzycski, eds., *Oral History Off the Record: Toward an Ethnography of the Record* (New York: Palgrave, 2013); Nan Alamilla Boyd and Horacio N. Roque Ramírez, eds., *Bodies of Evidence: The Practice of Queer Oral History* (New York: Oxford University Press, 2012).

28. See Marit Kathryn Corneil, "Citizenship and Participatory Video," in *Handbook of Participatory Video*, ed. E. J. Milne, Claudia Mitchell, and Naydene de Lange (New York: Rowman and Littlefield, 2012), 20.

29. Elizabeth Miller, "Going Places: Helping Youth with Refugee Experiences Take Their Stories Public," in Sheftel and Zembrzycski, *Oral History Off the Record*, 115.

30. Linda Tuhiwai Smith, *Decolonizing Methodologies: Research and Indigenous Peoples*, 2d ed. (New York: Zed, 2012). I must reemphasize here that Smith's work is written for and in direct conversation with indigenous peoples in and beyond Oceania. In part, I draw on her work to critically analyze the impact of prolonged war, militarization, and multiple colonialisms (specifically, Japanese and U.S. colonialism) on Koreans and Korean diasporic subjects.

31. Hong and Ferguson, "Introduction," 9.

32. Ibid., 11.

33. I am not attempting to obscure the traumatic implications associated with narrating experiences of war, displacement, and separation. In fact, during our interview Kim and Hong described a training for Intergenerational project members (facilitated by Ramsay Liem) to address potential emotional difficulties that emerge during the interview process. Yet as participants who are not professionally trained in clinical psychology or therapy— and as members committed to framing memories in relation to historical and social forma-

tion—Kim and Hong describe the exigency of cultivating a safe space for narration and expression without relegating these interview sessions to the confined realm of therapy, at least in the traditional sense of the term. For a recent collection that discusses the key differences between oral history and therapy, see Mark Cave and Stephen M. Sloan, eds., *Listening on the Edge: Oral History in the Aftermath of Crisis* (Oxford: Oxford University Press, 2014).

34. As Hong pointed out during the interview, participants across generations have very different levels of involvement in or exposure to political and social activism in Korea and the United States.

35. Leigh Patel, *Decolonizing Educational Research: From Ownership to Answerability* (New York: Routledge, 2016), 73.

36. Nina Eidsheim's scholarship has been particularly useful in identifying the subjective, multisensorial, and phenomenological elements of listening and sonic praxis: see Nina Eidsheim, *Sensing Sound: Singing and Listening as Vibrational Practice* (Durham, NC: Duke University Press, 2015), loc. 286 (Kindle).

37. President Park Chung-hee implemented the Yushin Constitution from 1972 to 1981. Modeled after the Japanese Meiji Restoration, the constitution consolidated Park's authoritarian power, including the removal of limitations placed on reelection, more stringent anticommunist surveillance policies, suspensions of constitution freedoms, and a crackdown on the public press: see Namhee Lee, *The Making of Minjung: Democracy, and the Politics of Presentation* (Ithaca, NY: Cornell University Press, 2007); Paul Chang, *Protest Dialectics: State Repression and South Korea's Democracy Movement, 1970–1979* (Stanford, CA: Stanford University Press, 2015).

38. As the next chapter details, my reading of "emotion" and "affect" in this book are entwined. That is, although theoretical distinctions are often made between affect and emotions (affect is often described as an "intensity" or a "potentiality" that precedes social classification and linguistic categorization, while emotions are the sociolinguistically fixed names given to materialized intensities), these terms are blurred and are used interchangeably in this book. In part, I conceptualize the emotional as an always already shifting and unstable formation that fluctuates between the unarticulated and the defined. For an elaboration of the blurry edge between emotion and effect, see Sianne Ngai, *Ugly Feelings* (Cambridge, MA: Harvard University Press, 2007).

39. For a discussion of the meanings of "cultural memory," see Marita Sturken, *Tangled Memories: The Vietnam War, the AIDS Epidemic, and the Politics of Remembering* (Berkeley: University of California Press, 1997); Macarena Gómez-Barris, *Where Memory Dwells: Culture and State Violence in Chile* (Berkeley: University of California Press, 2008).

40. Ann Cvetkovich, *An Archive of Feelings: Trauma, Sexuality, and Lesbian Public Cultures* (Durham, NC: Duke University Press, 2003), 18.

41. Michel Foucault, *The History of Sexuality, Volume 1: An Introduction*, reissue ed. (New York: Vintage, 1990), 27.

42. Passerini, "Memories between Silence and Oblivion," 249.

43. Hong shared this point during her presentation at the February 18, 2015, oral history roundtable discussion held at the University of California, Riverside.

44. As the next section of this chapter discusses, all narrators within the Intergenerational project remain nameless out of concern for project participants' safety and confidentiality.

45. Passerini, "Memories between Silence and Oblivion," 248.

46. Ann Laura Stoler, *Along the Archival Grain: Epistemic Anxieties and Colonial Common Sense* (Princeton, NJ: Princeton University Press, 2009), 20.

47. While the "open" movement has very different meanings across various disciplines and fields of study (e.g., media studies, education, archival studies), my concerns and

questions about "open" access (as it aligns with neoliberal notions of privatization, ownership, and market logics) draw primarily from and address oral history and archival studies scholarship. Particularly among scholars and archivists who work closely with indigenous peoples, there is an established body of literature concerning "public access" to indigenous lives and experiences. See Michelle Caswell, Ricardo Punzalan, and T-Kay Sangwand, "Critical Archives Studies: An Introduction," *Journal of Critical Library and Information Studies* 1, no. 2 (2017); 1–8; Kimberly Christen, "Opening Archives: Respectful Repatriation," *American Archivist* 74 (Spring–Summer 2011): 185–210; David Kim and Jacqueline Wernimont, "'Performing Archive': Identity, Participation and Responsibility in the Ethnic Archive," *Archive Journal* (April 2014); Wendy Rickard Nikita, Sarah Evans, Saskia Reeves, and Gail Cameron, "What Are Sex Worker Stories Good For? User Engagement with Archived Data," *Oral History* 39, no. 1 (Spring 2011): 91–103.

48. After my initial Skype interview with Hong and Kim on June 27, 2016, our correspondence continued until February 2018. I also organized a series of oral history events related to the Korean War and memory collection, archival processes, and the problematics of "open" access. These events include the roundtable discussion "The Making(s) of Memory Archives: Korean/Americans and Oral History Praxis," University of California, Riverside, February 18, 2015, and the roundtable panel "Beyond Survival, toward Resistance and Alliance-Building: The Making of Intergenerational Queer and Trans of Color Activist Archives" Association for Asian American Studies Annual Meeting, San Francisco, March 30, 2018.

49. Audra Simpson, "On Ethnographic Refusal: Indigeneity, 'Voice' and Colonial Citizenship," *Junctures* 9 (December 2007): 78.

50. Ibid.

51. Most recently, the Intergenerational project shared enacted segments from aural histories through the multimedia performance *Trauma of War and Division: A Multimedia Look at the Korean Experience*, Queens Library, Woodside, November 18, 2017.

52. Schneider, *Performing Remains*.

53. Ibid., 6.

54. Ibid. As emphasized in the Introduction and Chapter 1, the reference to "homogeneous, empty" time relates to the critique of historicity and historicism in Walter Benjamin, "Theses on the Philosophy of History," in *Illuminations: Essays and Reflections*, ed. Hannah Arendt, trans. Harry Zohn, (New York: Schocken, 1968), 253–264.

55. Charles Armstrong, "The Destruction and Reconstruction of North Korea, 1950–1960," *Asia-Pacific Journal* 7 (March 2009): 1–9.

56. Vinh Nguyen, "Refugeography in 'Post-Racial' America: Bao Phi's Activist Poetry," *MELUS* 41, no. 3 (Fall 2016): 175.

57. The Korean *buk* resembles a low-pitched barrel drum.

58. Eidsheim, *Sensing Sound*.

59. Lisa Yoneyama, *Hiroshima Traces: Time, Space, and the Dialectics of Memory* (Berkeley: University of California Press, 1999), 91.

60. Grele, *Envelopes of Sound*, 75.

61. Taylor, *The Archive and the Repertoire*, 20.

62. Ibid.

63. Ibid.

64. Rebecca Schneider, "Performance Remains," in *Perform, Repeat, Record*, ed. Amelia Jones and Adrian Heathfield (Chicago: University of Chicago Press, 2012), 143.

65. Ann Laura Stoler, *Duress: Imperial Durabilities in Our Times* (Durham, NC: Duke University Press, 2016), 205.

Chapter 3

Epigraph: Nadine Attewell and S. Trimble, "Introduction," *Topia* 35 (Spring 2016): 9.

1. *Twinsters*, codirected by Samantha Futerman and Ryan Miyamoto, is a documentary produced by Netflix in 2015.

2. Samantha Futerman, quoted in Anaïs Bordier and Samantha Futerman, *Separated @ Birth: A True Love Story of Twin Sisters Reunited* (New York: Penguin Random House, 2014).

3. Kim Park Nelson, *Invisible Asians: Korean American Adoptees, Asian American Experiences and Racial Exceptionalism* (New Brunswick, NJ: Rutgers University Press, 2016); Catherine Ceniza Choy, *Global Families: A History of Asian International Adoption in America* (New York: New York University Press, 2013). For a broader context of Cold War Orientalism and paternalistic sentiments of "othering" that characterized Asian children (and especially Korean orphan-cum-adoptees) as desired objects that needed to be saved and rescued by Americans, see Christina Klein, *Cold War Orientalism: Asia in the Middlebrow Imagination, 1945–1961* (Berkeley: University of California Press, 2003); Susie Woo, "Imagining Kin: Cold War Sentimentalism and the Korean Children's Choir," *American Quarterly* 67, no. 1 (March 2015): 25–53.

4. Eleana J. Kim, *Adopted Territory: Transnational Korean Adoptees and the Politics of Belonging* (Durham, NC: Duke University Press, 2010), 21, 25. Official statistics are from the South Korean Ministry for Health, Welfare and Family Affairs (MIHWAF), 2009.

5. For details on the Overseas Korean Act (OKA) as it applies to transnational adoptees, see Eleana J. Kim, "Human Capital: Transnational Korean Adoptees and the Neoliberal Logic of Return," *Journal of Korean Studies* 17, no. 2 (2012): 299–327. For a more general critique of the OKA, see Jung-Sun Park and Paul Y. Chang, "Contention in the Construction of a Global Korean Community: The Case of the Overseas Korean Act," *Journal of Korean Studies* 10, no. 1 (Fall 20015): 1–27. As Park and Chang argue convincingly, the OKA is selective in that it defines only select groups of Korean diasporans as quasi-citizens of the South Korean nation-state, while others remain, legally, outsiders. In that sense, the OKA presents several perplexing questions about who, exactly, counts as a proper Korean in relation to perceived ethnic "qualities" and national identities.

6. Kim, "Human Capital," 305–306. Here Kim directly quotes Michel Feher, "Self-Appreciation: or The Aspirations of Human Capital," *Public Culture* 21, no. 1 (2009): 21–41.

7. Kim, "Human Capital," 306.

8. Ibid.

9. Here I refer to the scholarly work and writing of J. K. Gibson-Graham (the pen name of Katherine Gibson and Julie Graham), which emphasize that the discourse of neoliberal capitalism is overdetermined. In their co-written work, Gibson and Graham argue that there are always noncapitalist practices, as well as rupture points and refusals, that exist alongside, within, and against the dominant politics/policies of capitalism: see J. K. Gibson-Graham, *The End of Capitalism (as We Knew It): A Feminist Critique of Political Economy* (Cambridge: Blackwell, 1996); J. K. Gibson-Graham, *A Postcapitalist Politics* (Minneapolis: University of Minnesota Press, 2006).

10. While I explicitly focus on the work of Jane Jin Kaisen and kate-hers RHEE in this chapter, I also consulted with other key scholars and cultural producers for research purposes. Other interlocutors include Kim Stoker (interviewed in 2013 in Seoul), who provided a nuanced analysis of Korean transnational adoption and cultural production in South Korea since the early 1990s. Anna J. H. Borstam and Trine Mee Sook (interviewed in 2014 in Malmö and Copenhagen, respectively) also provided important social context for a better understanding of the political trajectory of transnational adoption in Scandinavia.

Finally, Tone Olaf Nielsen (interviewed in 2014 in Copenhagen) articulated the problematics of "multiculturalism" in Denmark and the crucial role that artists of color (including adoptee, refugee, and migrant artists) have played in foregrounding the blatant contradictions embedded in the Danish discourse of "racelessness" and "human rights."

11. Tobias Hübinette, "The Orphaned Nation: Korea Imagined as an Overseas Adopted Child in Clon's *Abandoned Child* and Park Kwang-su's *Berlin Report*," *Inter-Asia Cultural Studies* 6, no. 2 (2005): 227–244; Eleana J. Kim, *Adopted Territory: Transnational Korean Adoptees and the Politics of Belonging* (Durham, NC: Duke University Press, 2010); Nelson, *Invisible Asians*; SooJin Pate, *From Orphan to Adoptee: U.S. Empire and Genealogies of Korean Adoption* (Minneapolis: University of Minnesota Press, 2014). See also Jennifer Kwon Dobbs, "Ending South Korea's Child Export Shame," *Foreign Policy in Focus*, June 23, 2011, http://fpif.org/ending_south_koreas_child_export_shame (accessed December 29, 2015).

12. Kim, *Adopted Territory*, 60–61.

13. Hosu Kim, *Birth Mothers and Transnational Adoption Practice in South Korea* (New York: Palgrave Macmillan, 2016), 36. See also Byung Hoon Chun, "Adoption and Korea," *Child Welfare* 68 no. 2 (1989): 255–260; Kim, *Adopted Territory*.

14. Dobbs, "Ending South Korea's Child Export Shame."

15. Arissa Oh, "A New Kind of Missionary Work: Christians, Christian Americanists, and the Adoption of Korean GI Babies, 1955–1961," *Women Studies Quarterly* 33, nos. 3–4 (Fall 2015): 161–188.

16. Jane Jin Kaisen, "Translator's Notes," unpublished essay, 2016, 4. This essay is part of Kaisen's working dissertation in the Department of Art and Cultural Studies at the Royal Danish Academy of Fine Arts/University of Copenhagen.

17. The notion of "visual iconography" in relationship to orphan-cum-adoptees is a concept that Laura Briggs first developed in "Mother, Child, Race, Nation: The Visual Iconography of Rescue and the Politics of Transnational and Transracial Adoption," *Gender and History* 15 (2003): 179–200.

18. *Collection of Resources and Scrapbook of GOAL* (Seoul: Global Overseas Adoptees' Link, 2003), 76; Tobias Hübinette, "Asian Bodies Out of Control," in *Asian Diasporas: New Formations, New Conceptions*, ed. Rhacel S. Parreñas and Lok C. D. Siu (Stanford, CA: Stanford University Press, 2007), 180–181; Kim, *Adopted Territory*, 216–217; Steve Haruch, "In Korea, Adoptees Fight to Change Culture That Sent Them Overseas," *Code Switch: Frontiers of Race, Culture, and Ethnicity*, National Public Radio, September 10, 2014, http://www.npr.org/sections/codeswitch/2014/09/09/346851939/in-korea-adoptees-fight-to-change-culture-that-sent-them-overseas (accessed December 15, 2015).

19. In part, the emergence of vocal critiques of Korean transnational adoption was supported by South Korea's gradual transition to procedural democratic rule in the 1980s: see Kim, *Adopted Territory*.

20. Maggie Jones, "Why a Generation of Adoptees Is Returning to South Korea," *New York Times Magazine*, January 14, 2015, https://www.nytimes.com/2015/01/18/magazine/why-a-generation-of-adoptees-is-returning-to-south-korea.html (accessed February 15, 2015).

21. Kim, *Adopted Territory*, 217.

22. Ibid.

23. Advocacy groups include, for example, Global Overseas Adoptees' Link and Truth and Reconciliation for the Adoption Community of Korea. Since August 2012, birth mothers must receive counseling and wait seven days before placing their child(ren) for adoption; all adoptions are also registered through South Korean federal courts, which provide a means for adoptees to access their birth histories if they later so desire: see Jones, "Why a Generation of Adoptees Is Returning to South Korea."

24. Kim, *Adopted Territory*; Pate, *From Orphan to Adoptee*.

25. For a historical contextualization of the first decade of transnational adoption activism and cultural production during the 1990s and early 2000s, see Kim Stoker, "Beyond Identity: Activism in Korean Adoptee Art," *Duksung Women's University Journal* 34 (2005): 223–248. More recent cultural works by adoptees include Sun Yung Shin, *Unbearable Splendor* (Minneapolis: Coffee House, 2016); Patty Yumi Cottrell, *Sorry to Disrupt the Peace: A Novel* (San Francisco: McSweeney's, 2017); Julayne Lee, *Not My White Savior: A Memoir in Poems* (Los Angeles: Rare Bird, 2018).

26. Pate, *From Orphan to Adoptee*, 9.

27. As offered on RHEE's website, "Despite being in solidarity with the many adoption rights movements and activists worldwide, she does not identify with the word, Adoptee, and rather recognizes her abandonment and subsequent adoption as a past act that was done to her, but ceases to define her": http://www.estherka.com/works/missing-persons-project (accessed March 8, 2015). I am grateful for astute commentary offered by the activist and curator Kim Stoker, who during a conversation in Seoul in July 2013 identified the crucial overlaps *and* differences underpinning the aesthetic oeuvres of Korean transnational adoptees throughout much of the 1990s and early 2000s.

28. For more general critiques of transnational adoption as a global phenomenon and practice beyond South Korea, see Sara K. Dorow, *Transnational Adoption: A Cultural Economy of Race, Gender and Kinship* (New York: New York University Press, 2006); Laura Briggs, *Somebody's Children: The Politics of Transracial and Transnational Adoption* (Durham, NC: Duke University Press, 2012).

29. See kate-hers RHEE's *Sex Education for Finding Face in the 21st Century* and her experimental video short, which are posted on her personal website, http://www.estherka.com/currentprojects/sex-education-for-finding-face-in-the-21st-century (accessed March 12, 2015).

30. kate-hers RHEE, "Artist Statement," http://www.estherka.com/artistinfo/statement (accessed March 12, 2015).

31. For conceptualizations of affect in relation to public space, see Sara Ahmed, "Affective Economies," *Social Text* 79, no. 2 (Summer 2004): 117–139; José Esteban Muñoz, "Feeling Brown, Feeling Down: Latina Affect, the Performativity of Race, and the Depressive Position," *Signs* 31, no. 3 (Spring 2006): 675–688; Sianne Ngai, *Ugly Feelings* (Cambridge, MA: Harvard University Press, 2007).

32. Muñoz, "Feeling Brown, Feeling Down," 682.

33. Ibid., 677.

34. For a critical and conceptual reading of affective dynamisms as they relate to artistic practice, see Jill Bennett, *Empathic Vision: Affect, Trauma, and Contemporary Art* (Stanford, CA: Stanford University Press, 2005).

35. RHEE, "Artist Statement."

36. The remixed video of RHEE's performance is available at her personal website, http://www.estherka.com/works/sex-education-for-finding-face-in-the-21st-century (accessed March 12, 2015). For this chapter, I focus on the documentation of the live performance, rather than the remixed experimental short, of *Sex Education* (note that I was not present at the live performance).

37. kate-hers RHEE, interview by the author, Seoul, July 30, 2016.

38. Christopher Bedford, "The Viral Ontology of Performance," in *Perform, Repeat, Record*, ed. Amelia Jones and Adrian Heathfield (Chicago: University of Chicago Press, 2012), 78.

39. For an example of U.S. and South Korean media portrayals of adoptee deportees, see Choe Sang-hun, "Deportation a 'Death Sentence' to Adoptees after a Lifetime

in the U.S.," *New York Times*, July 2, 2017, https://www.nytimes.com/2017/07/02/world/asia/south-korea-adoptions-phillip-clay-adam-crapser.html?_r=0; Jeff Gammage, "Adopted from Korea as a Child, Deported as an Adult—Philly Man Takes His Life," *Philadelphia Inquirer*, June 4, 2017, http://www.philly.com/philly/news/pennsylvania/philadelphia/adopted-from-korea-as-a-child-deported-as-an-adult-philly-man-takes-his-life-20170602.html.

40. Jennifer Doyle, *Hold It against Me: Difficulty and Emotion in Contemporary Art* (Durham, NC: Duke University Press, 2012), loc. 562 (Kindle).

41. Ibid.

42. RHEE interview.

43. In April 2019, the South Korean Constitutional Court struck down the country's laws prohibiting abortion, a critical decision that reversed the sixty-six-year ban on abortion. Previously, if a woman chose to undergo an abortion, the potential costs (if she was "caught") were substantial, with emphasis placed on surveilling and punishing women's bodies. Women were threatened with a prison sentence of up to one year and fined the equivalent of $2,000: see Jane Kang, "To Abort or Not to Abort: That Is the Question in South Korea," *Voices in Bioethics*, October 14, 2013, http://voicesinbioethics.org/2013/10/14/abortion-south-korea. That said, note that South Korea certainly is not the only liberal democracy to impose restrictive and gendered measures. Within the past decade, the United States, too, has doubled down on and enforced antiabortion measures, particularly in the South.

44. Seungsook Moon, *Militarized Modernity and Gendered Citizenship in South Korea* (Durham, NC: Duke University Press, 2005).

45. Chung-in Moon and Byung-joon Jun, "Modernization Strategy: Ideas and Influences," in *The Park Chung Hee Era: The Transformation of South Korea*, ed. Byung-Kook Kim and Ezra F. Vogel (Cambridge, MA: Harvard University Press, 2011), 116; Moon, *Militarized Modernity and Gendered Citizenship in South Korea*.

46. Jin-Kyung Lee, *Service Economies: Militarism, Sex Work, and Migrant Labor in South Korea* (Minneapolis: University of Minnesota Press, 2010).

47. Choe Sang-huh, "South Korea Confronts Open Secret of Abortion," *New York Times*, January 5, 2010, http://www.nytimes.com/2010/01/06/world/asia/06korea.html.

48. Kim, *Adopted Territory*, 25. According to Kim, the original source of the data is the South Korean Ministry for Health, Welfare, and Family Affairs, 2009.

49. By 1980, the state had identified 40 percent of workers in Seoul's manufacturing sector as girls and women, with 72 percent of this population between age eighteen and twenty. In light industries such as textiles, clothing, food, and electronics assembly, approximately 77 percent of workers were women younger than twenty: see Min-Jung Kim, "Moments of Danger in the (Dis)continuous Relation of Korean Nationalism and Korean American Nationalism," *positions: asia critique* 5, no. 2 (Fall 1997): 362. See also Moon, *Militarized Modernity and Gendered Citizenship in South Korea*, loc. 1381.

50. Dobbs, "Ending South Korea's Child Export Shame."

51. Roderick Ferguson, *Aberrations in Black: Toward a Queer of Color Critique* (Minneapolis: University of Minnesota Press, 2004); Lee, *Service Economies*. See also Michael McIntyre, "Race, Surplus, Population, and the Marxist Theory of Imperialism," *Antipode* 43, no. 5 (2011): 1489–1515, esp. 1490.

52. Ferguson, *Aberrations in Black*, 15 (here Ferguson quotes Karl Marx).

53. As Kim argues in "Human Capital," adoptees who remain in South Korea for longer periods are questioned about their motivations (given the South Korean public's assumptions about Western privileges and cultural capital).

54. Note that *The Woman, the Orphan, and the Tiger* is co-directed by Jane Jin Kaisen and the visual artist and filmmaker Guston Sondin-Kung.

55. Literature on the relationship between the index and the documentary film is plentiful. For key works, see Erik Barnouw, *Documentary: A History of Nonfiction Film*, 2d ed. (New York: Oxford University Press, 1993); Brian Winston, *Claiming the Real Documentary: Grierson and Beyond* (London: British Film Institute 2008); Bill Nichols, *Introduction to Documentary*, 2d ed. (Bloomington: Indiana University Press, 2010). For important works that critique the documentary genre in relationship to its colonial ethnographic origins, see Trinh T. Minh-ha, "Documentary Is/Not a Name," *October* (Spring 1990): 76–98; Fatimah Tobing-Rony, *The Third Eye: Race, Cinema, and Ethnographic Spectacle* (Durham, NC: Duke University Press, 1996).

56. As captured in Deann Borshay Liem's autobiographical films *First Person Plural* (2000) and *In the Matter of Cha Jung Hee* (2010), unexpected circumstances, such as the missing status of identity documents and birth families reclaiming children before their adoption led orphanage employees to intermittently switch the paper identities of Korean children.

57. Kaisen, "Translator's Notes."

58. Ibid.

59. For discourses concerning racial formation in Western Europe, see Fatima El-Tayeb, *European Others: Queering Ethnicity in Postnational Europe* (Minneapolis: University of Minnesota Press, 2011); Kristin Loftsdóttir and Lars Jensen, eds., *Whiteness and Postcolonialism in the Nordic Region: Exceptionalism, Migrant Others and National Identities* (New York: Routledge, 2012); Jin Haritaworn, *Queer Lovers and Hateful Others: Regenerating Violent Times and Places* (Chicago: University of Chicago Press, 2015).

60. Regarding Kaisen's experiences in Demark and her insightful interpretations of racial assimilation in Scandinavia, see Laura Kina, "Crossfading the Gendered History of Militarism in Korea: An Interview with Jane Jin Kaisen," in *War Baby/Love Child: Mixed Race Asian American Art*, ed. Laura Kina and Wei Ming Dariotis (Seattle: University of Washington Press, 2013), 87. I am also grateful to Trine Mee Sook Gleerup (in Copenhagen) and Anna Jin Hwa Borstam (in Malmö), both of whom I was able to speak with during a research trip to Denmark and Sweden in November 2014. During my conversations with Gleerup and Borstam, both artists commented on the conflicting histories of migration policy, refugee policy, and transnational adoption in Denmark and Sweden.

61. Kaisen, "Translator's Notes."

62. Today, the nine thousand Korean adoptees residing in Denmark constitute more than 40 percent of all transnational adoptees in the country.

63. Within the limited body of critical literature on transnational adoption in Danish and English, see Tobias Hübinette, "Korean Adoption History," in *Community 2004: Guide to Korea for Overseas Adopted Koreans*, ed. Eleana J. Kim (Seoul: Overseas Foundation, 2004); Sigalit Ben-Zion, *Constructing Transnational and Transracial Identity: Adoption and Belonging in Sweden, Norway, and Denmark* (New York: Palgrave Macmillan, 2014); Youngeun Koo, "The Politics of Belonging: Transnational Korean Adoptees in Denmark," *Compas Forum*, October 27, 2015, https://www.compas.ox.ac.uk/2015/politics-belonging-transnational-korean-adoptees-denmark, http://www.huffingtonpost.kr/soyoun-park/korean-adoptee-story_b_7908510.html.

64. Koo, "The Politics of Belonging."

65. While several scholars refer to the practice of juxtaposition for critical analysis, I am explicitly referencing the conceptualization of "critical juxtaposition" as a methodological approach in Yen Le Espiritu's *Body Counts: The Vietnam War and Militarized Refugees* (Oakland: University of California Press, 2014), 21. There Espiritu refers to an assemblage of seemingly different objects, subjectivities, and phenomena interlinked through the project of U.S. militarized imperialism and the making of the legible refugee figure.

66. For critiques of the 1965 ROK-Japanese Normalization Treaty as it relates to Korean "comfort women," see Chungmoo Choi, "The Discourse of Decolonization and Popular

Memory: South Korea," *positions: asia critique* 1, no. 1 (Spring 1993): 77–102; Lisa Yoneyama, *Cold War Ruins: Transpacific Critique of American Justice and Japanese War Crimes* (Durham, NC: Duke University Press, 2016).

67. Lee, *Service Economies*, loc. 167. Also see Cheng, *On the Move for Love*.

68. Kaisen, "Translator's Notes."

69. Jane Jin Kaisen, *Dissident Translations Catalogue* (Åarhus: Kunsthal Åarhus, 2011), 54. Here, Kaisen cites from a description provided by the War Memorial staff.

70. Audre Lorde, "The Uses of Anger," *Women Studies Quarterly* 25, nos. 1–2 (Spring–Summer 1997): 280, 282.

71. Ibid., 280.

72. For a critical engagement with the notion of disidentification within performance studies, see José Esteban Muñoz, *Disidentifications: Queers of Color and the Performance of Politics* (Minneapolis: University of Minnesota Press, 1999).

Chapter 4

Epigraph: Seong-nae Kim, "The Work of Memory: Ritual Laments of the Dead and Korea's Jeju Massacre," in *A Companion to the Anthropology of Religion*, ed. Janice Boddy and Michael Lambek (Oxford: John Wiley and Sons, 2013), 236.

1. See the United Nations World Heritage entry for "Jeju Volcanic Island and Lava Tubes," http://whc.unesco.org/en/list/1264, and "Introduction to Jeju," Imagine Your Korea: Visit Korea website, https://english.visitkorea.or.kr:1001/enu/SI/SI_EN_3_6.jsp?cid=256109.

2. See Heonik Kwon, *The Other Cold War* (New York: Columbia University Press, 2010); Dong-choon Kim, *The Unending Korean War: A Social History*, trans. Kim Sung-Ok (Larkspur, CA: Tamal Vista, 2009).

3. Kim, *The Unending Korean War*.

4. Sang-hun Choe, "Island's Naval Base Stirs Opposition in South Korea," *New York Times*, August 18, 2011, http://www.nytimes.com/2011/08/19/world/asia/19base.html.

5. Originally published (in German) as Sigmund Freud, "Trauer und Melancholie," *Internationale Zeitschrift für Ärztliche Psychoanalyse* 4, no. 6 (1917): 288–301; republished in English as "Mourning and Melancholia," in *The Standard Edition of the Complete Psychological Works of Sigmund Freud*, trans. James Strachey, vol. 14 (London: Hogarth, 1955), 243–258.

6. Here Anne Anlin Cheng's study of the melancholic dynamisms of racial formation in the United States is a particularly compelling examination of the relationship between prolonged violence and the melancholic: see Anne Anlin Cheng, *The Melancholy of Race: Psychoanalysis, Assimilation, and Hidden Grief* (Oxford: Oxford University Press, 2001).

7. Jane Jin Kaisen's *Reiterations of Dissent* includes two different versions: a five-screen installation first showcased in 2011 and an eight-screen installation showcased in 2016. In this chapter, I engage the 2016 version of the work. In addition, while I focus on Kaisen's and Lee's works in this chapter, I should emphasize that several other Korean and Korean diasporic cultural producers and curators provided insights critical to my research and writing process. For instance, Cho Sunjung, Choi Chang Hyun, and Choi Hwajung (affiliated with the *REAL DMZ Project* and Art Sonje in Seoul) discussed the significant public role played by Korean and Korean diasporic cultural producers in South Korea who examine in their oeuvres controversial issues such as military sex labor, transnational adoption, and civilian atrocities that the ROK government committed. I am immensely grateful for their tremendous efforts and support of Cho, Choi, and Choi, who also organized a personalized tour of the Civilian Control Zone (CCZ) for me during the summer of 2016. While I do not take up Minouk Lim's cultural work in this book (although I discuss her oeuvre elsewhere), my conversations with

her via e-mail and in person (in an August 2016 interview) allowed me to identify the historical struggles (e.g., government surveillance, funding resources, and political alliances) faced by artists in South Korea who address the ROK's contested history of military dictatorship.

8. See Henri Bergson, *Duration and Simultaneity*, trans. Leon Jacobson (Manchester, UK: Clinamen, 1999), and Gilles Deleuze's engagement with Bergsonian concepts of temporality in *Cinema I: The Movement-Image*, trans. Hugh Tomlinson and Barbara Habberjam (Minneapolis: University of Minnesota Press, 1986).

9. Bergson, *Duration and Simultaneity*.

10. Bliss Cua Lim, *Translating Time: Cinema, the Fantastic, and Temporal Critique* (Durham, NC: Duke University Press, 2009), 11.

11. I draw on the definition of remediation that Jay Bolter and Richard Grusin provide in *Remediation: Understanding New Media* (Cambridge, MA: MIT Press, 1998). Remediation, in this chapter, refers to the incorporation or folding in of older media (i.e., archival footage) by a newer medium (i.e., digital film) to produce a distinct media object (i.e., the multichannel installation).

12. Judith Butler, *Notes toward a Performative Theory of Assembly* (Cambridge, MA: Harvard University Press, 2015), 23.

13. The Gangjeong Naval Complex was officially opened on February 26, 2016. For a detailed timeline and information about the construction of the naval complex, see the Save Jeju Now Campaign website, http://savejejunow.org/ (accessed April 25, 2017).

14. For a description of the Northwest League, a paramilitary group primarily composed of anticommunist refugees from North Korea, see Bruce Cumings, *The Korean War: A History* (New York: Random House, 2010), 101–147.

15. I am grateful for my conversations with Jane Jin Kaisen, which have continued via conversations in person and by phone since 2014. As discussed in several works in progress she shared with me, Kaisen emphasizes that "translating others" is a term that is always mobile and always shifting: Jane Jin Kaisen, "Translator's Notes" (unfiled Ph.D. dissertation, University of Copenhagen), 2–3, in my possession. See also Kaisen's description of "dissident translations" in "A Conversation between Cecilia Widenheim and Jane Jin Kaisen," in *Dissident Translations*, exhibition catalogue, Åarhus Kunstbygning, Åarhus, Denmark, 2011, 8.

16. Barack Obama, "Remarks by President Obama at Hankuk University," Seoul, March 26, 2012, White House Office of the Press Secretary, https://obamawhitehouse.archives.gov/the-press-office/2012/03/26/remarks-president-obama-hankuk-university.

17. Kaisen, "Translator's Notes," 2.

18. Ibid., 1.

19. The first two quotations in this sentence refer to Kaisen's practice of "translating otherwise" (Kaisen, "Translator's Notes"). The second two quotations refer to Kaisen's direct descriptions as she addresses the meaning(s) of dissident translations in "A Conversation between Cecilia Widenheim and Jane Jin Kaisen," 8.

20. Kaisen, "Translator's Notes."

21. Michael Rush, *Video Art* (London: Thames and Hudson, 2003), 11.

22. For an extended conversation about the role of film in relationship to (neo)colonial historiography and narrative construction, see Priya Jaikumar, "An 'Accurate Imagination': Place, Map and Archive as Spatial Objects of Film History," in *Empire and Film*, ed. Lee Grieveson and Colin MacCade (New York: Palgrave Macmillan, 2011), 182.

23. Marita Sturken, "Absent Images of Memory: Remembering and Reenacting the Japanese Internment," in *Perilous Memories: The Asia-Pacific War(s)*, ed. Lisa Yoneyama, Takashi Fujitani, and Geoffrey M. White (Durham, NC: Duke University Press, 2001), 39.

24. Choe, "Island's Naval Base Stirs Opposition in South Korea." For a deeper analysis of the connections between tourism and militarization, see Vernadette Vicuña Gonzalez, *Securing Paradise: Tourism and Militarism in Hawai'i and the Philippines* (Durham, NC: Duke University Press, 2013).

25. Sara Ahmed, *Queer Phenomenology: Orientations, Objects, Others* (Durham, NC: Duke University Press, 2006).

26. Seong-nae Kim, "Mourning Korean Modernity in the Memory of the Jeju April Third Incident," in *The Inter-cultural Studies Reader*, ed. Kuan-Hsing Chen and Chua Beng Huat (New York: Routledge, 2007), 199.

27. Ibid.

28. For an illuminating discussion of the performance of critical memories and "other" knowledges in relationship to the Asia-Pacific War(s), see Lisa Yoneyama, *Hiroshima Traces: Time, Space, and the Dialectics of Memory* (Berkeley: University of California Press, 1999), 115.

29. See Kwon, *The Other Cold War*, 105.

30. Kim, "Mourning Korean Modernity in the Memory of the Jeju April Third Incident," 194; Kwon, *The Other Cold War*, 103–105.

31. Kim, "Mourning Korean Modernity in the Memory of the Jeju April Third Incident," 194.

32. For a more nuanced and detailed reading of the heterotopic, see Michel Foucault, "Of Other Spaces," *Diacritics* 16 (Spring 1986): 22–27.

33. For a detailed account of the post-1990 investigations of the Jeju massacres, see Hunjoon Kim, "Seeking Truth after 50 Years: The National Committee for Investigation of the Truth about the Jeju 4.3 Events," *International Journal of Transitional Justice* 3 (2009): 406–423.

34. "Blood History Buried under Jeju International Airport," *Jeju Weekly*, March 26, 2011, http://www.jejuweekly.com/news/articleView.html?idxno=1383.

35. For a contextualization of debates about the inception of the 4.3 Massacre, see Kim, "Seeking Truth after 50 Years," 410.

36. During the most ferocious period of fighting, between 1948 and 1949, the U.S. military monitored the situation, interpreting the violent measures as necessary for containing communism in the "red island." In a message wired to Washington on May 13, 1949, the U.S. ambassador to South Korea noted that Jeju communist sympathizers and rebels had been successfully killed, captured, or converted: see Chalmers Johnson, *Blowback: The Costs and Consequences of American Empire* (New York: Owl Books, 2000), 100–101.

37. According to Christine Ahn, because the villagers were given short notice about the April 24, 2007, town hall meeting, only approximately 10 percent of the village population was present. Although the former village chief, Yoon Tae Jun, promised to hold another village committee meeting, no such meeting ever materialized: see Christine Ahn, "Naval Base Tears Apart Korean Village," *Foreign Policy in Focus*, April 19, 2011, http://fpif.org/naval_base_tears_apart_korean_village.

38. Ibid.

39. Sasha Davis, "The U.S. Military Base Network and Contemporary Colonialism: Power Projection, Resistance and the Quest for Operational Unilateralism," *Political Geography* 30 (2011): 215–224.

40. The United States maintained peacetime control in South Korea until 1994, when South Korea officially transitioned from a military dictatorship to civilian control. At this writing, the South Korean government will receive wartime command of the Korean military in 2020.

41. See Choe, "Island's Naval Base Stirs Opposition in South Korea."
42. Anders Riel Müller provides astute commentary on the "geopolitical curse" of South Korea: see Anders Riel Müller, "One Island Village's Struggle for Land, Life, and Peace," Korean Policy Institute, April 19, 2011, http://www.kpolicy.org/documents/inter views-opeds/110419andersmulleroneislandvillagesstruggle.html.
43. Hilary Rodham Clinton, "America's Pacific Century," *Foreign Policy*, November 2011, http://www.foreignpolicy.com/articles/2011/10/11/americas_pacific_century.
44. For instance, the International Women's Network against Militarism, which includes scholars and activists from Japan, Okinawa, the Philippines, the Marshall Islands, Guam, Hawai'i, Puerto Rico, Australia, and the U.S. West Coast, has expressed solidarity with the people of Jeju Island in an open letter from September 11, 2011. See http://www.genuinesecu rity.org/actions/lettertojeju.html. The Okinawan Women Act against Military Violence and the Committee against Heliport Construction have also expressed solidarity with and active support for the people of Jeju Island: see "Event Reports and Photos—East Asia," Global Day of Action on Military Spending, April 17, 2013, http://demilitarize.org/2012-reports-east-asia. For broader analysis of the intersecting histories among Pacific Islanders and Asian/Americans, see Setsu Shigematsu and Keith Camacho, eds., *Militarized Currents: Toward a Decolonized Future in Asia and the Pacific* (Minneapolis: University of Minneapolis Press, 2010); Davis, "The U.S. Military Base Network and Contemporary Colonialism."
45. See Sasha Davis, "Repeating Islands of Resistance," *Human Geography* 5, no. 1 (2012): 1–18.
46. See Jennifer Hyndman, "Mind the Gap: Bridging Feminist and Political Geography through Geopolitics," *Political Geography* 23 (2004): 307–322. It is also important to note that these outlined principles are part of a statement the Women for Genuine Security offered in 2011: see Davis, "Repeating Islands of Resistance," 4–5.
47. Mayor Kang Dong-kyun delivered his talk on June 1, 2013, in Berkeley, California. For the complete address, see http://www.youtube.com/watch?v=_CW4ZFA4hss.
48. These critical points are also encapsulated in the International Women's Network against Militarism's redefinition of security. For a specific definition, see the organization's website, http://iwnam.org.
49. Macarena Gómez-Barris, "Reinscribing Memory through the Other 9/11," in *Toward a Sociology of the Trace*, ed. Herman Grey and Macarena Gómez-Barris (Minneapolis: University of Minnesota, 2010), 235–256. In the chapter, Gómez-Barris explicitly engages Tzvetan Todorov's concept of *exemplary* memory.
50. David Scott, *Conscripts of Modernity: The Tragedy of Colonial Enlightenment* (Durham, NC: Duke University Press, 2004), 21.
51. Dohee Lee, interview by the author, September 22, 2015, San Francisco.
52. For an English text on the significance of the mythic figure of the goddess Mago, see Helen Hye-Sook Hwang, *The Mago Way: Re-discovering Mago, the Great Goddess from East Asia*, vol. 1 (Lytle Creek, CA: CreateSpace, 2015).
53. Lim, *Translating Time*, 2. Lim's work is in conversation with Bergson's, Deleuze's, and Dipesh Chakrabarty's critiques of modern time and temporality and with Frederic Jameson's and Tzvetan Todorov's engagement with the genre of the fantastic.
54. Lee interview.
55. Carter J. Eckert, Ki-baik Lee, Young Ick Lew, Michael Robinson, and Edgar W. Wagner, *Korea Old and New: A History* (Cambridge, MA: Harvard University, 1990).
56. Koh Sunhui and Kate Barclay, "Traveling through Autonomy and Subjugation: Jeju Island under Japan and Korea," *Asia-Pacific Journal: Japan Focus* 5, no. 5 (May 2007): 6.
57. Ibid. See also Koh Sunhui, "Jeju Islanders Living in Japan during the Twentieth

Century: Life Histories and Consciousness" (Ph.D. diss., Chuo University, Tokyo, 1996); Karen Wigen, "Culture, Power and Place: The New Landscapes of East Asian Regionalism," *American History Review* 104, no. 4 (October 1999): 1183–1201; Epeli Hau'ofa, "Our Sea of Islands," *Contemporary Pacific* 6, no. 1 (1994): 148–161.

58. Kwon, *The Other Cold War*.

59. Ibid.; Kim, "Mourning Korean Modernity in the Memory of the Jeju April Third Incident."

60. Nirmala Nataraj and Dohee Lee, "The *MAGO* Project," Dancers Group, November 1, 2014, http://dancersgroup.org/2014/11/mago-project.

61. José Esteban Muñoz, *Cruising Utopia: The Then and There of Queer Futurity* (New York: New York University Press, 2009), 3.

62. Ibid.

63. Ibid.

64. I am grateful for Feng-Mei Heberer's suggestion to engage the presence of Lee's body in relation to the screen. For a critical reading of the *haptic* or sensual elements of cinema and media, see Laura Marks, *The Skin of the Film: Intercultural Cinema, Embodiment, and the Senses* (Durham, NC: Duke University Press, 2000). For a provocative reading of the relationship between the racialized gendered body, skin as surface, and performance, see Anne Anlin Cheng, *Second Skin: Josephine Baker and the Modern Surface* (Oxford: Oxford University Press, 2011). For incisive readings of the relationship between the exploitative dimensions of neoliberal labor and speculative cultural productions that exist beyond the damaging confines of capital, see Aimee Bahng, *Migrant Futures: Decolonizing Speculation in Financial Times* (Durham, NC: Duke University Press, 2017), and David Roh, Betsy Huang, and Greta A. Niu, eds., *Techno-Orientalism: Imagining Asia as Speculative Fiction, History, and Media* (New Brunswick, NJ: Rutgers University Press, 2015).

65. For readings of the romanticized rendering of the *haenyeo* as idealized feminist figures within Korean history and the tourism industry's popularization of female divers, see Anne Hilty, "Haenyeo: The Truth behind Tourism: A Look into Jeju Diving Women's Not-So-Romantic Livelihoods," *Jeju Weekly*, March 11, 2013, http://www.jejuweekly.com/news/articleView.html?idxno=1314; Gui-Young Hon, "Becoming a 'Legitimate' Ancestor: A Sociocultural Understanding of a Sonless Jamnyeo's Life Story," *Forum: Qualitative Social Research* 5, no. 3 (2004), http://www.qualitative-research.net/index.php/fqs/article/view/565/1227; Gwi-Sook Gwon, "Changing Labor Processes of Women's Work: The Haenyeo of Jeju Island," *Korea Studies* 29, no. 1 (2005): 114–136.

66. Kim, "The Work of Memory," 237. See also Roger L. Janelli and Dawnhee Yim Janelli, *Ancestor Worship and Korean Society* (Stanford, CA: Stanford University Press, 1982); Inchu Pyo, "War Experiences and Community Culture," in *Chonjaeng kwa saramdul [Korean War, Community, and Residents' Experience]*, ed. Inchu Pyo et al. (Seoul: Han'ul, 2003), 145–169.

67. Kim, "The Work of Memory," 231; Heonik Kwon, "New Ancestral Shrines in South Korea," in *Korea Year Book*, vol. 1, ed. Rüdiger Frank, James E. Hoare, Patrick Köllner, and Susan Pares (Leiden: Brill, 2007), 194–214.

68. Kim, "The Work of Memory," 230.

69. Ibid.

70. See Hon, "Becoming a 'Legitimate Ancestor,'"; Gwon, "Changing Labor Processes of Women's Work."

71. Helen Hye-Sook Hwang, "Old Traditions as New Revelation: Magosim and Its Nostalgic Ethos Expressed in Pan-East Asian Primary Sources," paper presented at the Academy of Korean Studies Congress Gathering, 2008, 1. See also Helen Hye-Sook Hwang, "Issues in Studying Mago, the Great Goddess of East Asia," in *The Constant and*

Changing Faces of Goddess: Goddess Traditions of Asia, ed. DeePark Shimkhada and Phyllis K. Herman (London: Cambridge Scholars, 2008), 10–32.

72. Hwang, "Old Traditions as New Revelation," 1.

73. Ibid.

74. Here my reference to "revised" versions underscores how Lee revises *MAGO* to reflect both the space of the performance venue and the agenda of the performance program. While *MAGO* is originally conceived of as a ninety-minute performance, Lee at times performs abbreviated iterations of *MAGO* or specific "chapters," depending on the performance venue (e.g., anti-military conferences, dance festival, public performance in open spaces, or artist talk). Lee also maintains digitized clips from her varied performances on her website. For an updated list of Lee's performances of *MAGO*, see http://www.doheelee.com/index.htm.

75. Diana Taylor, *The Archive and the Repertoire: Performing Cultural Memory in the Americas* (Durham, NC: Duke University Press, 2003), 187.

76. Frazer Ward, *No Innocent Bystanders: Performance Art and Audience* (Hanover, NH: Dartmouth College Press, 2012), 19.

77. Ward, *No Innocent Bystanders*, 21.

78. Maureen Turin, *Flashbacks in Film: Memory and History* (New York: Routledge, 2013), 1–2.

79. For texts that investigate the connective tissue between the history of domestic racial violence in the United States and militarized interventions abroad, see Derek Gregory, *The Colonial Present: Afghanistan, Palestine, Iraq* (New York: Wiley-Blackwell, 2004); Derek Gregory and Allan Pred, eds., *Violent Geographies: Fear Terror, and Political Violence* (New York: Routledge, 2006); Deborah Cowen, *The Deadly Life of Logistics: Mapping Violence in Global Trade* (Minneapolis: University of Minnesota Press, 2014).

80. Ward, *No Innocent Bystanders*, 18. Ward's "horizon of experience" phrasing is borrowed from the critique of Jürgen Habermas's concept of the public sphere in Oskar Negt and Alexander Kluge, *Public Sphere and Experience: Toward an Analysis of the Bourgeois and Proletarian Public Sphere*, trans. Peter Labanyi, Jamie Owen Daniel, and Asseka Oksiloff (Minneapolis: University of Minnesota Press, 1993).

81. Scott, *Conscripts of Modernity*, 21.

An Opening

Acknowledgments: I thank Niana Liu and Cristiana Baik, who provided nearly all of the photographs included in "An Opening": photographs of a bus stop crowd and a rivulet (by Niana Liu) and photographs of an empty room, a fruit stand, a street mural of young women, and a street mural detail (by Cristiana Baik). The only exception is the last image, the photograph of the notebook page, which is my own. I am also grateful to Cristiana Baik for writing the poem "Wreckoning" for inclusion herein.

1. Donald Rumsfeld, U.S. Department of Defense Report, 2006, as quoted in David Shim, *Visual Politics and North Korea: Seeing Is Believing* (London: Routledge, 2014), 3–4.

2. Édouard Glissant, *Poetics of Relation*, trans. Betsy Wing (Ann Arbor: University of Michigan Press, 1990), 193.

3. Don Mee Choi, *Hardly War* (New York: Wave, 2016), 4.

4. Caren Kaplan, "Sensing Distance: The Time and Space of Contemporary War," *Social Text* online (*Periscope*), June 17, 2013, https://socialtextjournal.org/periscope_article/sensing-distance-the-time-and-space-of-contemporary-war.

5. Glissant, *Poetics of Relation*, 189.
6. Ibid., 190.
7. Ibid., 192.
8. In regard to my engagement with partial knowledges, I am deeply indebted to Donna Haraway's "Situated Knowledges: The Science Question in Feminism and the Privilege of Partial Perspective," *Feminist Studies* 14, no. 3 (Autumn 1988): 575–599.
9. Glissant, *Poetics of Relation*, 193.
10. Ibid., 194.
11. Ibid., 192.

Index

Page numbers in italics refer to illustrations.

Abraham, Nicolas, 189n38
adoptees, Korean transnational: assimilability of, 46–47, 116–117; counterpublic of, 106–107, 117, 122–123, 125; as cultural translators, 100; as *dongpo*, 111; emigration of, 45; as human capital, 100–101, 121; and model minority discourse, 100; Scandinavian, 116–117, 210n60; as temporary returnees, 111; and visibility, 111. *See also* orphans, Korean; returnees, Korean
adoption, Korean transnational, 43, 198n47, 207n23; and affect, 101–102, 106, 113, 125; and American exceptionalism, 122; and benevolence, rhetoric of, 114; critiques of, 105, 207n19; to Denmark, 210n60, 210n62; and factory worker mothers, 113; and homogenization of South Korea, 103; and identity forgery, 115, 210n56; and South Korean development, 112; and South Korean laws, 209n43; and teen pregnancy, 113; and U.S. immigration laws, 43–44; in *The Woman, the Orphan, and the Tiger*, 120–121
adoption rights, 208n27
aesthetics, 8–10; and perception, 188n15

affect: and aural history, 82; and Cold War discourse, 11; and emotion, 204n38; and Intergenerational project, 82, 86–87; and Korean transnational adoption, 101–102, 106, 113, 125; and Korean War, 14, 16, 63, 95, 182; in performance art, 108–109, 111, 113, 152; and silence, 95; and time, 108
affect studies, 9
Agamben, Giorgio, 15
Ahmed, Sara, 109, 138
Ahn, Christine, 56, 142, 213n36
American exceptionalism: and Cold War, 10–11, 13; discourse of, 73; and Korean transnational adoption, 122
American studies, transnational, 13, 32
anticommunism: and Americanism, 47; and Cold War, 52, 57, 61; discourse of, 62, 73; and 4.3 massacre, 213n36; and immigration, 52; and immigration policy, 47; and Korean migration, 46; and migration, 46, 68; and red-baiting, 86; in South Korea, 7, 54–56, 59, 80, 102, 104, 130, 138; and surveillance, 47, 49, 80, 83, 104; and war brides, 46–47
April 3 massacre. *See* 4.3 massacre

April 3rd Peace Memorial Park, 139, *157;* and critical remembering, 156–158
Arirang (film), 105
Armstrong, Charles, 54
army base stew, 3; gendered origins of, 5; as symbol of Korean War, 6. *See also* BooDaeChiGae
Arndt-Johns, Jennifer, 106
Asian/Americans: and model minority discourse, 60, 100; red-baiting of, 86
Asian American studies: cultural studies, trauma in, 7; literary studies, dominance of, 23
Attewell, Nadine, 97, 101
aural history, 72, 93–94; and affect, 82; collaborative dimensions of, 72, 74–75, 90; intersubjectivity of, 73, 90; listening practices of, 71–72; as memory-making process, 76–77; as participatory process, 74–75; and silence, 73, 83; and women of color feminism, 78–79. *See also* Intergenerational Korean American Oral History Project; oral history
aurality as diasporic methodological praxis, 72–73

Baik, Cristiana Kyung-hye: photography of, *174, 176, 178;* "Wreckoning," 161–164, 184
Barthes, Roland, 15
Battle Hymn (film), 18, 104
Bedford, Christopher, 110
benevolence, discourse of: and Korean immigration, 63, 75, 125; and Korean transnational adoption, 114; and U.S. Cold War discourse, 28, 63, 75, 125
Benjamin, Walter, 12–13
Bennett, Jill, 188n15; on aesthetics, 9
Bergson Henri, 131, 132
biopower, 101
Boed, Charlotte Kim, 106
Bolter, Jay, 212n11
BooDaeChiGae (Yoo video installation), 3, *4,* 5, 9–10, 13
Bordier, Anaïs, 99, 115, 126
Borshay Liem, Deann, 40, 50, 59, 61, 106, 195n9, 199n65; autobiographical films of, 210n56
Borstam, Anna Jin Hwa, 106, 206n10, 210n60
Briggs, Laura, 207n17
Brink, Suzanne, 105

Browne, Simone, 15
budae jjigae, 3; gendered origins of, 5; as symbol of Korean War, 6. *See also* BooDaeChiGae
Butler, Judith, 133; on performativity, 189n35; on recognition, 14–15

Camacho, Keith, 20
camptowns (*gijichon*), 42, 48, 120; sex workers in, 196n15
capitalism: and decolonization, 27; human capital, 100–101, 114, 121; neoliberal, 206n9
Caruth, Cathy, 15, 201n3
Chakrabarty, Dipesh, 189n28
Chang, Paul Y., 206n5
Chen, Kuan-Hsing, 194n89
Cheng, Anne Anlin, 211n6
Cho, Grace, 5, 14, 121–122
Cho, Margaret, 184
Cho, Maria (Chang Sook Kim), 46, 196n17
Cho Sunjung, 211n7
Choi Chang Hyun, 211n7
Choi, Chungmoo, 194n89
Choi, Don Mee, 181, 185
Choi Hwajung, 211n7
chrononormativity, 38; of Cold War, 90, 131–132, 139; and heteronormativity, 29; and immigration, 58
Chu, Tammy, 106
Chun Doo-Hwan, 105, 112; economic development model of, 112–114
citizenship: and Cold War, 131; and gender, 40; and model minority discourse, 58–60; and race, 40; and sex difference, 40
Civil Rights Act of 1964, 49
Clay, Philip, 111
Clinton, Hilary Rodham, 144
Cold War: and American exceptionalism, 10–11, 13; and anticommunism, 52, 57, 61; chrononormativity of, 90, 131–132, 139; and citizenship, 131; and heteronormativity, 37–38, 45; historiography of, 10, 136, 139; and immigration policy, 43–47, 57; and knowledge production, 10, 17, 20, 73, 89; and Orientalism, 74; and refugees, 195n5; and South Korean economic growth, 53–54; and surveillance, 57; and violence, 11–12; and white supremacy, 45

Cold War discourse, 21; and affect, 11; and diasporic memory works, 23; and Korean War, 18, 19, 28, 184; North Korea in, 183; United States as savior in, 51, 74, 91; of U.S. benevolence, 28

colonialism: Japanese, 191n62, 192n65; of Jeju Island, 146, 155; in *Mago*, 154–155; and the nation-state, 193n89; and violence, 78

comfort women, 14, 20, 190n40; in *The Woman, the Orphan, and the Tiger*, 117–119; Women's International War Crimes Tribunal on Japan's Military Sexual Slavery and, 118–119

Committee against Heliport Construction, 214n44

Committee for Preparation of Korean Independence, 22

Corneil, Marit, 77

Crapser, Adam, 111

Crenshaw, Kimberlé, 193n82

Cumings, Bruce, 20

Cvetkovich, Ann, 82

decolonization, 193n89; and capitalism, 27; of Korea, 7, 26–27, 144; and *MAGO*, 133, 155; and true justice, 27

de la Cadena, Marisol, 13

Democratic People's Republic of Korea (DPRK). *See* North Korea

Denmark: transnational adoption to, 210n60, 210n62; white supremacy in, 116

desegregation, 45

diasporans, Korean, 5; as immigrants, 28, 48, 49; and memory production, 41, 75; militarized migration of, 29, 49; as refugees, 28–29, 48, 49. *See also* adoptees, Korean transnational; returnees, Korean

diasporic, the: and aurality, 72–73; and differential listening, 25; and disidentification, 25; as feminist analytic, 24–27, 72; and oral history, 70–71; and re-performance, 93–94; and translation, 136; and true justice, 22; and women of color feminism, 25

diasporic memory works, 6, *179*, 182; as aesthetic meditations, 8; and Cold War discourse, 23; and re-performances, 93–94

differential listening: as diasporic practice, 25, 95; and women of color feminism, 95

disidentification: and the diasporic, 25; in

The Woman, the Orphan, and the Tiger, 125

Dobbs, Jennifer Kwon, 106, 119, 122–123

double consciousness, 116

Doyle, Jennifer, 111

DPRK (Democratic People's Republic of Korea). *See* North Korea

Du Bois, W. E. B., 116

Dudziak, Mary, 6

durational memory, 132; and folkloric mythology, 147; and *gut*, 139; and Korean War, 156, 158; in *MAGO*, 145, 150, 152, 155, 156; and participatory engagement, 132; in *Reiterations of Dissent*, 133, 135, 137, 141, 145, 152, 156

Eidsheim, Nina, 204n36

El-Tayeb, Fatima, 25

Enloe, Cynthia, 42

Espiritu, Yen Le, 28, 210n65

family reunification, 49, 194n3

Fanon, Frantz, 116

Felman, Shoshana, 15

feminism and the diasporic, 2, 24–27, 72. *See also* women of color feminism

Ferguson, Roderick, 79, 114

Foucault, Michel, 101; on silence, 83, 84; on subjugated knowledge, 51

4.3 massacre, 31, 129–131, 133, 136, 139; and anticommunism, 213n36; diasporic memory practices of, 131; Jeju Special Law of Restitution for the Victims of the April 3rd Incident, 150; in *MAGO*, 149, 152–153; in *Reiterations of Dissent*, 134, 137–145; and silence, 140–141

Freeman, Elizabeth, 29

Freud, Sigmund, 130–131

Frisch, Michael, 77

Futerman, Samantha ("Sam"), 99, 115, 126

Gangjeong naval base, 31, 130–134, 138, 142–145, 156, 212n13

gender: and *budae jjigae*, 5; and citizenship, 40; and Korea-U.S. relations, 46, 151; and labor, 150–151; and the nation-state, 24–26, 29, 47, 138, 151; social construction of, 189n35; in South Korea, 123, 150–151; and violence, 80–81

Gibson, Katherine, 102, 206n9

Gibson-Graham, J. K. (pen name for Katherine Gibson and Julie Graham), 102, 206n9
gijichon. See camptowns
Gillem, Mark, 42
Gleerup, Trine Mee Sook, 106, 210n60
Glissant, Édouard, 31, 185
Global Overseas Adoptees' Link, 207n23
Gluck, Sherna Berger, 72
Gómez-Barris, Macarena, 8, 204n39, 214n49
Gonzalez, Vernadette Vicuña, 138
Graham, Julie, 102, 206n9
Grele, Ronald, 50
Grewal, Inderpal, 11
Grusin, Richard, 212n11
gut, 139; as durational memory practice, 139; in *MAGO,* 149
Gwangju Uprising, 19

Harney, Stefano, 76
hauntings, 14; intergenerational, 189n38
healing, 6–7; and violence, 6–7
heteronormativity: and Cold War, 29, 137–138, 145; and immigration, 58; and the nation-state, 24–26, 29, 47, 138, 151
hibakusha, 93
Hirsch, Marianne, 15
historiography, Cold War, 10, 136, 139
Holocaust studies, 15–16
Holt, Bertha, 43
Holt, Harry, 43, 198n47
Hong, Christine, 21–22, 95–96, 195n9
Hong, Grace Kyungwon, 24–25, 79, 193n82
Hong, Sukjong, 6, 72, 73–95 passim, 201n7, 202n15; on cross-generational approach, 84–87; on debriefing, 80; on familial silence, 83–84; "My Mother Used to Tell Me," 202n17; on "official" knowledge, 88. *See also* Intergenerational Korean American Oral History Project
Hübinette, Tobias, 43, 103, 117
Hurh, Won Moo, 196n18
Hwang, Helen Hye-Sook, 150

immigration: and anticommunism, 47, 52; and chrononormativity, 58; and heteronormativity, 58; occupational, 194n3; and war brides, 196n24, 197n29
immigration, Korean, 37–41; and American benevolence discourse, 63, 75, 125

immigration laws, U.S.: Alien Fiancées and Fiancés Act (1946), 197n29; Immigration and Nationality Act of 1952, 44, 57; Immigration and Nationality Act of 1965 (Hart-Celler Act), 38, 44, 49; War Brides Act, 44, 197n29
immigration policy, U.S., 37; and anticommunism, 47; during Cold War, 43–47; and Korean adoption, 43–44
Intergenerational Korean American Oral History Project, 29, 72–73, 202n15; accessibility, ethics of, 78; affect in, 82, 86–87; collaborative praxis of, 78–80, 90, 93; cross-generational approach of, 84–87; differential listening in, 81; intersubjectivity in, 73; and knowledge production, 73, 76–78, 88, 89–90; member training of, 203n33; and oral history, 202n20; origins of, 73–78; reflecting back in, 79; re-performances of, 90–93, *92,* 205n51; silence in sessions, 84–86, 94–95; temporal elasticity of, 73; translation in, 81–82; vernacular knowledge of, 76; and women of color feminism, 78–79; working paradigm on, *75,* 76–77, 202n18. *See also* aural history; oral history
International Women's Network against Militarism, 214n44, 214n48
intersectionality, 24–25, 193n82
intersubjectivity, 201n9; of aural history, 73, 90; in Intergenerational project, 73; and oral history, 50
The Interview (film), 183–184

jamnyeo, 149–150
Japan's trans-Pacific arrangement with the United States, 20
Jeju Island, 22, 28, 30–31; colonization of, 146, 155; local mythologies of, 146; in *MAGO,* 145; and masculinity, 29; mourning on, 149–150; occupation of, 146; remilitarization of, 130, 133, 141–144, 152; as tourist destination, 15, 129, 138, 150
Jimmy Kimmel Live, 165

Kaisen, Jane Jin, 30, 102–103, 104–106, 206n10; biography of, 115–116; dissident translation of, 136, 212n15, 212n19;

and durational memory, 132; visuality, critique of, 136–137. *See also Reiterations of Dissent* (Kaisen video installation); *The Woman, the Orphan, and the Tiger* (Kaisen film)
Kang Dong-Kyun, 143, 144
Kang, Laura Hyun Yi, ix, 23
Kaplan, Caren, 182
Kim, Christine Sun, 69, *70*, 95
Kim Dae-jung, 21
Kim, Daniel, 14
Kim, Danny, 72, 73–95 passim, 201n7, 202n15; on aural history, 93–94; on cross-generational approach, 84–87; on debriefing, 80; on distance from Korean War, 79; on "official" knowledge, 88. *See also* Intergenerational Korean American Oral History Project
Kim Dong-choon, 21, 192n65
Kim, Dong-man, 134–135
Kim, Eleana J., 43, 100, 103, 105–106, 209n53
Kim, Jodi, 10, 53
Kim Jong-il, 21, 184
Kim Jong-un, 12, 21, 184
Kim, Joo Ok, 201n8
Kim, Mimi, 60
Kim, Seong-nae, 127, 131; on "straightening up," 138–139
Kim Young-sam, 138
Klein, Christina, 45
Klein, Melanie, 7
knowledge production: and Cold War, 10, 17, 20, 73, 89; and Intergenerational project, 73, 76–78, 89–90; and Korean returnees, 122; and Korean War, 17–20, 31–32, 73; limits of, 95; and North Korea, 31
Kondo, Dorinne, 6–7
Korea: decolonization of, 7, 26–27, 144; Japanese colonial rule of, 191n62, 192n65; reconciliation of, 26–27; U.S. occupation of, 20, 39, 41, 54. *See also* Korean War; North Korea; South Korea
Korean/Americans: oral histories of, 49–50; red-baiting of, 57–58
Korean armistice, 41, 187n4
Korean National Revolutionary Party, 57
Korean-ness, 26, 30, 121
Korean-U.S. gendered relations, 46, 151

Korean War, 3, 61–62; affects of, 14, 16, 63, 95, 182; and American benevolence, discourse of, 62, 75, 104; and anticommunist discourse, 62; *budae jjigae* as symbol of, 6; Cold War framing of, 18–19, 28; and durational memory, 158; as ever-present, 13; as forgotten war, 13, 18; and knowledge production, 17–20, 31–32, 73; *longue durée* of, 17; naturalized portrayals of, 78; and non-normative bodies, 25–26; in popular media, 18; reencountering of, 182–183; Scandinavian humanitarian work in, 117, *118*; and silence, 70, 83; and subject formation, 102; as transnational war, 5; as unending, 16, 183; as unfinished war, 5, 158; United States as savior in, 91; U.S. bombing in, 170–171; and vernacular of everyday life, 87–88
Korean War memory studies, 17–18; trauma in, 13–16
Korean War Veterans Memorial, 18, *19*
Koshy, Susan, 47, 197n44
Kumi, Yun, 11
Kwon, Heonik, 10, 54
kyopo (*gyopo*), 190n44

Langvad, Maja, 117, 122–123
Laub, Dori, 15, 71
Lee, Dohee, 30, 131, 145, 211n7; and durational memory, 132; on mythologies and folklore, 146–147. *See also MAGO* (Dohee Lee performance)
Lee, Eun-Joung, 69–70; oral history of, 40, 48, 50–51, 58–63, 198n52
Lee, Jin-kyung, 54, 114
Lee, Kyung-hui, 202n17
Lee, Min Yong, 61, 69–70, 199n65; CNN interview, 62; on Korean War, 61–62; oral history of, 40, 48, 54–58, 63
Lee Myung-bak, 139
Lee, Namhee, 20, 56, 195n9
Lee Yong Soon, 35–38, *36, 37,* 42, 47, 63, *64*
Legacies of the Korean War (oral history archive), 40–41, 55, 70, 95–96, 195n9; silence in, 83
Le Guin, Ursula, 67
Lemoine, Mihee-Nathalie, 106
Levi, Primo, 15

Leys, Ruth, 14
Liem, Ramsay, 49, 59, 67, 95–96, 195n9, 199n65
Life (magazine), 35–37, 63, *64*
Lim, Bliss Cua, 132, 133; on the fantastic, 145–146
Lim, Minouk, 212n7
listening, 80; and aural history, 71–72; collaborative, 76; diasporic memory practice of, 96; differential, 25, 81, 95
Liu, Niana, photography of, *175, 177*
Lorde, Audre, 24, 124
Loving v. Virginia, 47
Lutz, Catherine, 17

MAGO (Dohee Lee performance), 30–31, 133, 145–156, *148;* audience participation in, 153–154; and body, hypervisibility of, 148; colonialism in, 154–155; and decolonization, 133, 155; durational memory in, 145, 150, 152, 155, 156; 4.3 massacre in, 149, 152–153; *gut* in, 149; "Invited Ritual: Crow" chapter, 153, *154,* 155; Jeju Island in, 145; mourning rituals in, 149–152; mythologies and folklore in, 153; remediation in, 153; revised performances of, 151, 216n74; shamanistic ritual in, 139, 147, 149; the supernatural in, 145. *See also* Lee, Dohee
Melamed, Jodi, 45
melancholia and racial formation, 211n6
memory: and aural history, 76–77; and the diasporic, 6, 70–71, 96, 131, 182; and forgetting, 137; and Korean diaspora, 41, 75; and mourning, 130; postmemory, 14, 16, 86; as practice, 88–89; rememory, 73, 202n11; re-performance of, 93; translation as diasporic mode of, 136. *See also* durational memory
Memory of Forgotten War (documentary), 40–41, 54, 61, 70; silence in, 83
Mignolo, Walter, 193n89
migration: and anticommunism, 46, 68; militarized, 9, 42–45, 48–49, 60, 62–65; refuge migration, 38–39. *See also* immigration
migration, Korean, 29, 41, 49; and anticommunism, 46; of military brides, 39, 41, 42; multiracial children, 42. *See also* immigration, Korean

militarized migration, 29, 42–45, 48–49, 60, 62–65; as American immigration history, 182; of Korean diaspora, 29, 49; of Min Yong Lee family, 50–54
military-industrial complex, 17, 191n53
Miller, Elizabeth, 77
Miller, Wayne, photography of, *36, 37,* 63, *64*
Min, Pyong Gap, 194n3
Minjung (People's) movement, 19–20, 188n10
miscegenation, 47, 65
mixed-raced GI children, 29, 41, 43, 100; hypervisibility of, 121; in *The Woman, the Orphan, and the Tiger,* 121–122
model minority discourse, 39–40, 45; and Asian/Americans, 60, 100; and citizenship, 58–60; and Korean adoptees, 100; and Korean refugees, 63; and silence, 83
Moon Jae-in, 12, 21
Moon, Katherine, 42
Moon, Seungsook, 112
Moraga, Cherríe, 24
Morgan, Johnie M., 35, *36, 37,* 63, 65
Morrison, Toni, 73
Mortensen, Jette Hye Jin, 106
Moten, Fred, 76
mourning: on Jeju Island, 149–150; in *MAGO,* 149–152; and melancholia, 130–131; and memory, 130
multichannel video installations, 137, 212n11. *See also Reiterations of Dissent* (Kaisen video installation)
Muñoz, José Esteban, 109, 147

nation-state: as arbiter of justice, 188n10; as enforcer of violence, 188n10; heteronormative logics of, 24–26, 29, 47, 138, 151
Nelson, Kim Park, 43, 103
neoliberalism: and capitalism, 206n9; and human capital, 100–101
Nevins, Allan, 202n20
Ngai, Sianne, 109
Nguyen, Mimi Thi, 11, 28
Nguyen, Vinh, 91
Nielsen, Tone Olaf, 207n10
Niranjana, Tejaswini, 136
Nodutdol for Korean Community Development, 74
Noh Moo-hyun, 192n65

North Korea: caricaturization of, 31, 183–184; in Cold War discourse, 183; and denuclearization, 26; and knowledge production, 31; and Orientalism, 183; as part of axis of evil, 12, 166; reencountering of, 184–186; U.S. bombing of, 170–171
Northwest Youth League, 134, 140, 199n65

Obama, Barack, 26
Oishi, Eve, 202n11
OKA (Overseas Korean Act), 100, 206n5
Okinawan Women Act against Military Violence, 214n44
opacity, 185; as provocation, 31
oral history: as diasporic memory practice, 70–71; and ethics of access, 77; history of, 202n20; and intersubjectivity, 50, 201n9; of Eun-Joung Lee, 40, 48, 50–51, 58–63, 198n52; of Min Yong Lee, 40, 48, 54–58, 63; shared authority in, 77; as testimonial, 71. *See also* aural history; Intergenerational Korean American Oral History Project
orphans, Korean, 44, 46–48, 103–104, 198n47, 207n17. *See also* adoptees, Korean transnational
Overseas Korean Act (OKA), 100, 206n5

Page, Lawrence Edward, 172
Paik Nak-Chung, 188n9, 194n89
Paik, Nam June, 137
Panmunjom Declaration, 26
Park, Chung-hee, 52, 53–54, 56, 198n55; economic development model of, 112–114; and transnational adoption, 103; Yushin Constitution of, 80, 204n37
Park Geun-hye, 26, 56, 188n10; and 4.3 massacre, 139; and Korean adoption returnees, 99
Park, Jung-Sun, 206n5
Park, Randall, 184
Park, Sarah, 5, 9–10
Passerini, Luisa, 71–72, 74
Pate, SooJin, 43, 103, 105–106
Patel, Leigh, 80
performance and public participation, 151–152
performativity, 189n35
photography and trauma, 15–16
Pianoiss . . . issmo (Worse Finish), 69
postmemory, 14, 16; and blood kinship, 86

Rancière, Jacques, 203n21
recognition, 14–15, 182; and legibility, 15
Reddy, Chandan, 11, 40
reencounters, 6–8, 182; of Korean War, 82–83; with North Korea, 184–186
refugee laws, U.S.: Migration and Refugee Assistance Act of 1962, 44; Refugee Act (1980), 44; Refugee Relief Act (RRA), 44–45, 46
refugees: and anticommunism, 195n5; and Cold War, 195n5; Korean, 63; Korean diasporans as, 28–29, 48, 49; as model minorities, 63; refugee migration, 38–39, 53; UN Convention Relating to the Status of Refugees, 44, 194n5; UN definition of, 38, 194n5
Reiterations of Dissent (Kaisen video installation), 30–31, 131, 134–145, *135, 143,* 211n7; and decolonization, 133; and dissident translation, 137, 145; durational memory in, 133, 135, 137, 141, 145, 152, 156; as excessive, 135; 4.3 massacre in, 134, 137–145; Gangjeong in, 143; "Ghosts" short, 140–141; "History of Endless Rebellion" short, 141–142, 143; "Island of Endless Rebellion" short, 141; "Lamentation of the Dead" short, 137–138, *139;* multiple temporalities in, 140; "The Politics of Naming" short, 137–138, *139;* remediation in, 134; "Retake: Mayday" short, 134–135; visualization of history in, 137
remediation, 132, 212n11; in *MAGO,* 153; in *Reiterations of Dissent,* 134
rememory, 73, 202n11
reparative creativity, 7
re-performance, 73; diasporic practices of, 93–94; of Intergenerational project sessions, 90–93, *92,* 205n51; of memory, 93
Republic of Korea (ROK). *See* South Korea
returnees, Korean, 99–125 passim; assimilability of, 111; as diasporic memory analytic, 101; as expendable excess, 114; as human capital, 101–102, 114; and knowledge production, 122; and motherland trips, 105; unassimilable bodies of, 122; in *The Woman, the Orphan, and the Tiger,* 115, 117, 119. *See also* adoptees, Korean transnational; orphans, Korean
Rhee, Juyeon, 56

RHEE, kate-hers, 30, 102–103, 105, 206n10, 208n27; and spectatorship, 108, 110–111; and surveillance, 108. *See also Sex Education for Finding Face in the 21st Century* (RHEE performance)
Rhee Syngman, 43, 187n4; and transnational adoption, 103
Robinson, tammy ko, 106
Roh Moo-hyun, 138
ROK (Republic of Korea). *See* South Korea
ROK-Japan Normalization Treaty, 119
Roosevelt, Franklin D., 53
Rumsfeld, Donald, 167
Ryan, John L. ("Jack"), 57, 200n76

Sakai, Naoki, 20, 192n63
Schlund-Vials, Cathy, 28
Schneider, Rebecca, 73, 90
Scott, David, 144–145, 158
See, Sarita, 23
Separated @ Birth: A True Story of Twin Sisters Reunited (Bordier and Futerman), 99
Sex Education for Finding Face in the 21st Century (RHEE performance), 30, 102–103, 107–114, *108,* 115; excessive feelings in, 109–110, 114, 123, 125; extensions of, 110–111; "failure" of, 111–112; remix of, 110, 208n36; and RHEE's body, hypervisibility of, 112; and spectatorship, 110–111; teen pregnancy in, 112. *See also* RHEE, kate-hers
sex workers, 14; in South Korea, 122, 196n15
Shigematsu, Setsu, 20
Shin, Jungran, 55
silence: and affect, 95; and aural history, 73, 83; familial, 83–84; and 4.3 massacre, 140–141; in Intergenerational project sessions, 83–85, 94–95; and Korean War, 70, 83; and model minority discourse, 83; and violence, 83, 84
Simpson, Audra, 89, 95
Singh, Nikhil, 45
SKIG. *See* South Korean Interim Government
Small House Burning (video short), 91, *92*
Smith, Linda Tuhiwai, 78, 203n30
SOFA (U.S.–South Korean Status of Forces Agreement), 11
Sommers, Ben, 126

Sook, Trine Mee, 206n10
South Korea, 187n4; abortion in, 112; adoption laws in, 209n43; anticommunism in, 37, 54–56, 59, 80, 102, 104, 130, 138; asymmetrical relationship with United States, 19–20; democratization of, 20; economic development of, 112–114, 122; and economic growth during Cold War, 53–54, 112; emigration policies of, 52; gendered labor in, 113, 150–151, 209n53; gender in, 123; homogenization of, 103; industrialization of, 52; militarized modernity of, 112–113, 117–118; and National Security Act, 55–56; 1962 coup in, 56; red-baiting in, 86; sex workers in, 122, 196n15; surveillance in, 55–56, 79, 80, 104, 113–114; unwed pregnancy in, 113; women factory workers in, 113, 209n53
South Korean Interim Government (SKIG), 130, 134–135, 140–141, 143, 153; and occupation of Jeju Island, 146
Spam, 3, 5
Stalin, Joseph, 53
Still Present Pasts (exhibit), 5, 50, 74, 187n1 (intro.)
Stoker, Kim, 106, 206n10, 208n27
Stoler, Ann Laura, 62–63, 88, 95
Sullivan, Sady, 72
surveillance: and anticommunism, 47, 49, 80, 83, 104; and Cold War, 57; in RHEE's performances, 108; in South Korea, 55–56, 79, 80, 104, 113–114

Takagi, J. T., 50, 61
Tauscher, Ellen O'Kane, 142–143
Taylor, Diana, 94, 151
Tempo, Carl J. Bon, 47
Theiler, Kim Su, 106
30 Rock (sitcom), 184
Torok, Maria, 189n38
TPP (Trans-Pacific Partnership), 192n63
translation: as diasporic mode of memory, 136; in Intergenerational project sessions, 81–82
Trans-Pacific Partnership (TPP), 192n63
trauma: in Asian American cultural studies, 7; in Korean War memory studies, 13–16; and photography, 15–16
trauma studies, limits of, 14, 16–17

Trenka, Jane Jeong, 106, 119, 122–123
Trimble, S., 97, 101
Trinh T. Minh-ha, 136
true justice, 7; and decolonization, 27; nation-state as mediator of, 26; and the sovereign state, 22
Truman, Harry, 45
Trump, Donald, 16, 53
Truth and Reconciliation Commission, 21, 192n65
Truth and Reconciliation for the Adoption Community of Korea, 207n23
Turim, Maureen, 153
Twinsters (documentary), 99–100, 126

UFOLab (Unidentified Foreign Object), 106
UN Convention Relating to the Status of Refugees, 44
U.S. Army Military Government in Korea (USAMGIK), 20, 41, 129, 191n62; and occupation of Jeju Island, 146; protests against, 142
U.S. foreign policy: in Southeast Asia, 17, 53–54; and violence, 11–12
U.S. military: and occupation of Korea, 20, 39, 41, 54; and remilitarization of the Pacific, 143–144; sexualized violence of, 78, 192n65
U.S.–South Korean Status of Forces Agreement (SOFA), 11
U.S. state: as arbiter of justice, 17, 24; as enforcer of violence, 17, 24

Vang, Ma, 28, 72, 201n8
violence: and Cold War, 11–12; colonial, 78; gendered, 80–81; and healing, 6–7; militarized, 39, 78, 154–155, 182, 192n65; sexualized, 78, 117–119, 192n65; and silence, 83, 84; state, 80–81; and U.S. foreign policy, 11–12, 17, 24; in *The Woman, the Orphan, and the Tiger*, 117–119
visibility, 15

Walsh, Catherine, 193n89
war: and neoliberalism, 17; as profit-making industry, 101. *See also* Korean War
war brides, 42–43, 65; and anticommunism, 46–47; emigration of, 45; and immigration, 196n24; War Brides Act, 44
Ward, Frazer, 152
War Memorial of Korea, 122–123; and masculinity, 124–125
War on Terror, 11, 12
The Woman, the Orphan, and the Tiger (Kaisen film), 30, 102–103, 115–125, *124,* 133; comfort women in, 117–119; excessive feelings in, 123–125; mixed-race people in, 121–122; racialized sexual violence in, 117–119; returnees in, 115, 117, 119; transnational adoption in, 120–121
women, Korean: assimilability of, 47, 65; as military brides, 39, 41; unassimilability of, 65
women of color feminism, 24; and aural history, 78–79; and coalitional politics of difference, 25, 76; and the diasporic, 25; and differential listening, 95; and Intergenerational project, 78–79; and intersectionality, 24–25
Woo, Susie, 47–48, 196n18
Wynter, Sylvia, 8–9, 188n15, 193n89

Yoneyama, Lisa, 10, 13, 20, 60; on postredress moment, 21–22; on testimony, 93; on true justice, 7, 192n71
Yoo, Ji-Young, 3, 5, 9. *See also* BooDae ChiGae (Yoo video installation)
Yoon Tae Jun, 213n37
Yuh, Ji-Yeon, 38; on camptown workers, 48; on Korean migration, 28; on military wives, 196n24; on refuge migration, 53; unassimilability of, 65
Yushin Constitution, 80, 198n55, 204n37

Zinn, Howard, 202n19

CRYSTAL MUN-HYE BAIK is an Assistant Professor in the Department of Gender and Sexuality Studies at the University of California, Riverside.

Also in the series *Asian American History and Culture*:

Shelley Sang-Hee Lee, *Claiming the Oriental Gateway: Prewar Seattle and Japanese America*
Isabelle Thuy Pelaud, *This Is All I Choose to Tell: History and Hybridity in Vietnamese American Literature*
Christian Collet and Pei-te Lien, eds., *The Transnational Politics of Asian Americans*
Min Zhou, *Contemporary Chinese America: Immigration, Ethnicity, and Community Transformation*
Kathleen S. Yep, *Outside the Paint: When Basketball Ruled at the Chinese Playground*
Benito M. Vergara Jr., *Pinoy Capital: The Filipino Nation in Daly City*
Jonathan Y. Okamura, *Ethnicity and Inequality in Hawai'i*
Sucheng Chan and Madeline Y. Hsu, eds., *Chinese Americans and the Politics of Race and Culture*
K. Scott Wong, *Americans First: Chinese Americans and the Second World War*
Lisa Yun, *The Coolie Speaks: Chinese Indentured Laborers and African Slaves in Cuba*
Estella Habal, *San Francisco's International Hotel: Mobilizing the Filipino American Community in the Anti-eviction Movement*
Thomas P. Kim, *The Racial Logic of Politics: Asian Americans and Party Competition*
Sucheng Chan, ed., *The Vietnamese American 1.5 Generation: Stories of War, Revolution, Flight, and New Beginnings*
Antonio T. Tiongson Jr., Edgardo V. Gutierrez, and Ricardo V. Gutierrez, eds., *Positively No Filipinos Allowed: Building Communities and Discourse*
Sucheng Chan, ed., *Chinese American Transnationalism: The Flow of People, Resources, and Ideas between China and America during the Exclusion Era*
Rajini Srikanth, *The World Next Door: South Asian American Literature and the Idea of America*
Keith Lawrence and Floyd Cheung, eds., *Recovered Legacies: Authority and Identity in Early Asian American Literature*
Linda Trinh Võ, *Mobilizing an Asian American Community*
Franklin S. Odo, *No Sword to Bury: Japanese Americans in Hawai'i during World War II*
Josephine Lee, Imogene L. Lim, and Yuko Matsukawa, eds., *Re/collecting Early Asian America: Essays in Cultural History*
Linda Trinh Võ and Rick Bonus, eds., *Contemporary Asian American Communities: Intersections and Divergences*
Sunaina Marr Maira, *Desis in the House: Indian American Youth Culture in New York City*
Teresa Williams-León and Cynthia Nakashima, eds., *The Sum of Our Parts: Mixed-Heritage Asian Americans*
Tung Pok Chin with Winifred C. Chin, *Paper Son: One Man's Story*
Amy Ling, ed., *Yellow Light: The Flowering of Asian American Arts*
Rick Bonus, *Locating Filipino Americans: Ethnicity and the Cultural Politics of Space*

Darrell Y. Hamamoto and Sandra Liu, eds., *Countervisions: Asian American Film Criticism*
Martin F. Manalansan IV, ed., *Cultural Compass: Ethnographic Explorations of Asian America*
Ko-lin Chin, *Smuggled Chinese: Clandestine Immigration to the United States*
Evelyn Hu-DeHart, ed., *Across the Pacific: Asian Americans and Globalization*
Soo-Young Chin, *Doing What Had to Be Done: The Life Narrative of Dora Yum Kim*
Robert G. Lee, *Orientals: Asian Americans in Popular Culture*
David L. Eng and Alice Y. Hom, eds., *Q & A: Queer in Asian America*
K. Scott Wong and Sucheng Chan, eds., *Claiming America: Constructing Chinese American Identities during the Exclusion Era*
Lavina Dhingra Shankar and Rajini Srikanth, eds., *A Part, Yet Apart: South Asians in Asian America*
Jere Takahashi, *Nisei/Sansei: Shifting Japanese American Identities and Politics*
Velina Hasu Houston, ed., *But Still, Like Air, I'll Rise: New Asian American Plays*
Josephine Lee, *Performing Asian America: Race and Ethnicity on the Contemporary Stage*
Deepika Bahri and Mary Vasudeva, eds., *Between the Lines: South Asians and Postcoloniality*
E. San Juan Jr., *The Philippine Temptation: Dialectics of Philippines–U.S. Literary Relations*
Carlos Bulosan and E. San Juan Jr., eds., *The Cry and the Dedication*
Carlos Bulosan and E. San Juan Jr., eds., *On Becoming Filipino: Selected Writings of Carlos Bulosan*
Vicente L. Rafael, ed., *Discrepant Histories: Translocal Essays on Filipino Cultures*
Yen Le Espiritu, *Filipino American Lives*
Paul Ong, Edna Bonacich, and Lucie Cheng, eds., *The New Asian Immigration in Los Angeles and Global Restructuring*
Chris Friday, *Organizing Asian American Labor: The Pacific Coast Canned-Salmon Industry, 1870–1942*
Sucheng Chan, ed., *Hmong Means Free: Life in Laos and America*
Timothy P. Fong, *The First Suburban Chinatown: The Remaking of Monterey Park, California*
William Wei, *The Asian American Movement*
Yen Le Espiritu, *Asian American Panethnicity*
Velina Hasu Houston, ed., *The Politics of Life*
Renqiu Yu, *To Save China, To Save Ourselves: The Chinese Hand Laundry Alliance of New York*
Shirley Geok-lin Lim and Amy Ling, eds., *Reading the Literatures of Asian America*
Karen Isaksen Leonard, *Making Ethnic Choices: California's Punjabi Mexican Americans*
Gary Y. Okihiro, *Cane Fires: The Anti-Japanese Movement in Hawaii, 1865–1945*
Sucheng Chan, *Entry Denied: Exclusion and the Chinese Community in America, 1882–1943*

www.ingramcontent.com/pod-product-compliance
Lightning Source LLC
Chambersburg PA
CBHW061252230426
43665CB00026B/2916